# CARL SCHURZ
## GERMAN-AMERICAN STATESMAN

Best wishes for a "good read"

Peter Lubrecht Sr.

# CARL SCHURZ

## GERMAN-AMERICAN STATESMAN

### *My Country Right or Wrong*

PETER T. LUBRECHT SR.

AMERICA
THROUGH TIME®
ADDING COLOR TO AMERICAN HISTORY

America Through Time is an imprint of Fonthill Media LLC
www.through-time.com
office@through-time.com

Published by Arcadia Publishing by arrangement with Fonthill Media LLC
For all general information, please contact Arcadia Publishing:
Telephone: 843-853-2070
Fax: 843-853-0044
E-mail: sales@arcadiapublishing.com
For customer service and orders:
Toll-Free 1-888-313-2665

www.arcadiapublishing.com

First published 2019

Copyright © Peter T. Lubrecht Sr. 2019

ISBN 978-1-63499-140-7

Typeset in 10pt on 13pt Sabon
Printed and bound in England

# *Dedication*

*Encouragement he needs not, for nobody has known better than he, and taught all his life that, though it suffice for the average man to do no wrong, he whose wagon was ever hitched to a star, looks at duty from an ideal point of view, unserved by the inducements, motives or passions of smaller men.*

Dr. Abraham Jacobi
Banquet to the Honorable Carl Schurz at Delmonico's
on his seventieth birthday.

This book is dedicated to the immigrants in my family and friends who like Carl Schurz left Germany and adopted America as their homeland:

Heinz D. "Harry" Lubrecht; Gesine Ehlers
Christian Grueninger: Mayor in Valhalla, New York
August Schwartze, hat maker in Brooklyn, New York
Charles T. Lubrecht, Forty-Eighter, nineteenth-century lithographer, and publisher
Dr. Hans Kudlich, physician at the German Hospital, New York
Dr. Martin Rehling, pioneer thoracic surgeon
Marie Pauline Sassin Rehling, first nursing class at the German Hospital
Dr. Thomas Darlington, health commissioner of New York, Tammany Hall

# Contents

*Dedication*                                                                      5

*Foreword*                                                                        9

*Preface*                                                                        11

1    Introduction                                                                13

2    Humble Beginnings                                                          15

3    The Education of a Revolutionary Romantic                                  17

4    Early End to Boyhood—The Dark Years (1838–1840)                            22

5    Sculpting a Rebel                                                          24

6    The Baden Revolution: Escape                                              37

7    The Miraculous Kinkel Escapade                                            44

8    Expatriates in London                                                     57

9    Marriage and America                                                      62

10   Introduction to American Politics (Washington, 1854)                      67

11   The American Journeys (1854–1856)                                         72

12   Watertown, Wisconsin                                                      76

13   Lincoln                                                                   81

14   Ambassador to Spain                                                       92

15   Emancipation                                                              96

16   General Schurz                                                            98

17   "The Flying Dutchmen," Chancellorsville                                  103

18   Gettysburg                                                               109

19   The End of the War                          111

20   Years of Turmoil                            116

21   The Political Journey to Congress           121

22   Senator Schurz                              127

23   Losses                                      135

24   Secretary Schurz                            139

25   Fanny Chapman                               145

26   New York and the Gilded Age                 150

27   Elder Statesman—The Final Years             157

28   Epilogue                                    164


*Appendix: Schurz's Cast of Characters*          167

*Endnotes*                                       171

*Bibliography*                                   183

*Index*                                          188

# Foreword

The 175th anniversary of the Revolutions of 1848 in Germany will take place in a few years, in 2023. Therefore, it is more than appropriate to focus on those who came to the U.S. after its failure—the colorful group of German-speaking immigrants known as the Forty-Eighters—and reassess their impact. Foremost among them was Carl Schurz.

After playing a dramatic role in the Revolution, he came to America and immersed himself in the life of his new homeland. Schurz made an indelible imprint on it throughout his life. He wrote in his memoirs:

> The Forty-Eighters brought something like a wave of spring sunshine…They were mostly high-spirited young people, inspired by fresh ideas which they had failed to realize in the old world, but hoped to realize here; ready to enter upon any activity profitable but also to render life merry and beautiful; and, withal, full of enthusiasm for the great American Republic, which was to be their home and the home of their children.[1]

His well-chosen words aptly describe his compatriots as well as his own life and work in America. The contributions of the Forty-Eighters were great and none more so than those of Carl Schurz. He also stands preeminently as one of the most prominent German-Americans, if not the most prominent himself, in American history.

Unsurprisingly, much has been written about Schurz. In completing work on the *Catalog of the German-Americana Collection* (1990), I was struck by how many publications there were about him. There were even more than those on Friedrich Wilhelm von Steuben (1730–94), another noteworthy German-American. So the challenge of researching and writing a biography of Schurz is no easy task.

Given the forthcoming 175th anniversary of the Revolutions of 1848, however, the time is ripe for a re-examination and reassessment of the life and work of

Schurz. Historian Peter Lubrecht has risen to the task and completed a stellar biography that breaks new ground in illuminating our understanding of this amazing Forty-Eighter.

Peter Lubrecht has thoroughly researched his subject, even traveling throughout Germany and the U.S., following in the footsteps of Schurz, from his birthplace to various sites relating to the Revolutions of 1848 to places he lived and worked in America. His interesting contacts with the descendants of Schurz have also been fruitful for his research. In addition, he has uncovered letters and other materials that previously have not been explored, which greatly enrich his work.

The basic dates, facts, and events in the life of Schurz are relatively well-known, but by means of his travels and in-depth research, Peter Lubrecht has gained a unique perspective on him. His goal has been not to simply retell what we already know about Schurz, but to dig deeper below the surface and explore what kind of person he was and what "makes him tick." This has resulted in a fully rounded biography of Schurz that is at once multi-dimensional as well as absorbing, and it brings us closer to an understanding of Schurz as a person.

I got to know Peter Lubrecht at the "Legacy of 1848" conference, which was coordinated by Joachim Reppmann and myself, taking place on March 31–April 2, 2017, in Northfield, Minnesota. Since that time, we have been in touch with one another regarding his research on the Revolutions of 1848 in general and Carl Schurz in particular. Based on our frequent discussions, I know that readers and researchers will benefit greatly from this book and gain new insight into the life and work of Carl Schurz.

Dr. Don Heinrich Tolzmann

Dr. Tolzmann is a German-American historian, author, and editor. He has been the recipient of Germany's Federal Cross of Merit; Ohioana Book Award; Distinguished German-American of the Year Award; and Outstanding Achievement Award from the Society for German-American Studies. He is the curator of the German-Americana Collection, director of Emeritus German-American Studies at the University of Cincinnati, president of the German-American Citizens League of Greater Cincinnati, book review editor for *German Life Magazine*, and an advisor for PBS on "*German-Americans* and *Zinzinnati Reflections.*"

# Preface

*The streak or the strain of German liberalism which Carl Schurz represented
stood for human dignity and individual freedom....*

Henry Kissinger, address on March 8, 1979,
on the 150th anniversary of Carl Schurz's birth

I have been fascinated with the life of Carl Schurz since my cousin, "Aunty"
Florence, a pioneer in women's rights, told me that her father, Charles T. Lubrecht,
fled from the German Revolutions of 1848 and came "*mit* Schurz" when refugees
from the Revolution flooded the United States in 1849. The Prussian Military had
chased his family across Lake Constance to Switzerland. He fled to Brooklyn,
New York, in 1860, where he became a mapmaker, lithographer, and publisher of
the first German-language biography of Lincoln. Charles T. Lubrecht knew Schurz
there since they had mutual friends and acquaints. The connections to my
family and Carl Schurz grew increasingly interesting and more than coincidental.
I grew up in the German-American world in New York City; my family doctors
were on staff at Lenox Hill Hospital on 77th Street and Lexington Avenue,
formerly the German Hospital founded by Dr. Abraham Jacobi, the pioneering
first pediatrician, and Carl Schurz's best friend. I was born in the Jacobi Pavilion.
German immigrants, in nineteenth- and twentieth-century New York trusted only
German doctors. My first physician was Dr. Hans Kudlich, whose grandfather
carried Schurz's coffin.

The Liederkranz of the City of New York German Club, now on 85th Street off
Fifth Avenue in New York, supports German and operatic music as it did when
William Steinway was its president and where Schurz's portrait hangs in the large
lobby. My uncle Carl was a member, and as a youngster, I performed at Christmas
shows at the club where, during the nineteenth century, the politics of the rich
and famous were hashed out over fine food, drink, and *gemütlichkeit*.

During the research for my last "German and Civil War" themed books, Carl Schurz's name came up repeatedly.[1] I visited the Chancellorsville, Virginia, battlefield where the Union Army lost the battle to the Confederacy; the guide pointed to the area where the XI Corps, composed of German immigrants, ran with Schurz and became known as the "Flying Dutchmen." When I decided to write about Major General Schurz, the research had to start at the source—Germany—as I wanted to see where this man had lived.

Genealogists who research family trees and church records of births and deaths speak of a "silent" hand on the shoulder" that makes one turn the page or look again in unusual places. I found that this silent, spooky cue occurred during my own family research. Therefore, with my Ancestry.com version of Carl Schurz's *Stammbaum* (family tree), I packed to go to Germany, but before I left, I received an e-mail from two of Carl Schurz's living relatives. One kind cousin (Schurz had no direct descendants) offered to meet me and my wife at the airport, in Frankfurt am Main, and take us on a tour of Schurz's early student experience there. She found me through the online family tree where she had also been researching her famous ancestor in London and Hamburg.

I traveled to Rastatt, in the Black Forest, to look into Schurz's escape route from Prussian capture. Fortunately, a local historian, an expert on the 1848 revolutionary activities in Rastatt, was able to meet me one morning, pulling up to the old *Rathaus* on her bicycle. My wife and I had been staying at Bildungshaus St. Bernhard, a former Catholic boy's school converted to a hotel, and our guide told us that it had been the fort during the Baden Revolution where Schurz was stationed. She was also able to show us the spot from which Schurz escaped from a storm drain, which is now marked by a faded plaque.

We then went to Schurz's home town of Liblar, now merged with the town of Erftstadt, and booked into the hotel Schloss Gracht next to the *Schloss* itself, which was once owned by the Metternich family. The hotel manager greeted me as we arrived and told me that the town archivist was waiting to give me a tour of Schurz's birthplace, which turned out to be the hotel itself. Our room was a few doors down from the spot where Carl Schurz was born. Along the way, we found vestiges of his German journey, and maybe Carl Schurz was looking over my shoulder.

Schurz's personal story needs to be told in relation to his accomplishments and, more importantly, his motivations for them. Therefore, special thanks go to his cousin, Sabine Bishop Klaus; the Rastatt historian, Irmgard Stamm; Erftstadt and Liblar historian, Dr. Frank Bartsch; Don Heinrich Tolzmann; Gerd Winard-Meyer; Hans and Charlotte Arndt for translation help; Yogi Reppmann; Fred Ulfers; and my good wife, Thea, for all their support and patience.

# 1

# Introduction

Separating the public figure from the private man of this nineteenth-century giant is difficult and, at the same time, intriguing. Carl Schurz was either politically praised or reviled. His contemporaries and colleagues wrote about him in a complimentary or uncomplimentary way depending on the situation; with each little bit of information, more of a portrait of the man emerges. The need, therefore, is to place Schurz in his time and place while looking for the man and not the one-dimensional cartoon character drawn by his political enemies. His actions were very much those of a reformer who did not care what others thought of or about him—at least, not publicly.

The *Diary of William Steinway* (a close friend), the letters of Abraham Jacobi (probably more like a brother), and Schurz's letters to his girlfriend, Fanny Chapman, reveal more of the personal side of his life. Other accounts of Schurz's "doings" by Henry Adams, Mary Chapman Lawrence, Lilli de Hegermann-Lindencrone, Mark Twain, James Michener, and Booker T. Washington relate the humor, artistry, and passion missing from the newspaper articles and political and professional writings.

The task, therefore, was to assemble clues to his character and make-up. What was behind the stern stentorian aspect that was pictured to the world in art and statuary? Carl Schurz performed on the largest stage in the world, spanning two continents and the terms of twelve American presidents. He met kings and queens, prime ministers, generals, Native American chiefs, musicians, educators, pioneer medical men, and the Gilded Age millionaires. Yet he remains just a name on a park and in some books, denigrated as a Civil War general who ran with his troops to the rear. Where are the man and his nature behind the professional mask of his writings? Who was he?

His works, and speeches, printed after he died, encompass ten volumes. Although Schurz had started a three-volume autobiography (*Erinnerung*), he did not live to finish it. He wrote the first volume in German at Bolton Landing,

New York, when he was seventy-six years old, in which he self-admittedly reported a memory gap for some of his reminiscences. He had them translated into English by Eleonora Kennecott, whose husband, Frank, was the president of the Association of American Physicians and the head of Columbia Presbyterian Hospital in New York. Both Eleonora and Frank, members of New York Society's upper crust, were fluent in German. After Schurz's death, his daughter, Agathe, carefully combed through and edited, and omitted from the German text, snippets of information that she thought would be detrimental to his memory and legacy. There are no letters included from his children. Frederic Bancroft, who edited all six volumes of Carl Schurz's letters and speeches, admittedly deleted the "personal references" including greetings salutations and intimate notes. His papers were published in 1913, seven years after his death. They were carefully edited to remove personal material between the copyright of 1906 and the release for publication in 1908; the work itself was then published seven years later by his son, Carl Lincoln Schurz. The major biography by Hans L. Trefousse, written in 1982, relies heavily on the earlier works. New information, including writings about and by Schurz, including some of his more intimate letters, have been found in the last few years; these, hopefully, will reveal a better picture of the motivations and ideals that drove him.

The formality of the manners in the writing spanning from the Civil War until the end of the nineteenth century hides the persona of the writer and the recipient. Soldier's wartime letters written to families from the battlefield address the wife as "Mrs." and are signed with a full signature, not a nickname or a first name. Men handed *cartes de visite* to the father and mother of the young woman that they were courting. Personality and passion were carefully shielded from family members, particularly among the wealthy. Carl Schurz's "intimate letters" published in 1929 omit the salutation in every instance. In addition, as is the case in many historical documents, fire plagues the researcher; Carl Schurz's ephemera and personal possessions were lost in a railroad fire in Detroit in 1866, and his souvenirs perished. After his death, a fire consumed a summer home of his friend Dr. Abraham Jacobi, destroying everything related to their friendship.

# 2

# Humble Beginnings

*I was born in a castle ...*[1]

Carl Schurz was born March 2, 1829, in Liblar, Germany, which was then, as it is now, a quaint Rhineland town with a single main street winding through its middle. The small weekly market is held in the parking lot of strip mall right in front of the "Carl Schurz Grill," in Erftstadt-Liblar. He was baptized in the Catholic Church of St. Barbara as Carl (with a "C") Christian Schurz. His mother, Marianne (born Jüssen), gave birth to him in a second-story room, not in the castle, as he wrote in his autobiography, but in the servants' quarters facing Count Metternich's *Schloss*, which still dominates the town with its presence. The outbuilding housed cows, horses, farmhands, servants and the estate manager's family. The site of the castle dates from the middle 1400s; today, it is a business school for executive training operated as a branch of the University of Berlin.

The actual building in which Carl Schurz was born is now the hotel Schloss Gracht, which has retained many of the original features of earlier days. In his autobiography, Schurz described the complex:

A large compound of buildings under one roof, surrounding on three sides a spacious courtyard, tall towers with pointed roofs, and large iron weather vanes at the corners that squeaked when moved by the wind; a broad moat always filled with water, encircling the whole, and spanned by a drawbridge which led through a narrow arched gateway into the court. In the wall above the massive gate, which was studded with bigheaded nails, there was a shield bearing the Count's coat of arms, and an inscription which I puzzled out as soon as I could read, and which has remained in my memory through all vicissitudes of my life.

*In the old days in Hessenland*
*I was called the Wolf of Gutenberg;*
*Now by the Grace of God,*
*I am Count Wolf Metternich of the Gracht*[2]

The entrance and the moat surrounding the castle complex are intact; the portcullis is closed at night. A light shines on the Count's crest over the entranceway. Schurz's childhood memories of the castle are fragmented and disconnected. He was raised in the castle's operating offices, outfitted for cooking, cleaning, laundry, and livestock. The rings for the horses' harnesses are still mounted on the cement columns in the modern bar, which were the stables in Schurz's day; the large family room was adjacent to the horse barn, where the farmhands and family ate with wooden spoons, three-pronged forks, and their own pocketknives.

Christian Schurz, Carl's father, served in the army as a conscripted soldier in the Napoleonic Wars, arriving at the Waterloo battlefield the day after Wellington defeated Bonaparte. He married Marianne Jüssen, the daughter of the "Burghalfen," or manager of Count Metternich's estate.[3] Christian Schurz was the village of Liblar's schoolmaster; although it was a prestigious position, it was a poorly paying job. The newlyweds had to move in with Marianne's parents at the castle. Carl's father was a product of the Prussian educational institutions implemented in 1748, requiring compulsory education, but also keeping teacher training closely connected with the Church. The German education system remains the same today, with the traditional German *Abitur* as a culminating examination for completion of studies.

Carl's mother, Marianne (Jüssen), was raised on the Metternich's farm estate and her education was at the Parish School of the Catholic Church. She could read and write and took an active part in the chores of the daily mechanics of the large estate that bred her skill of common sense and organization. Her son saw her as a bright ray of hope and love supported by a strict moral character that never produced any trait but modesty, virtue, and kindness. She married Christian later in life; she was thirty years old and her husband was thirty-two. They had started the family immediately, with Carl the eldest, followed by Heribert a year later, and then two girls, Anna and Antoinette. Schurz wrote of his mother: "Whether in the blossom time of her life she would have been called beautiful we never knew, but her countenance was to us all love and goodness and sunshine."[4] She sang as she worked about the house, and, according to Schurz's sister, "Toni" Schurz's musical talent came from her.[5]

Schurz lived in the shadow of the castle for four years, until his father, concerned with the family finances and the close living quarters with his in-laws, moved up the street into the town of Liblar. The schoolmaster's salary was not sufficient to support a large family; therefore, he rented living space and opened a hardware store in his house. Young Carl often visited his grandparents in the castle, which was a short distance from his home. The town of Liblar, today, paired with Erftstadt, has only the one main street, which is a short walking distance from any part of the town. The local Romantic setting fueled the imagination of a boy in those years to dreams of knights, jousting, and fair maidens in distress

3

# The Education of
# a Revolutionary Romantic

*The source of genius is imagination alone, the refinement of the senses that sees
what others do not see, or sees them differently.*

Eugène Delacroix

The years in the eighteenth century preceding Carl Schurz's birth produced revolutions not only in a national and military sense but also in art, politics, and music. "Romanticism and Revolution" was a new theme inspired by the American and French Revolutions, which was nurtured by political unrest across Europe. The artists and writers embraced a rejection of Neoclassicism and the rational ideal of Enlightenment. More simply stated, the artistic community in all genres believed that the senses and emotions, and not only reason and order, were important in understanding and experiencing the world. The French Revolution caused the quest for freedom, equality, and justice, all of which were part of the formational structure of the relatively new United States of America; it also spurred an interest in nationalism, as well as in intellectual and individual freedoms.

Revolutions in religion continued to foster an increased rejection of the organization and structure of the church; connections with God were found in nature and beauty where faith in a deity was relegated to the acceptance of a higher pantheism or finding God in nature. Many artists and philosophers believed that the "noble savage" was the purest most unspoiled person that walked the earth.

The most famous advocate of this movement in Germany was Johann Wolfgang von Goethe, whose novel *The Sorrows of Young Werther* became a model for tales of the young man detached from society who dies for an impossible love.[1] Goethe wrote of his friend the South German poet, Friedrich Schiller: "Yet the tocsin of Liberty and Nationality had been sounded in Germany to Schiller during the Napoleonic Wars."[2] Schiller's two dramas—*The Robbers* and *William*

*Tell*—were all about the individual in conflict with the law and the Romantic ideal of individual liberty and nationalism.[3]

Carl Schurz was born into this intellectual climate; however, the idea that a boy of humble and relatively poor beginnings could not be educated both academically and artistically did not apply in his case. Although he grew up in a small town, and apparently had no connection to higher education, the boy's family embodied a respect for learning and art. Schurz's mother, though minimally educated, was described by her son as "a woman of excellent mental qualities—in a high degree sensible, of easy and clear perception and discernment." He said the chief strength of her character "lay in her moral nature." She was a devout Roman Catholic and inculcated this strict moral character in her young son.

Carl Schurz's father was from the pre-Enlightenment school of learning. He took his son with him to the village school, where Schurz was the teacher even when the boy was a toddler. Carl wrote that he never remembered learning how to read or write, although it was very early in his life that he did. After a year, and after his father left his position as a schoolmaster, plans were made for Carl's formal education; initially, he would attend the village school until he was ready for the *Gymnasium*. However, the education that he garnered from his family and from his surroundings influenced his thinking and character for the rest of his life.

His father believed that all his children should study music and, therefore, found a "queer little piano" for him, which had no pedals or damper. It was good enough for learning the keyboard and Carl thought it beautiful. The teacher was another matter; since the local organist was not competent to teach, the boy had to walk 4–5 miles to his father's hometown of Brühl twice a week for lessons. Carl's younger brother, Heribert, later joined him later. The brothers, a year and two months apart in age, were close companions, traveling through their boyhoods in the tiny town, which was, as Schurz wrote later, void of intellectual stimuli.[4] Their father bombarded them with his literary heroes. Any books that he could find, and which he read voraciously, were shared with his sons. Even if they were too young to understand them, the exposure to Becker's *Universal History* and to translations of Voltaire and Rousseau stayed with Schurz for his whole life.[5]   The images of heroes danced in the heads of many boys before the days of film and video games; a vivid imagination created pictures of the mighty heroes and independent fighters for right. Carl Schurz was no different; his boyhood pictures of literary legends were the beginnings of an incurable German Romanticism enhanced by his father reading to him; When he had the measles, for example, his father read the poems and dramas of Schiller, adding more "heroes" to his fertile imagination.

His mother's four brothers, who visited the house regularly, regaled him with military tales of valor and bravery; they were living "Romantic influences". They were called "*Ohm*," from the old High German word "*oheim*" for a maternal uncle; each one was over 6 feet tall and had different occupations in the area.

Uncle Peter had served in a French Grenadier regiment during the last years of Napoleon's reign; he had married the daughter of a "*Halfen*" (old term for overseer or deputy) and became a "*Halfen*" of a large estate in Lind near Cologne. Uncle Ferdinand was the superintendent of a peat works belonging to Count Metternich; he lived in Liblar and had been a lieutenant in the *Landwehr* in the Prussian Military. When he appeared in his uniform with a giant "shako" hat, he was the living image of a small boy's "superhero." Although a military man, he was also a "free thinker, a Voltairian," who belonged to one of the oldest Freemason Lodges in Germany, which was rumored to be practicing "devil worship." This connection made him more mysterious and fascinating for the younger children. He never went to church on Sunday, even in a devout family led by Schurz's mother.

Uncle Jacob, the *Bürgermeister* of the nearby town of Jülich, brought gifts and stories to the family. The youngest brother was Uncle Georg, who had served in a Berlin regiment of cuirassiers and lived with his father to help with the castle affairs. Schurz called these uncles, who brought him fantastic tales from the outside world, a "tall stately group."[6] They encouraged a path of personal independence and morality. They were his early boyhood heroes.

Little Carl was taken to the castle daily, even after the family moved out of it; he became his grandfather's favorite helper and was allowed to play hunter with an old flintlock rifle in the large serving house. He learned firsthand the life of a farmer, and most importantly, to him, that of a hunter—at least in his imagination. A tragic paralytic stroke turned his hero grandfather into an old unhappy man confined to an armchair in front of a window from which he continually tried to run the estate. The "old man" was left to content himself by spreading sugar on the arm of his chair and killing the flies that were attracted to it. His only joys were the visits from his grandson who listened avidly to the tales of the "French Times" (when the Rhineland was governed by the French, 1794–1813). It was here that Carl learned of the Napoleonic era and the invasion of the Cossacks and the Napoleonic armies; he would ask to hear these stories over and over again, claiming, later in life, that these tales were connected to the future history of Germany, and more importantly, they were the foundation to his later political life and beliefs.

When he was six years old, Schurz's idyllic boyhood of tales of "derring-do," hunting, and history ended. His father was a stern taskmaster, even for his own children; now in the hardware business, he focused on the education of his boys. Carl could read and write at a very early age; he was also informed that his educational path would be through the *Gymnasium* and then the university. He continued music lessons, singing and walking to Brühl with an occasional ride from the postman; Heribert was a blond contrast to the red-headed Schurz, and he was more interested in plants and the outdoors than his studious brother was; therefore, the family decided he would be a trained gardener. They stayed out of trouble and harm's way, only straying once when they secretly drank too much wine at a funeral celebration and had to be carried home, which Schurz wrote gave him a "loathing for drunkenness."

Education continued with a strong background in Classical and Romantic literature. His father hung portraits of the south German poet, physician, and philosopher Friedrich von Schiller; his friend, Johann Wolfgang von Goethe; novelist Christopher Martin Wieland; soldier poet Theodor Körner; sixteenth-century Italian poet Torquato Tasso; and William Shakespeare in the living room of the "new" house. Schurz recalled, "Poets, historians and scientists" were his father's heroes. He heard stories from folklore, legends, and mythology from the library in Brühl. He was told of the Emperor Octavian of Rome, the *Four Sons of Haimon* by Tieck, and of the German hero Roland. The Count's old head gardener, "*Herr Gartner*," gave him a copy of *Robinson Crusoe* by Daniel Defoe, and it became his favorite book. Years later, he could picture the binding, the woodcut illustrations, and the ink spots in the cheap edition he had read and reread as a boy.

Eduard Breier's *Der Landwehrmann*, a popular history of the War of Liberation of 1813, combined with the family military history, turned Schurz, as he wrote, into a "fiery German patriot."[7] The effect of Schiller's *Sturm und Drang* and poetry (which questioned personal liberty, power, and the fight between good and evil) read to them by his father was joined by the family circle's fascination with America. The talk of the town was that a Liblar family emigrated there complete with a village farewell to them as their wagon loaded with trunks and boxes.

Carl's father believed that George Washington, whose portrait and biography appeared in the December 17, 1842, edition of *Das Pfennig-Magazin: der Gesellschaft zur Berbreitung gemeinnütziger Kenntnisse,* was "the noblest of men in all history."[8] *The Penny Magazine* arrived weekly on Sundays; the Schurz family used it to discuss their admiration for George Washington leaving the presidency and returning to the life of a simple farmer. They became obsessed with the American way of life that they imagined as a "log cabin romance."

The small village of Liblar was an island of serenity in a chaotic world. To Carl Schurz, it was a Romantic, Grimm's fairy tale setting. Many of the local "characters" told wondrous tales to the young boy, exposing him to philosophy, history, and religion. Schurz remembered those who influenced him, as many do, and perhaps the memory was colored by the passing of the years, but the mark made on him remained for life.

Georg van Bürk was a messenger forced into a menial job by failing eyesight, ending his career as a shoemaker. He befriended young Carl. He delivered and chatted whenever employed by Carl's father. He was self-educated and had very quaint and odd ideas, but everyone liked him. In the face of a very devout Roman Catholic population, Master Georg, as he was called, argued, "Why if we are to believe blindly and never think for ourselves, did the all wise Creator give us our reason?" He went as far as to tell the youngster to avoid the priesthood. He also told him stories about witches and ghosts that the boy knew were untrue; however, this was shaky knowledge in a town where superstitions were believed and accepted. It was here, however, that Schurz got his "picture" of a philosopher, seen via Master Georg who looked like a "queer" old man wearing a tri-cornered hat and a monocle. He had a large library in his home that villagers called a "haunted deserted house."[9] The impression was so strong that Schurz saw, in his mind's eye, this image whenever the word or term "philosophy" appeared. The most important lesson Carl learned was to keep sight of a "beautiful" world. Master Georg could have cried and tormented himself over his unfortunate lot, but instead, he preached of the pleasures that life gives and not the sufferings. "In fact all that was required for earthly happiness was a few wants and a good conscience."[10]

Carl Schurz's tolerance of minorities and people of "difference" started in his early childhood. The irony lies in the fact that he lived during a small-minded intolerant period in which the women of his circle were devout Catholics while many of the men tended to offer lip service to the church, pursuing the freethinking spirit of the age. The youngster repeatedly heard from the pulpit that the Catholic religion was the "only saving one," and that all of different beliefs including Protestants, Jews and heathens, were "hopelessly condemned to everlasting Hell fire."[11] Only one Protestant passed though Liblar in those days, who the children knew was doomed. There was one Jew in the village: the neighborhood butcher. Another Jew named Aaron, from a neighboring town, visited Carl's father and talked with him in a friendly fashion. When the boy asked about him, the father replied that he was a good and honest wise man, more honest than many a Christian. The youngster, now about six and a half years old, was further troubled when his father read Lessing's *Nathan the Wise* to him which taught a lesson of tolerance. These experiences began to shake his faith in the organized church and were only the beginning of issues with religion. Carl Schurz, the choirboy, went to Mass regularly but could not, even at a young age, reconcile the conflict between the "true" church and tolerance of those outside of it.

The happy and idyllic years of boyhood end for every man, and in this young boy's village life, there was a very sudden change in his ninth year. It started when the schoolmaster in Liblar, who had replaced his father, was accused of "taking illicit liberties" with one of his female students (one of Schurz's cousins). The girl reported the event to her mother, brothers, and sister. They believed her. The Parish priest and the Count did not. The disagreement caused an irreparable schism between the extended Schurz family and the townspeople that supported the innocence of the teacher. The arguments grew in intensity and both parties came to blows, causing a bloody riot. Schurz recalled the event as his first exposure to "revolution" and, even as a choirboy, the start of his questioning the teachings of organized Catholicism.

# Early End to Boyhood
# The Dark Years (1838–1840)

During 1838, the schoolmaster left the town in disgrace. Although Carl was only nine years old, his father decided that Liblar was providing an insufficient education for his son. The local lower school was allowed to give younger students a grade for trying hard even if they were not capable of success; however, that system and weaker instruction motivated Christian Schurz to send his son to Brühl to a "model" school connected to a teacher training facility. The journey was about a 10-mile round trip, and young Carl was expected to walk to the house of a butcher's widow where he stayed during the colder months; in the summer, he made the trip daily. He was to be "first" in each class—not only in the "first chair" in each subject, but he was expected to be the student with the highest grade. German schools, even today, use a six-point grading system where "one" is excellent (*sehr gut*) and "six" is insufficient (*ungenügend*). Carl's father demanded that he achieve the first seat for each subject and that only the grade of excellent would suffice.

On one occasion, Schurz, although in that first seat, only achieved a grade of *gut* (two). When he reached home to tell his father, he hid for a whole day before he could confess his "failure." "You failed to do your duty and you tried to conceal the truth from me; don't you think that you deserve a whipping?" said his father. Carl consented but begged that the punishment be meted out in the more private "cow stable" so that no one else would be aware of his "shame."

The blows from his father's punishment were insignificant compared to "another heavy blow." His little brother and companion, Heribert, was dead. The boy, perfectly healthy on Monday, suffered and died at 5 p.m. on Thursday evening. His death was caused by "pneumonia" and sadly, he probably had contracted bronchitis, which was often mistaken for the fatal lung infection. Heribert was seven and a half years old. His father had traveled to Brühl to tell Carl the sad news and to walk home with him to Liblar. Schurz remembered:

For a long time I could not console myself over this loss. Whenever, I was alone in the woods I would call my brother loudly by name, and pray God, if he would not give him back, at least allow his spirit to appear to me.[1]

The lonely walk between towns became a literary refuge for the ten-year-old boy who had conquered the skill of walking and reading at the same time. His book of choice was the poems of Friedrich Gottlieb Klopstock, whose difficult, epic work, *Der Messias (The Messiah)*, was one of the elder Schurz's required readings. It is a poem of redemption and Christian mythology, modeled after John Milton's *Paradise Lost*, which was read and reread by young Carl on his journey from home to school. His father ordered other poems committed to memory. He learned Christoph August Tiedge's *Urania* über *Gott, Unsterblichkeit und Freiheit*, a poem inspired by the ethics of Immanuel Kant on the rights and wrongs of actions fulfilling a duty. He added verse after verse of poems by Christian Fürchtegott Gellert, a writer whose poetry was an attempt to raise religious and moral character; Johann Gottfried Herder, a Romantic revolutionary; Gottfried August Bürger, a German balladeer famous for his poem *Lenore*; August Friedrich Ernst Langbein, a German humorist; and Carl Theodor Körner, one of his father's favorites. The motivation of this rote learning was twofold: one as preparation for the *Gymnasium* and the other for a performance. His father found a local hall where the ten-year-old boy was required to recite his memorized poetry with proper emphasis for an audience. It was here in Liblar that Schurz began training for his career as an orator. With all the Romantic and revolutionary poetic philosophy committed to memory, speaking became easier and easier for him. In the earlier days of schooling, "reciting" was an art and a skill required of many pupils; the more skilled and less frightened children were frequently paraded for public performance.

The conflict with the old schoolmaster's actions left a permanent communal rift. At the same time, the sixty-nine-year-old Count or *Graf* Maximillian Werner Wolff Metternich zur Gracht, loved by the populace, died in March 1839. His son, Levin Wilhelm Anton Maria Herbert Wolff Metternich zur Gracht, aged twenty-two, took over and began a general removal of the old servants. Schurz's beloved grandfather, *Burghalfen* Heribert Jüssen, and his wife, Anna were relieved of their positions. She died that December, after they moved out of the family housing in the *Schloss*. Her husband joined her on January 1, 1840. Carl Schurz was heartbroken at everything he had lost over that two-year period: his brother, his grandparents, and, most of all, his boyhood.

# Sculpting a Rebel

In the modern world, it is hard to imagine a ten-year-old boy wandering freely in a large city, even for an education; however, at this age, Carl Schurz was taken to the *Dreikönigsgymnasium* in Cologne—informally, the Jesuit *Gymnasium* named after a cleric involvement in 1582. This very old school, founded in 1450, is still operating. It was named after the Three Wise Men who are interred in a golden casket behind the altar of the nearby *Kölner Dom*.

Carl, as much as he had learned memorized and studied, was a country boy who had to be told not to remove his cap to every passerby in the city. He carried his slate under his arm on the first day of school, not knowing that paper and pen were used in the city schools. Naturally, his new schoolmates made fun of him and his mistakes.

He boarded with a locksmith and shared a bed with the locksmith's son. It was a difficult time for him; in the nineteenth century, children were to be seen and not heard. Only the master of the house was supposed to speak. The children were required to remain silent; however, schooling was another matter. Schurz believed that people should not be concerned with what they learn, but rather how they learn, and that they must discover this process on their own. The head of the lower school, Heinrich Bone, a famous German educator and hymn writer, taught young Schurz how to write simply and clearly, which was not the fashion of the day. He shared with the boy stories that he was writing for his *Lesebuch*.[1] Bone encouraged and challenged the youngster's readings, unknowingly influencing the life of his student. Schurz was already acquainted with moral philosophy and could now at an early age apply his earlier studies to the classics and to the writers that helped to formulate his philosophy of the Romantic revolutionary.

He reread Becker's *Universal History* as well as Homer's *Iliad* and *Odyssey*. He wrote that he was inspired to learn Greek so he could read Homer's poetry in the original; however, that study became difficult for him as it does for many who attempt it. Bone assigned Cornelius Nepos: *De Viris Inlustribus,* and Julius Caesar's *Gallic Wars* for him to learn about the history of Ancient Rome.

His host, the stern locksmith, introduced him to the city theater in Cologne. Friedrich Schiller's trilogy *Wallenstein* inspired Schurz to write his own play, choosing the tenth-century Anglo-Saxon King Edwy's love for the beautiful Elgiva and his struggles with St. Dunstan as his focus. His creative urge satisfied, Schurz turned to poetry, helped by Professor Wilhelm Pütz, a professor and author of several works on German and Roman history and ancient geography. He introduced Schurz to Cervantes' *Don Quixote*, the plays of Pedro Calderon de la Barca and Shakespeare, and the complete works of Goethe.

The poetic and literary learning also led Schurz to continue questioning the Catholic Church. He was probably not agnostic, but, like Martin Luther, he was a dissatisfied member of a Church that, in his mind, preached intolerance and eternal damnation to those not in its folds as "true believers." His doubts started when his brother died, and then in the *Gymnasium*, his readings and lifestyle led to a questioning and discussions of faith that were based on the damnation of the classical literary figures. Although he was an enthusiastic and believer at his first communion, the fervor festered within him, leading him to a lifetime of rejection of organized religion.

Family misfortunes only made it worse. His grandparents' ejection from Schloss Gracht, followed by his father's loss of the business in a faulty sale, which landed him in debtor's prison, left Carl without money for tuition or the chance of returning to school. His fall from the town "boy who studied" to loss of his place was earth-shattering to the young man.[2] However, by tutoring, he finally earned enough to continue for a while, working his way to the highest class but one. His uncles would have helped, but they too had fallen on to hard times. Seventeen-year-old Carl was unable to enroll for his last year in school. The family was forced to move to Bonn after his father's creditor was persuaded to help and get his father out of prison.

Christian Schurz came up with a plan that would allow his son to attend classes at the University of Bonn, and then return to the *Gymnasium* to take his final tests, which, although a more difficult path, was possible. Carl did not matriculate at Bonn but he could attend classes there.

During September 1845, Carl Schurz, at home in Liblar, was awaiting the determination of his educational path. His father's financial woes were being settled, and while his fate was being decided, Schurz, like any other sixteen-year-old, was worried about his future. He wrote to his friend, Petrasch, that he was "frittering his life away."[3] This period not only brought unrest to his family but illness to him. He was sick off and on, and the loss of his brother increased his stress. By January 1846, he turned to poetry, but mostly in the self-centered melancholy phase of adolescence. He was depressed because he could not produce the poetry that he desired. He wrote:

'Melancholy (Phantasy)'

*Oppressive fall the burning rays*
*Upon the weary valley ways.*
*The brooklet creeps, and mute the breezes all;*
*Upon their stems the blossoms droop and fall.*
*A single rose, all withered, faint and frail,*
*Looks yearning tow'rd the sky's mysterious*
*darksome pale.*[4]

'Schwermuth (Phantasie)'

*Schwer drückte der Sonne Gluthenstrahl*
*Hernleder, auf das müde Thal.*
*Es schlecht der Bach, und alle Lüfte schweigen,*
*Die Blüthen senken sich an Ihren Zweigen.*
*Und eine Rose, matt und welk bleich*
*Starrt sehnend indes Blau's geheimer dunkles Reich.*

At this point in his young life, Schurz dreamed of becoming a writer of poetry, novels, and dramas. He wrote his versions of literary criticism back and forth to his friend, Theodor Petrasch. He began to smoke cigars when he was sixteen or seventeen years old. In response to one letter, he responded that Petrasch's protestations of melancholy and remorse were self-induced and that he should make life more agreeable to himself. In February 1846, Schurz was suffering from a cold and runny nose again, considering material for his writing "career" including poetry, epics, and retelling of Rhineland legends. His writing, streaked with hyperbole, included grand philosophical statements: "Time is too glorious and youth too fleeting. With it (youth) the heaven aspiring flame sinks, sinks, murkily down in the ashes."[5]

Fervently young Carl, in a letter to his friend in February 1846, questioned the existence of God, which was a topic he could not approach with his very devout Catholic parents. He continued to distrust organized religion, but he also did not deny the existence of God. He believed that everyone carried their morality in their heart, and there was no need to have children "nonsensically recite them." He wrote:

This is my belief, and morality is my religion. I believe the beliefs of all nations and have religion of humanity. Do not speak of the manifold gods of the peoples; their distinction rests merely upon the manner of regarding them upon the stage of development of all nations; and all gods together are but one and the same deity, and the names can all be united under the sublime name "All Father."[6]

Schurz began a *Sorrows of Young Werther* mode, as many a young man in Germany did. Their only concerns were self, school, and mood. However, his depression was real and his situation, both educationally and personally, was filled with anxiety. His father tried to right his financial status by opening a boarding house for students in Bonn, which was not as successful as he might have liked. Both of Schurz's sisters suffered: Anna dropped out of school and Antoinette (Toni) had to help around the inn before and after classes. Carl was confined to a small fourth-floor room, studied for his exams, and wrote his drama and poetry while wallowing in his philosophical, melancholy discussions with Petrasch. Schurz was concerned with finishing his *Gymnasium* final examination and his entrance into the University at Bonn.

During the academic year 1846–1847, he was a "guest student" at Bonn, comparable to "auditing" courses in the American universities. At the same time, he was studying for his *Abitur* in August 1847. He wrote that he passed all his exams and was fortunate that he had memorized Book Six of the *Iliad* for his Greek examination and therefore translated it easily; however, in reality, the examiner reported that his "knowledge of the Greek language is still a bit spotty."

His two friends, Petrasch and Weise, who had already matriculated, helped him to become a member of *Burschenschaft* Frankonia (fraternity), an organization that furthered his Romantic and patriotic ideals. These student societies still exist in the modern German university; in particular, the *Bonner Burschenschaft Frankonia*, to which Carl Schurz belonged, has a website and is still active.

Carl Schurz, in his later memoirs, omits the conflicts and history of the *Burschenschaft* that had occurred before and after his entry into the fraternity. Founded in 1818 and 1819, by the winter of 1819–20, it had 280 members; among them were August Heinrich Hoffmann von Fallersleben and Heinrich Heine. The political conflict at the university was between the Conservatives, who wanted to restore a governmental monarchy, and the Liberals, who wanted to change to democratic constitutional government. Heine and Hoffmann were radical Liberals. They suffered a mandated dissolution of their organization forced by the university. They re-formed as "*Cervesia*" and renamed themselves *Germania*, proudly wearing black red and gold, hiding their colors, to become a secret society because the University formally dissolved them. In 1828, they were restored to their former position. Their new statutes focused on physical and mental educational development by living a morally grounded life. In 1845, the fraternity Franconia was founded as a split of the older units under the leadership of Gottfried Kinkel and his wife, Johanna. They developed it into a radical revolutionary leftist movement in favor of a Germany united by a constitutional democracy. Although Schurz downplayed his role and involvement with this fraternity, it became one of the most important organizations in his life. He was unable to be a full member for the first year because he was a non-matriculated student; all first-year students were novices called a "*Fuchs*" for their term of probation. Once a full member, the "brother' was given a student cap (*Studentenmütze*) and a tri-color ribbon of black, red, and gold worn over the right shoulder, the same one used in the modern German flag, which honors the student movement in the revolution of unification. Schurz's chapter—the Frankonia Unit at Bonn—was not involved with dueling (*Mensur*) and scarring traditions popularly associated with these organizations.

Finally, in the fall of 1847, Carl Schurz could say "*Ich studiere*" at the University of Bonn. Although he still lived at home in newly rented larger family quarters, he entered student life with full vigor. Much of this early happiness does not appear in his later written works, but here are indications of celebrations outside of his studies. He donned the cap and colors of the *Burschenshaft* and went to "*Kegel abends*" (nine pins bowling held in various inns accompanied by much drinking), songfests, and general happy camaraderie. His reddish blonde hair was now long in the student fashion, and he had grown an inch or two in height.

Although he had not been made a member of the *Franconia Burschenschaft*, while he was "auditing" courses, Schurz was able to present some of his writing to the fraternity brothers. He had written a parody on the famous "Leipzig Auerbach's cellar" scene from Goethe's *Faust* (Scene V), which was ready at *Kneipenzeitung* (a university humor publication), which he had read aloud by Petrasch. Both it and he were well-received.

His life changed in many ways after he met Professor Gottfried Kinkel at the beginning of his first full year in 1847. Kinkel began at Bonn, in 1836, as an instructor of church history. While teaching at different universities, he met and married a Catholic divorcee, Johanna Mockel, who had been unhappily married to a Cologne bookseller named Matthieux. Their marriage, and her divorce, forced Kinkel out of his theology professorship at Bonn: however, he was reinstated as a professor of culture and art.

Kinkel was a thirty-two-year-old popular pedagogue when Schurz first met him. He was a living symbol of the Romantic ideal; he was tall, beautifully spoken, with a mellifluous voice. He charmed the students; his "Art of Speech" classes were always full. Mrs. Kinkel was, as Schurz put it, "not at all handsome, since she was somewhat masculine with a sallow complexion" and did not understand "the art of dressing." She was, however, an expressive, highly intelligent woman who could hold her own in conversation with anyone. She was a brilliant musician, having studied with Felix Mendelsohn. An impressionable Carl Schurz worshipped the philosophical discussions presented in the warm intellectual circle of the Kinkel home. He kept at his studies and writings, determined to be a poet or playwright, working on a tragedy about Ulrich von Hutten, a fifteenth-century scholar, poet, satirist, and reformer. As a critic of the Church, and an Imperial Knight of the Holy Roman Empire, he represented a humanist in a medieval world to young Carl, who at this point was considering a personal schism with the high Catholic church. He found a literary friend in Friedrich Althaus of Detmold, who listened to his writing ideas with great interest and later continued as a German literary critic and translator of Charles Dickens' works. The intellectual world of a university can become an "ivory tower" isolated from the world outside of it. Bonn was no different; however, in February 1848, as Schurz had finished his *magnum opus*, word reached from the streets below that Louis Phillippe had been overthrown and France had been proclaimed a republic.[7]

This new republic, in the young German men's minds, was a duty call for the unification of the "Fatherland" into one country, with a national parliament, demands for civil rights and liberties with free press, the right of free assembly, equality before the law, elected representatives, and the right to carry arms. These ideals were student dreams and in their peculiar concept of the real world, the town of Bonn was turned into a "party in the streets" to celebrate the French Republic. Other cities and towns, separated from University life were rumbling with discontent. Arrests and disturbances happened in Koblenz, Düsseldorf, Aachen, Krefeld, Cleves, and other towns on the Rhine. In the southern German towns of Baden, Hesse, Nassau, Württemberg, and Bavaria, demonstrations erupted, causing some success of raising the awareness of the rulers. Bloody violence in the streets of Vienna proclaimed the downfall of Prince Metternich. The Prussian cities of Breslau, Königsberg, and Frankfurt an der Oder sent deputies to Berlin to beg the king to give in to the populace's demands.

Meanwhile, on March 18, the students of Bonn held a mass demonstration led, in a flashing dashing fashion by Professor Kinkel, who wore the tricolor colors (black, red, and gold) in open display to a cheering mob of students. Kinkel spoke passionately in the market square of Bonn about a new German unity and equal rights for all. The crowd, cheering and yelling, burst forth with the tricolors all over the town. Schurz wrote, "In no time the city was covered with black-red-gold flags, and not just the *Burschenschaften*, but almost everyone soon wore the black-red-golden cockade on cap or hat."[8] This was a definitive life-changing event for nineteen-year-old student Schurz.

The happiness of independence was short-lived; the rumors that the King of Prussia, Frederic William IV, ordered troops to fire on the "rebels," turning the streets of Berlin into a blood bath were found to be true. On the afternoon of March 18, the people of Berlin had gathered in the square of the royal palace, ready for a victory party; instead, the King from his balcony, as far as anyone could tell, ordered the military to fire on the crowd. A bloody riot ensued. Barricades were erected, and the conflict took to the streets. After failed promises from the monarch, the battle ended on March 19, when the citizens captured high commander General Möllendorf and held him hostage. A peace was negotiated, which included the army's retreat from Berlin, freedom of the press, and the creation of a Prussian democratic constitution.

The demonstrations were not over. A silent processional from all parts of Berlin approached the royal palace. The people marching were carrying the bodies of the 180-murdered citizenry on litters high above the heads of the crowd which were then placed in long rows in front of the "*Stadtschloss*," where the crowd of crying, yelling, and weeping people called for the King. When he appeared, they shouted for him to remove his hat, and as if on cue, a single bass voice from the crowd started the old hymn "*Jesus meine Zuversicht*" ("Jesus: My Refuge").

The consummation of the deaths and the riot was a graveside funeral service, with the King (garbed in the black, red, and orange of the revolutionaries) declaring that he wanted nothing more than a "constitutional and unified Germany."[9] The students were excited, and on the campus of the University of Bonn, quite by accident, Carl Schurz began his "political" career. First, at an assembly in the Aula, the great hall of Bonn, at a student meeting, Schurz felt compelled to enter a "debate" with the pro-Prussian monarchist Constitutional Civic Association. Caught in the fervor of the moment, he made his first public speech, which was highly complimented by Professor Friedrich Wilhelm Ritschl, one of the leaders of the opposition, who thought him brilliant.[10] However, at nineteen years old, Schurz was too young for the coming German Parliament.

In 1842, the students had been confronted with a government official, Moritz August von Bethmann-Hollweg, appointed to watch over the student activities of the University.[11] He was a "born again" right-wing Christian, opposed to any concept of democracy and as a result was highly unpopular with the students, who organized an impromptu protest meeting at the Bonn riding academy. Later on, when Schurz was elected president of the Democratic Club because of his earlier speech in the Aura, the students voted to ask the higher officials to remove Bethmann-Hollweg. According to Schurz's memory, the men in the meeting ("seven or eight hundred strong") marched to the house of the Rector Friederich Calker, carrying a petition demanding the removal of the "*Regierungsbevollmächtigter*" (government authority).[12] The demonstration caused Bethmann-Hollweg to resign. The petition was well received; Schurz had developed a leadership and an oratorical reputation with his fellows and cemented a closer relationship with Kinkel. The event turned Schurz away from poetry and drama, instead heading toward political and historical studies. He helped organize a radical democratic club (*Demokratische Verein*), serving as a platform for the "Constitutionalists" who were opposed by Conservatives seeking the slow restoration of order and authority. Professor Johann Wilhelm Löbell, a German historian, was the faculty advisor.[13] The club's offshoot was the development of a newspaper under the aegis of Kinkel, with Schurz as a writer, called the *Bonner Zeitung*. This newspaper was distributed by students locally once or twice a week. On July 13, 1848, at a meeting of the Central Citizen's Assembly, Schurz's Democrats defeated a conservative motion to instruct the delegates of an upcoming Frankfurt Assembly to oppose Republicanism.

This journalistic venture and political success were the start of a long writing career and joined with his introduction to oratory, the nineteen-year-old had unwittingly started his journey. It almost ended before it was in full swing when, in March 1848, there was a revolt in Schleswig-Holstein, where the populace was trying to join the German Federation and separate itself from Danish Rule. Schurz immediately started packing to join the large number of students joining up with volunteer organizations to go to the embattled area. Kinkel stopped him, believing that the new German Parliament would recognize Schleswig-Holstein and that Schurz would serve better at the University. Kinkel was right. Seriously wounded student volunteers returned to the University from Schleswig-Holstein; one of them, Adolph Heinrich Strodtmann, became a friend of Schurz's for life and went on to become one of the literary lights of nineteenth-century Germany.[14]

The political maneuvers, fights, conflicts, and ideals were complicated; students and faculty alike supported factions. These were tenuous times of political unrest spurred on by Romantic ideals and ideas; Germany was being torn apart, causing politically minded students to debate, demonstrate, and drink. The University of Bonn had seen the presence of Karl Marx, Friedrich Nietzsche, and now Carl Schurz, who stepped into an academic potboiler of conflicting political philosophies.

Schurz's political star continued to rise as he began to speak publicly more and more. His public recitals in Liblar alongside Kinkel's tutelage in public speaking classes contributed to his propulsion into prominence in the university community. He must have been impressive. His friend and fellow student Friedrich Spielhagen used him as a model (Wolfgang) in his novel, *Die von Hohenstein*.

In the summer of 1848, Schurz, now often neglecting his studies, and Kinkel traveled to Cologne for a Congress of "democratic associations" where he remained, as he says a "shy and silent observer." This meeting was called by the Cologne Democratic Society and the Cologne Workers Association on August 13 and 14, 1848. By this time, the club members were addressing each other as "citizen" in the fashion started by the French Revolutionaries and were very conscious of equality in the communities. Schurz first encountered Karl Marx here, when he was planning secession from the clubs to form his own.[15] He wrote: "I have never met a man whose bearing was so provoking and intolerable. To no opinion which differed from his own did he accord the honor of even condescending considerations."[16] Schurz's view of Marx was clouded by his friendship with Kinkel, who hated Karl Marx as much as Karl Marx hated him.

The political and revolutionary climate of all of Germany became very confusing, if not active and disturbing. Carl Schurz was caught right in the middle of the conflicting factions at the university, at the same time enjoying his role as a "student revolutionary" who was received well in the towns nearby. He made a long trip on behalf of the student organization he had been chosen to represent. He left on a journey up the Rhine to Eisenach, filled with hope until he heard of the revolt in Frankfurt and the King's complete turnaround, bending to pressure from other European powers to conclude a truce with Demark called the Treaty of Malmö. The victorious German troops in Schleswig-Holstein were to be withdrawn, and the duchy would lose its own government; it would instead have to be overseen by a commission composed of two Prussians, two Danes, and a fifth member selected by the new organization, which would eventually govern the entire state. The assembly of Schleswig-Holstein protested, which caused a reaction across the country. The National Parliament in Frankfurt resolved on September 5, 1848, to refuse recognition of the so-called "Truce," but after this initial rejection, and to avoid repercussion from the Prussian Government, the body reversed its stance and resolved further to now support the Treaty of Malmö Treaty. The decision caused an immediate reaction and the area surrounding Frankfurt was filled with inflammatory speeches encouraging mass meetings and fueling the citizen's anger, calling the members of the Frankfurt Parliament traitors to a Republican Germany. Armed "democratic" troops tried to get the Parliament to overturn the latest ruling or to drive out those that supported it. There were moments of bloody violence on the streets of Frankfurt following the parliament's decision. There was a mass demonstration on September 17, 1848, which was led by a "leftist" member of the parliament: Dr. Franz Heinrich Zitz. the head of the Mainz Militia who declared the Conservatives were traitors to the fatherland, freedom, and honor. The next day, there was further violence when a mob went looking for *Reichsminister* Heckscher and Prince Felix Lichnowsky.[17] The Prince was elected to the national parliament in 1848 and was a right-wing conservative who supported the Treaty of Malmö. On September 18, he took General von Auerswald to meet the troops coming from Württemberg; on the way, he met a mob on the Bornheimer Highway who recognized him. The two men were chased and finally captured on a dead-end garden path where Auerswald was shot to death and the Prince was beaten so severely that he died the next day.

On his way to Eisenach, young Schurz passed through the bloody streets of Frankfurt, through remaining barricades and military bivouacs. Later historians and accounts, including that of Schurz himself, minimized the dangers that this young student reformer encountered. His was not the Romantic crusade for justice and right, but he was on a very bloody and divided path for German unity. The three factions of the political parties remained in conclave in St. Paul's Church in daily sessions when he arrived and he decided, along with friends, to attend one.

Schurz described the major players in this drama. Joseph von Radowitz, whose "finely chiseled face, somewhat oriental in character, looked like a sealed book containing the secret of reactionary politics" was on the far right representing the Prussian concept of unification under a monarchy.[18, 19] In the center was Heinrich von Gagern, president of the assembly, representing a moderate faction, which encouraged the formation of a parliament under the control of the Grand Dukes.[20] He had an "imposing stature and heavy eyebrows," wrote Schurz. On the far left was the "Silenus Head Robert Blum," who was a virtual early communist and spokesperson against ethnocentrism.[21] Finally, he saw "the little shriveled figure of the old poet Ludwig Uhland."

The great hall in Frankfurt's St. Paul's Church was used for the Parliament because of its size and central location. The original structure, lost to Allied bombing during the Second World War, has been reconstructed, retaining the large room with the flags of every modern German state lining the walls. Today, it houses events including the award of the Peace Prize of the German Book Trade during the Frankfurt Book Fair. In the museum surrounding the hall, there are exhibits demonstrating a timeline and display of the history and events in the original building, while the outer wall of the church contains plaques commemorating the 1848 assembly, which was Carl Schurz's first exposure to the conflicting revolutionary factions.

The speakers, although in disagreement, provided an overview of the politics of the time. The long-haired, colorfully dressed student revolutionaries of the *Burschenschaft* took it all in and moved on to the friendly town of Eisenach and a student Congress there in September 1849.

Schurz's recollection of the gathering was a fond one, happily telling of the good times and progress he felt that the congress made by uniting all the university societies towards the common cause of German national unification. He was elected president of his chapter of the "brotherhood" and proposed a local administrative code in Bonn. This journey remains a bit of a mystery; the accounts and letters are focused on the good times in Eisenach and very briefly mention the presence of the Prussian Military. When the students reached Wartburg on their return, they encountered a rally, featuring political speeches and a Prussian Military presence joining the celebrating crowd. The celebration continued into the next day; Schurz began to worry about the effect of it with the consequences of officers watching a demonstration that attracted the lower ranks. The "guardsmen" had to be convinced that this was a lighthearted student party and there had been no harm to anyone.

However, these were dangerous and ugly times. Somewhere in the recollection, the absolute horror of an internal conflict is overlooked. The events of the students were leading to a very sad ending without the desired result of a successful change in government and ways of life. On his return home to Bonn, Schurz reflected sadly on the fact that his speech in Eisenach had been published fostering the possibility of a serious set of consequences. It appeared to him, too, that bloody unrest in Austria Hungary and the public mob lynching of the Austrian Minister of War would cause a domino effect across Germany.[22] He was right. In October 1848, the Prussian Constituent Assembly supported the people of Vienna and asked the Prussian Government to help restore peace there to protect the people in the German districts of Austria. After supporting the resolution, the president, General Ernst von Pfuel, was forced to resign by the King who had different ideas. The appointment, by his majesty, of Friedrich Wilhelm Count of Brandenburg as Prussian Minister President and with the help of Interior minister Otto Theodor von Manteuffel, they dissolved the Prussian National Assembly on December 5, 1848.[23, 24] Attempts at keeping the assembly were futile and finally resulted in a tax revolt, which involved the students in Bonn. Schurz minimized his involvement with the overall tax issues, but since students did not pay taxes, he was helping to convince those who did pay to stop. They did this by attacking the tax collectors which led to police actions, because of the student "takeover" of the tax department much like nineteen sixties America where "sit-ins" and "takeovers" were protesting the war in Vietnam. These events produced additional police and military presence. As Schurz became heavily involved, he was paying very little attention to his education.

The educational process was important for more than one reason, as the protection of the student protestors, was insured by the threat, presented to the local authorities, that all the students would leave the city if harmed. Nothing happened and the students in question, including Schurz, could safely come out of hiding, with the hope on the government's part that they would go back to normal. Schurz, now attending lectures on a less frequent basis, continued to edit the *Bonner Zeitung* and to address meetings.

His position in writing of the *Bonner Zeitung* was never clearly defined. Johanna Kinkel, instrumental in the control of the paper, increased her participation when her husband was elected to the King's newly created diet in Berlin. The Kinkels left Bonn, but they sent articles back to the only editor, which was now Carl Schurz. The paper is in the archives of the University of Bonn, but the writers of each of the articles during this time are not identified. This responsibility as an editor and producer of a newspaper marked the beginning of Carl Schurz's full-time journalistic career and marked the end of his academic one.

The political situation in Germany in 1848 and into 1849 was a complicated maze of political idealism, conservatism, and nationalism. The princes of the various German states did not want a united Germany, which under a single monarch would limit the powers of the individual states. The Kaiser wanted a single controlling Emperor of these unified states. The direct opposition to his idea was the National Parliament, a product of the revolutionary movements earlier in the year, which represented the "will of the people" and wanted a fully democratic government. A long debate continued over the creation of a constitution and a leader. The scholars and philosophers in the parliament bogged down its progress with discussion and indecision; however, finally, on March 28, 1849, they declared a hereditary Kaiser as a constitutional head of State and offered the crown to the King of Prussia, Frederick Wilhelm IV. He was never a supporter of a constitutional monarchy, and, much to the populace's chagrin, he turned the offer down. The Kaiser did not support the right of the people to govern or even to be involved in the unification of the German states. He believed that the only way that could happen was by an agreement between the King and the princes. The National Parliament continued to get the states to ratify the constitution that it had prepared. The German people now tired of talk; dissent and intellectual debate spread the ratification from one part of the country to another—first, the Bavarians, through rallies and mass meetings said that they would stand behind the new constitution and then placed a provisional government to replace the King of Bavaria's officers. This action spread to Baden, literally the next-door neighbor, where the state army surrendered to the people in the fortress of Rastatt. A provisional government was formed while the Grand Duke of Baden fled. When the new revolution spread to Saxony, and then to in Dresden, the King of that state appealed to the Prussian Government for aid, which came in the presence of troops and bloody fights in the Dresden streets. Uprisings were suppressed in Berlin and Breslau, and by the time the revolt began in Cologne, the military presence was such that there could be no revolutionary actions. The Prussian army was prepared to deal with revolutionists.

One mistake that the Prussian Government made was to try to mobilize the reservists (*Landwehr*) of the Rhine provinces to quell the uprisings in Bavaria and Baden. These men, aged between twenty-five and thirty-five, were farmers and tradesmen who would have to leave their families to fight in their own country. Instead of going into the army, they started to gather in Bonn and under the leadership of Kinkel, and now Schurz; they held meetings and assemblies to determine what they would do. The decision was to arm and fight the Prussians. Schurz's father attended the Democratic Club meetings and supported his son's decision; his mother, according to Carl, gave him his sword and told him to "use it with honor."[25] Schurz had been instrumental in resisting the mobilization orders and spoke at Neunkirchen and again with Kinkel at another meeting. They decided to arm, mobilize, and attack the armory at Siegburg. They met at 1 a.m.; after saying goodbye to his family in Bonn, Schurz set out to join the revolutionary army up the Rhine in Siegburg. He rowed across the river to join the men who were to attack the arsenal there. The plan met with disaster. Prussian dragoons scattered the would-be rebels without a casualty.

On March 23, 1849, Schurz wrote to Petrasch, about being drafted into the Prussian Army. He had evidently had a physical examination, which measured his height at 5 feet 8.25 inches; he grew taller later. He did not want to leave Bonn and the political activities, and in light of his revolutionary fervor, he did not want to face an army of rebels with the Prussian Army. He asked Petrasch for his father's help to use his connections to postpone his service for three years. Petrasch's father was a stipendiary magistrate in Cologne, who Schurz hoped could help with his cause. Three letters went to the Prussian Government, but there appeared to be no success. There are no letters published from March 27 until July 21, 1848; either he did not write any or they were removed from later collections. There was one note of disagreement between Theodor and Carl in earlier letters, which were about poetry and literary theory. When Petrasch married in Liverpool, England, in 1862, his occupation was listed as a captain in the Prussian Army. It is possible that they were on different sides of the revolution. There are no letters left from Schurz's friend to help understand this conflict of ideas; Petrasch left Germany to settle in New York in 1863 where he met Schurz at different events, although disagreed with him over the election of President Lincoln.

Was Carl Schurz, therefore, a "draft-dodger" or was he excused from the army for three years? The issue is a cloudy one, and later reports of his notoriety of "being" wanted as a revolutionary and a draft-dodger are tangential to his journey and cannot be substantiated but can only be considered supposition. It is during this period that he went into battle with the student-driven revolutionary army. He signed on with an artillery company commanded by Fritz Anneke, who had been dismissed from the Prussian Army for his "democratic" activities.[26] He was a friend of Karl Marx and Friederich Engels; after some jail time in 1848, he formed the company to which Carl Schurz was his adjunct officer.

The objective was to take over the armory in Siegburg; however, this unit was a ragtag outfit constructed of peasants and Democrats, most of them without weapons. Schurz noted that although he was issued a rifle, he had no ammunition. The expedition was destined to failure, and it came to what Schurz called an "unfortunate "and a "ridiculous and disgraceful end." They set out on the ferry over the River Sieg, but they neglected to destroy the ferry on the way over, enabling a small unit of Prussian dragoons reportedly followed them. They were few in number and were not in hot pursuit; however, Anneke halted the revolutionaries and told them to scatter because he believed they would be unable to face trained military. Schurz and his friend, Ludwig Meyer, decided to set out for Elberfeld, where they thought there was fighting and where they could help. To their chagrin, there was nothing going on there but leaderless milling about and a lot of talk. They decided to head for the Palatinate, and after writing home to his parents asking them to send, "necessary things," Schurz wrote that the time he spent with his friends Meyer and Wessel discussing matters was significant, but when they returned home, and he was left alone he felt that his student years were over. "*Die Lehrjahre waren zu Ende, die Wanderschaft begann. Meyer und Wessel fuhren rheinabwärts nach Bonn zurück, ich allein rheinaufwärts nach Mainz.*"[27]

Not only was Carl Schurz's apprenticeship to politics over but so was his university education.

# The Baden Revolution: Escape

After saying goodbye to Meyer and Wessel, Schurz headed up the River Rhine to Mainz to find Kinkel and to see where he could be of use. His professor, however, had already passed through there. The members of the Democratic Club told him that Franz Zitz, in the town of Kircheimbolanden, would know more.[1] He found Zitz, who sent him on to find Kinkel in Kaiserslautern. After a beer in the local *Bierstube*, Kinkel commissioned him to edit the *Bonner Zeitung* while he was there. He followed closely the rumblings of revolutionary activities. Most of the populace realized that all rationale, hope, and negotiations for a unified Germany were no longer possible; demonstrations by angry armed citizens began across the country. In Kaiserslautern, for example, a mass meeting of liberal clubs elected a committee for the "defense of country," which wanted to seize the government of the province by creating an armed force.[2] One argument with the Princes after another led to the mustering of Prussian troops by the very King who had earlier refused the throne of a unified country. The attitude of the kings of Prussia, Bavaria, Hannover, and Saxony made it clear that unity for Germany was to be forgotten or ignored. Unfortunately, the reaction to this action caused more creation and mustering of troops by the citizens of the Palatinate and of Baden-Württemberg. Volunteers in all towns stepped forward for "army service" but had no actual arms. There was a rifle shortage, and an attempt to import guns from Belgium was intercepted by the Prussians. There simply were not enough.

The command of troops that could be formed was left to former Prussian Officers now joined to a "rebel" army. Gustav Adolph Techow (Chief of the General Staff of the Baden Palatinate Army), Friedrich Beust, Alexander Schimmelfennig, and Fritz Anneke took on various commands.[3,4,5] The army was under the general command of General Franz Sznayde, an experienced Polish General and a veteran of Napoleon's army who was, however, a lackluster organizer.[6] His continued efforts created a disorganized mass of confused would-be soldiers.

There was better news in Baden and in Württemberg where the fortress of Rastatt and its munitions were in the hands of the insurrectionists. Schurz wanted to sign up as a private, but Anneke commissioned him as his *aide-de-camp* and a lieutenant in the artillery. His duties were limited and he had time to follow political activities. The army, however, did not look like anything military; most men were in street clothes, with one old uniform spotted here or there. There were, according to Schurz, only maybe a dozen muskets; the rest of the "soldiers" were armed with spears and scythes fastened to the top of poles. Schurz had a pistol in his belt but with no ammunition.

His first task was to arrest a priest who was rallying peasants against the "rebels," doing this with an unloaded gun. Schurz talked the Father into dispersing the crowd, did not arrest him, and took him to the local inn for a drink. The ragged army eventually started to move, via Frankenstein Castle, and on to Neustadt an der Haardt, a Jewish town in the heart of wine country. The residents welcomed them with pails of wine on their doorsteps for the thirsty soldiers. There they met Colonel Blenker and his smarter-looking units.[7] Blenker later reunited with Schurz during the American Civil War, when they were both generals in the Union Army. Eventually, the units were sent into Baden to support other troops there; they arrived in Ubstadt and, for the first time, Schurz faced a real battle. In a later letter, he wrote that he was grazed by a bullet in his shin; the action, considered a skirmish, was dangerous enough. Schurz had just learned to ride and was an adequate equestrian. The next day, his unit engaged the Prussians, again, nearer the town of Bruchsal but was forced to retreat. Schurz was sent, after the skirmish, to get artillery ammunition from the fortress at Rastatt 35 miles away, where the Baden revolutionary forces were fighting their last defensive battle on June 28, 29, and 30, 1849, against larger Prussian forces. Schurz's orders, from Anneke, were to meet him there and observe the battle from a good vantage point. Once inside the barricades, Schurz wearied after the long ride, tied his horse to a cannon wheel, and fell asleep. He awoke at sunset, and went to find Anneke who was not anywhere to be found; Schurz tried to leave but was turned back at the gate because the Prussian troops had surrounded the town. One rebel officer at the gate said to him as he was trying to get out: "I do not belong here, and have tried and have tried all possible points where I thought I might slip through, but all in vain. We have to submit and remain."

Anneke, in charge of a small artillery battalion, was out of communication with the battle raging in Rastatt. Some 13,000 revolutionary forces, under the command of Ludwik Mieronowski, were divided into three divisions of about 4,000 men each; they were lined up on both sides of the river Murg.[8] Fierce fighting with the Prussians ensued, forcing the remaining revolutionaries back into the walls and fortress of Rastatt. At the same time, a smaller part of the rebel forces—under the command of Franz Sigel, Gustav Becker, and August Von Willich—was on the edge of Swiss territory.[9] Any action there would be considered a breach of neutrality by the Swiss; therefore, Von Willich, on July 11, 1849, declared the revolution was over. The news arrived in Rastatt too late for those under the Prussian siege.[10]

The small town of Rastatt has not changed much over the 160 plus years since the battle; its centerpiece is still the pale reddish orange *Schloss* on a hill a block above the town square. The fortress, which was under siege, is further up a slight hill from the castle; it has been replaced by the hotel Bildungshaus St. Bernhard, sponsored by the Catholic Church. There is only one exterior gate to the town still standing near the river. The old *Rathaus* (town hall), from Schurz's day, is at the end of a large market square.

Schurz decided to report to the governor of the fortress. Colonel Gustav Tiedemann found a place for him on his staff and found "officer's quarters" for him in a local *Bäckerei und Konditorei* (bakery/sweet shop) owned and occupied by a revolutionary sympathizer named Gustav Nusser, his wife, Katharina, and their two-year-old son. Schurz's *Bursche* (a fraternity pledge assigned to a brother) named "Adam" had accompanied him to Rastatt.[11, 12] The baker's family welcomed them to a nice room on the second floor overlooking the busy square below. From his window Schurz could see a sprawling array of oddly outfitted foot soldiers sleeping, eating and drinking on the pavement of the crowded market where they were bivouacked.

The next day, Lieutenant Schurz, equipped with a telescope, was assigned to the highest tower in the castle to watch the Prussians who had circled the whole town. His duties included the inspection of gates and the watches until one day, cannon fire besieged the town, and the inhabitants quickly filled the large yard in front of the castle for refuge. A company was sent out to repel the Prussian artillery which they did with success. For three weeks, the town resumed a normal life, until a Prussian officer, under a flag of truce, brought a summons to surrender because the revolutionary army, now in Switzerland, had ceased to exist.

Schurz had known for several days that the situation was hopeless; he wrote and delivered his "noble last letter" to his parents via Gustav Nusser in the bakeshop. This long letter of apology for his actions said:

> Fate has played me a sorry trick, raising the suspicion that our family is been to misfortune. All this, however I saw long ago, if not in all its details, at least in its results. I knew my life would be full of storms and dangers because I was too proud to evade them. But I always imagined that I should die like a man whose memory should encompass a rich life charged with distinguished achievements.
>
> All captured Prussians will be subject to martial law and, according to overwhelming probability, will suffer the penalty of death. Among these am I.[13]

He told them that Kinkel had been sentenced to death in a military court in Karlsruhe. Sadly, his estimate of Prussian retribution came true for ninety-four soldiers who died, were imprisoned, or executed after the surrender. Twenty-six men were captured (with three executed) in Freiburg. Twenty-one men were imprisoned in Mannheim (of which five were executed). In Rastatt, forty-seven officers were captured and twenty-two were executed. Schurz's mentor, Kinkel, was tried for high treason in Freiburg and was sentenced to life imprisonment in a fortress. Schurz's belief that Kinkel was originally sentenced to death was incorrect. However, Schurz, who, if he had not slept, could have left earlier when he could not find Anneke, faced certain imprisonment. His destiny, if captured, was the firing squad because of his newspaper involvement, his status as an officer, and his connection to Tiedemann.

Schurz, when surrender was imminent, stretched out on a couch in the castle, pondering his fate, when a Prussian officer and Otto von Corvin arrived to report that the revolution was officially over.[14] There was to be no negotiation for amnesty or the release of the revolutionaries; the rebel staff discussed their fate: their plans ranged from dying to the last man or unconditional surrender. Finally, after a much-debated decision to surrender to the Prussians, the order was given to leave the fort on the next morning. Schurz, still thinking on his couch as he stared at a ceiling painting of Greek gods and goddesses, concluded that he would write the farewell letter to his parents. On his way back to the castle after delivering his letter to the bakeshop, he realized that he had passed an incomplete drainage ditch for street gutter overflow, which emptied at the bottom of the hill in the town and began outside the fortress on the top of the hill.

After the surrender, the captured troops were marched in close order to the market place. Schurz, Adam, and an artilleryman named Neustädter made a quick turn into a side lane; at 2 p.m. on July 23, they entered the drain. The escape route was uphill through ankle-deep water, which after a while grew a bit deeper, hindering their progress. They found a board that they could jam against the walls of the drain and sit on to rest. The plan was to wait until midnight and then escape down the road to Steinmauern (about 4 miles away on the Murg River); however, it started to rain, flooding the drain and bringing the water to the fugitives' chests. The water brought rats; the men had to get out, but the sound of the wheels and footsteps of the Prussian army over their heads kept them frozen in place. They decided to push forward in the darkness, and they soon found that a grating blocked the passageway. Their first thought was that it was a barrier to keep the sewer cut off from the town during the siege; however, by accident, Schurz discovered that it was movable, being installed for cleaning; they were able to crawl under it even though submerged in the dirty water. When they reached the end of the tunnel, they heard voices of a sentry, peeking out they saw that the road to Steinmauern was closed. They retreated to their "bench" with cold feet and hunger pangs. Upon the realization that they would have to wait for a better opportunity, Adam opened the "wine" bottles that they brought along, only to discover them filled with rum. They finished them. At 3 a.m., they started to leave the tunnel, but Schurz dropped his carbine into the water, making a loud splash. A Prussian guard overhead heard the noise; he stuck his bayonet into the grate as they ducked back in and they remained safely in the water. Eventually, the three wet and muddy refugees were able to surface and creep down the road via backyard gardens. Their destination was a house belonging to one of Adam's cousins. When they arrived there, she wanted no part of them; she was afraid that the Prussian soldiers billeted at her house would make trouble for her family. She threatened to turn them in if they did not leave, which they did.

Luckily, they found a hollow square of firewood surrounded by brush where they could hide. A farmer passed by their refuge, took pity on them, and led them to a shed, where they could climb into a small loft where they would not be discovered if they lay still tightly next to each other. He brought them food, but to their horror, the Prussian cavalry was housing its horses in the shed under their roost. Hunger, thirst, and sleep overtook them; rain coming through the leaking roof quenched their thirst. By taking turns sleeping, they could avoid noise. After three days and two nights of no food, Neustädter went to a neighboring house to buy some, returning with a loaf of bread and an apple. The farmer promised to deliver supplies and the next day returned with provisions and the news that the Prussian guards were leaving. However, the Prussians decided to celebrate in the shed. After most of them left, one soldier remained trying to convince a local girl that he "really loved" her; she must have believed him for there was no quiet until they left at midnight.

They were still not safe. The Prussians had posted sentinels that prompted their return to the drain to hide and back to the makeshift bench where they waited until the man who had hidden them reported that the road was free. The sewer exit was very close to this road, and a hasty escape was possible. Off they went and were led by their guide, who later introduced himself as August Löffler, to a man sleeping in his boat.[15]

The odyssey was just beginning. Löffler would not take any of the money they offered him. The surly boatman took five florins and took the refugees to what they thought was the French shore and safety. The next morning, they realized that they had been had and were stranded on an island a distance from the French shore. Eventually, they were taken to it; two customs officers pointed them to a town named Selz, where there were many German refugees. After a necessary cleanup in a nearby stream, they joined a party of Germans, none of whom had escaped from Rastatt. Schurz learned of Kinkel's fate; rumor had it that his professor had joined the volunteers as a private, and in a fight on the River Murg, he was wounded, captured, and imprisoned in a tunnel (casemate) in Rastatt waiting for a court-martial. The three were not in the clear; the French police arrived, asking their names and whether or not they intended to stay; on the condition that they move on, the mayor of the town gave them a kind of passport. They said they wanted to go to Strasbourg; however, they really wanted to get to Switzerland, where they heard that Anneke and other refugees were.

Ironically, Schurz's father arrived days later in the same inn in Selz where the three escapees had had a night's rest and a full day of sleep. He went to Rastatt to search for his son's body, having received the last letter predicting a sure end. Schurz left the inn several days earlier. When his father arrived in Rastatt and asked for his son at the Prussian command, he was given permission to visit all the prisoners in the casemates. It took him three days and all he found was Kinkel. Everyone knew of Schurz, though no one knew where he was. Christian Schurz left after hearing from the residents in Rastatt that there were several escapees. He found the inn in Selz where he heard the story of his son's flight; he journeyed to Bonn to bring the good news to Carl's mother. The mistaken report of his son's death was so traumatic that it was described in his American obituary in 1876.

When Schurz and his compatriots stopped in Strasbourg, the local police took them to headquarters; they were told either to go deeper into France or to leave the country. They chose, instead, to go to Switzerland even without French or any other passports. News came of the release of the Baden common soldiers who were let out of prison and sent home without penalty; Adam the orderly was safe to go home, and Schurz, still not knowing his last name, never saw him again, no matter how hard he tried to find him in later life.

Schurz and his companion "Neustädter" found a man in a tavern that appeared to know the way to get over the Swiss border without a passport.[16] They followed his instructions and landed in Bern. Schurz stopped in Dornachbruck, Germany, where he fell into a ten-day malaise, contemplating the experiences and failures that he had just experienced. Toward the end of his depression, he was surprised to find his old friend, Adolph Strodtmann from Bonn, who was sent by the Schurz family with news, letters, and (most importantly) money. Schurz took a mail coach to Zurich, where he miraculously found his old friends Anneke, Techow, Schimmelfennig, and Beust standing at the coach stop as if they were waiting for him. They helped him find an unheated room at a baker's house in Dorf Enge. When winter came, Schurz and a *Bierstube* comrade, a forester named Emmermann, took two rooms in the house of a merchant in Schanzengraben. He joined a democratic club with all the old refugees from Germany coming to the slow realization that the unification and democratization of Germany and the revolution "might delay its coming much longer than we believed."[17] Schurz, at twenty years old, realized that he had to plan for his own future and could not depend on a path that he came to believe was "utterly illusory." There were rumors, he writes in his "memoirs," of the founding of the University of Zurich and that he thought of enrolling there, or becoming a professor of history. Actually, the arts and science division of the university, which was founded in 1833, did not become a reality until 1859—ten years after Schurz left.

Finally, to make some money, he started to write articles for Dr. Hermann Becker, nicknamed "Red Becker" not for his communist connections, but because of his red hair and beard.[18] The paper was called the *Westdeutsche Zeitung*, a journal that was denounced by Karl Marx and his fellow editors. Schurz wrote to his father in October 1849, saying that he could prepare and pass the exam for a history degree at the University of Zurich and commenting that it did not much of a difference where he made his living. His parents had sent him money and he was homesick but hopeful. He had asked for a passport, only to be delivered when and if he needed it, and by February 1850, he found that he needed it. His friend and mentor Gottfried Kinkel (who once been tried by the Prussians) was moved twice from one prison on to another and was finally incarcerated in a tower in Spandau Prison.

# The Miraculous Kinkel Escapade

There is a pencil sketch by an unknown artist (included in the English edition of the three-volume Carl Schurz's *Reminiscences*) of Gottfried Kinkel sitting in a chair next to a small pile of straw, wearing formal clothing and bedecked with links of heavy chains. Critics have noted that he would have been wearing prison clothing and not a formal coat. This picture accompanied a romanticized account of his trial and capture; it was widely distributed by Mrs. Johanna Mockel Kinkel across Europe and America. She left Germany in 1850 and, at the time of her husband's prison term, was living with a group of fellow refugees in the Bloomsbury district of London, which had become a haven for the revolutionaries including Karl Marx and Friederich Engels.

Some contemporaries saw her as a strong feminist, while others, including Marx, saw her as a "she-devil." Schurz initially had a great deal of respect for her. Johanna Kinkel, five years older than her husband, was somewhat slovenly and not attractive. The question arose: was she a brilliant musician or merely moderately talented? Schurz never writes about her music. After she left Germany and while in London, she started her widespread "money to free Kinkel campaign."

Gottfried Kinkel was arrested in Karlsruhe; after the surrender of Rastatt, he was transferred to the prison in the casements and tried for treason on August 4, 1849. It is here that the legend of the "Professor Patriot" becomes unclear. According to Schurz, Kinkel was on trial for his life since there were trials and executions being ordered daily. They began in Rastatt on August 6; according to legend, Kinkel represented himself with "wonderful eloquence" and changed the sentence of death to one of life imprisonment. This trial story was spread across America in 250 extant newspaper articles, reporting Kinkel as a victim.

Kinkel was not a battlefield leader; however, he was a very vocal leader in the press. When he ran for a seat in the Parliament in Bonn, the Catholic Church condemned his candidacy, telling women in the confessional, "Kinkel wants to abolish the Catholic religion. He wishes freedom for sect (Kultus) and separation of church and state."[1] He was applauded wildly as he addressed the Cologne Democratic Society, calling Germany's revolutionary future a "social democratic republic."[2] During elections for the Frankfurt National Assembly, Kinkel wrote: "The five fingers of despotism, clergy, nobility, moneybags, soldiers, officials, have triumphed and will dominate parliaments."[3] He left the Baden Revolution and fled to the Palatinate where he commanded a "People's Guard" in support of local "revolutionary regimes". At Zweibrücken, and at the failure of the uprising in Siegburg, Kinkel began a fiery berating of the city council and followed that with a public speech in the market place complete with cheering crowds who supported his "proposal that the Provisional Government not be bound by the Frankfurt constitution but act as a revolutionary dictatorship."[4] The German press repeatedly documented Kinkel's proposal for restoration of the medieval guild system to a democratic Germany. His high-profile activities during the months of the revolution were enough to make him a symbol of the conflict. He had painted a target on his back. His military activities were limited to enlistment as a private in the Bensançon Company under the command of Willich; therefore, as a private, and not as an officer, he would not have been executed as some of the officers and leaders were, but if convicted he would have been sentenced to six years in prison and released after one month in jail. Kinkel, however, was tried for high treason because of the *Bonner Zeitung* and his blatant anti-government speeches and campaigns.

Kinkel's works were published throughout Germany; his speeches, well-delivered in a mellifluous voice, became subjects of editorials and were published in local newspapers. His wife promoted his fame, and by the time he was arrested and brought to Rastatt, he was a rebel celebrity. However, not all of the "revolutionaries" offered friendly support. Karl Marx and Friedrich Engels wrote scathing rebukes and severe character assassinations of Kinkel and Schurz. In an article called "Heroes of the Exile," Marx called Schurz "a little intriguer with great ambitions and limited achievements."[5] In the *Rheinische Politisch-ökonomische Revue* of 1850, Marx quotes from Kinkel's self-defense at his trial.[6] However, as in other reports culled from a newspaper, in this case, the April 6 and 7 editions of the *Berlin Abendpost,* they are taken out of context.

There are few records of Kinkel's trial, but it occurred before the officers were tried and executed. The records of prison journeys are unclear. The accounts in the contemporary and later American newspapers continued to see him as a wonderful mistreated democratic voice. The image of the brave imprisoned poet was exaggerated in many articles. Kinkel, in his writing, exhibits a self-righteous arrogance. He wrote to the Royal Prussian commandant at Rastatt on August 9, 1849:

I request the following:

1. To send the enclosed letter to my wife, after the same has been censored, sealed and addressed in ink to Mrs. Johanna Mockel, Baden, Baden as provided.
2. As the air in my prison causes a physical tension, I wish to enjoy some wine every day and therefore, at my last visitation I had to relinquish a Baden Ducat which I would like back and also the money bag which has value for me as it was made as a souvenir by a friend.
3. I would also request permission to have a pencil and paper to facilitate my lonely imprisonment by recording my thoughts.
4. Finally, when judgement is passed on me, before it is announced I would like permission to say good-bye to my wife having prevented from seeing her during my fourteen days in Baden, the refusal of such a natural demand would provoke harsh judgement from the educated classes.

With reverence,

Gottfried Kinkel.[7]

He got his answer two days later, and while he was waiting for his sentence, he may or may not have heard the early morning shots from the executions in the courtyard of the fortress starting on August 6, continuing daily until he got his answer on the 11th. There is no record of any contact that Kinkel may have had with the other condemned prisoners, including Gustav Tiedemann, before their deaths. The Commandant wrote:

Order of the Governor Rastatt: 11.8.1849

1. The letter you mention has not been sent, but shall be sent or returned at my discretion depending on the content.
2. The detainee may receive some Ducats from time to time to meet his needs.
3. To have writing material only for letters which will go to the Commandant
4. The attached note which is delivered today to Dr. Kinkel will contain the court's decision.

On behalf of The Adjutant General of the Governor:

Borstel, Captain and Adjutant.

Kinkel, Gottfried: Professor in Bonn convicted of High Treason to Life Imprisonment in a fortress. The martial law verdict confirmed by a civil institution.[8]

Karl Marx reported the sentence as a twenty-year detention, but in reality, the sentence stood, and Kinkel, turned martyr, began to write poetry that, according to Karl Marx, depicted himself as a Christ figure "shedding my blood for you." Marx's issue with him was that during his defense, he lied about his involvement in the revolution:

Also, I was never in command, so that I am not responsible for the actions of others either. For I wish to guard against any identification of my actions with the dirt and filth which recently, I know, unfortunately tagged on to this revolution.

My guilt is that in the summer I still wanted the same thing that you all wanted in March, that the whole German people wanted in March! And what happened to me because of this? During this my absence from home I received a second summons to appear in court, and since I was unable to appear to defend myself I was deprived, as I have recently been informed, of the franchise for five years. Five years deprivation of the franchise was pronounced over me: for a man who has already once had the honour of being a deputy, this is an exceedingly harsh punishment. (!)

How often have I heard it said that I am a 'bad Prussian'; these words have wounded me.... Well then! My party has for the present lost the game in our fatherland. If the Prussian Crown now at last pursues a bold and strong policy, if His Royal Highness our Crown Prince, the Prince of Prussia, succeeds in forging Germany into one by the sword, for no other way is possible, and giving it a great and respected place in relation to our neighbours, and ensuring real and lasting internal freedom, raising trade and intercourse again, sharing the military burden, now weighing too heavily on Prussia, equally over the whole of Germany, and above all providing bread for the poor of my nation, whose representative I feel myself to be-if your party succeeds in this, well, upon my oath! The honour and greatness of my fatherland are clearer to me than my ideals of state, and I know how to appreciate the French republicans of 1793 (Fouché and Talleyrand?) who afterwards voluntarily bowed to the greatness of Napoleon for the sake of France; now should this happen, and then my people once again do me the honour of choosing me as their representative, I should be the first deputy to cry with a glad heart: Long live the German Empire! Long live the Hohenzollern Empire! If one is a bad Prussian with such opinions, well! Then I really have no desire to be a good Prussian.

Gentlemen, think a little also of wife and child at home when you pronounce sentence upon a man who stands before you today in such deep misfortune as a result of the changing tides of human destiny![9]

The sentence for life in prison was short-lived; there were rumors of a new trial among the German press and population, but the government felt that the verdict was too mild. The royal auditor general brought the conviction and sentence to the King for rejection because of illegality, hoping to retry him for the death penalty. The King "graciously" affirmed the sentence but qualified it by moving Kinkel to a "civil prison" where any freedom that he would have had in the military facility would be removed. He was to be treated as a common criminal.

Kinkel was taken first to Bruchsal, and then to the penitentiary in Naugard, in Pomerania on the Baltic, as far from the revolutionary sympathies as the government could get him. His head was shaved, he was issued a number and a prison outfit; the day started at 4.30 a.m. and after washing as well as morning meal and prayers, the prisoners were required to "work" by spinning wool until lights out at 8.30 p.m. in the summer and until 4.40 p.m. in the winter. There was no writing or reading allowed. Kinkel, during his confinement from October 8, 1849, until April 1850 only received one pound of meat. During his prison stay, his wife was very active in soliciting support for her "martyred husband" even after, in 1850, she was expelled from Baden-Württemberg. The spinning wheel of wool became a symbol of his incarceration and poems by other authors appeared. In addition, there were rumors, started with the May 1849 trial of the revolutionaries in Cologne, that Kinkel would be retried and probably receive a harsher sentence.

Johanna Mockel Kinkel and the three children (aged one, four, and six years old) settled in the St. John's Wood area of London near "Little Venice" in the Bloomsbury district, where she began recruiting support, both politically and monetarily, for the release of her husband. The operation was highly successful; many offered escape plans and she collected money from such notables as Charles Dickens and Walter Savage Landor.[10] Despite the positive tone of Johanna Kinkel's letters and the relation of the distress of her family, and despite the money, no one would take the risk and try to free Kinkel.

In February 1850, Schurz received a letter from Johanna Kinkel begging the twenty-year-old student to take action and save his friend and mentor. She wrote that she would have taken on the "rescue" but was afraid that her appearance at the prison would cause suspicion. At this time, Kinkel was still spinning wool in Naugard. After a sleepless night of consideration, Schurz agreed to be the one who would save his close friend. He felt that as a young student, he could remain unnoticed. However, the Swiss Government was in the process of expelling the expatriates who could not pay to stay. An immigrant had to pay 400 francs per year for each year living in Switzerland. Obtaining citizenship was difficult; leaving and moving on would be a positive direction. The question was where they should go.

Carl Schurz had again reached a turning point in his life, and after his difficult decision to help Kinkel escape, he wrote to Frau Kinkel using an assumed name and sent the letter via a third person. He also needed to obtain a passport; he wrote to Heribert Jüssen, his maternal first cousin in Liblar, to get one and send it to him. There were no photographs used then; the bearer of the document had to match the description on all "essential points" and Schurz and Heribert resembled each other in coloring and stature. He told his friends and acquaintances that he was returning to Germany to organize branch democratic clubs and asked for a long list of people in Germany who could be trusted and would not turn him in. Armed with a forged passport and lists of "compatriots," Schurz set out for his home in Bonn with a stopover in Frankfurt am Main to meet with the "Democrats." He then visited Wiesbaden, Bad Kreuznach, Birkenfeld, and Trier, stopping in Koblenz to take the night train towards Bonn. Fearing recognition and a passport check Schurz got off in Bad Godesberg and walked the remaining ten miles to his parents' home, which he reached at 3 a.m. When his mother awoke, like every mother, she commented on how tired he looked and immediately set to making breakfast. His father, he related later, was "beyond" proud of him and told him so.

Fortuitously, Frau Kinkel paid a visit to Schurz's parents that morning. Schurz was able to have a confidential talk with her. He insisted that if he were to take on the rescue of her husband, he would have to have the matter completely in his own hands; he would speak to no one about it. She was never to mention his name or ask for any more information than he would "voluntarily give her."[11] She agreed to all his conditions.

The story of the Kinkel's escape and rescue became a worldwide spy tale of "cloak and dagger." Schurz instructed Frau Kinkel to use "magic invisible ink" on correspondence.[12] When a letter in real ink was written over it, there was no evidence of the original message. Once received, the letter had to be washed, removing the ink with a special chemical, and then heated for the real message to appear; Johanna Kinkel's oldest son, aged six years, remembered her hanging letters near the stove to dry.

Schurz's biggest fear was being caught. Prussian spies were rumored to be in the area, and after flowers were delivered for him to his parents' house from a would-be lady love (Betty), fearing recognition, he got Heribert to take him by carriage to Cologne at night, to avoid curious officials, spies, and police. He was most afraid of neighborhood and tavern gossip revealing his identity. He took a room in the upper story of his friend "Red Becker's" restaurant, where a fellow Democrat revealed to him upcoming plans to free Kinkel when he returned to Cologne for his trial. Schurz and Becker believed that an obvious plan like that would fail. Schurz still was worried that his presence in Cologne might become too public; therefore, he left at night via Brussels for Paris. Becker had suggested that he establish links with the German refugees living there to write about the present situation for his new newspaper *Westdeutsche Zeitung Democratic Politischer Tageblatt*; and for the sake of his scholarly studies, spend a long time in the French capital. More importantly, Becker would pay him for what he wrote.[13]

Schurz stayed in Paris for about four weeks, studiously learning French and finding fellow Germans. At the same time, Kinkel, taken from the prison at Naugard, under the guard of three police, arrived in Cologne for his trial on April 29, 1850. The trip was cloaked with secrecy; Kinkel clad now in a black coat with a hat pulled down over his face, was transported to the prison in Cologne, where he was redressed in traditional prison garb. Now gaunt and grim, still with a shaven head, his wife and son, Gottfried, hardly recognized him during an allowed visit before the trial.

Schurz was in danger while traveling with an assumed name and a false passport. He later omitted from his letters, and memoirs, the seriousness of the trial. Ten men were charged with "alleged assassination, storming of the Siegburg arsenal and incitement to the civil war." The list of charges and descriptions of the thirteen defendants were published later in a booklet for the benefit of Kinkel's children. The tribunal consisted of an appellate judge, a District Court consul, and an assessor.[14] The case was heard in front of a twelve-man jury.[15] Schurz was listed as one of the absent defendants along with six others including Fritz Anneke. His host, "Red Becker," probably knew what was coming to Cologne told him to leave. Fearing identification, he went off to Paris.

According to Schurz, Kinkel's personal defense was a brilliant one and after moving the entire assemblage to tears, according to an eyewitness, the jury immediately returned a verdict of not guilty. The truth of the matter was that of all seven defendants present—Anselm Ungar, a merchant in Bonn; Ludwig Meyer, a student who later became a renowned psychiatrist; Johann Bühl, a "carter" in Bonn; Anton Maximillian Toups, a barber from Bonn; Franz Fleischmann, a carpenter from Bonn; Leopold Ungar, an eighteen-year-old student in Bonn; and a relative of Anselm Ungar and Kinkel—were declared not guilty after the jury's thirty minutes of deliberation.[16] The book about the trial was written to raise money for Kinkel's children noted:

> The President of the tribunal ordered the immediate release of the accused, unless there were grounds for further detention for one reason or another. The prosecutor replied that this was the case only for Kinkel, and so Ungar, Meyer, and Buhl were at once released; Gottfried Kinkel again climbed into the car, which led him as a reward for his conviction, loyalty again to the desolate Moors of the penitentiary, so that he would finish his wool plucking life.[17]

Due to the political uproar, Kinkel was taken to a more secure prison near Berlin, where he was locked in the tower. On the way back to prison, Kinkel, according to Schurz, found an opportunity to escape when his guards stopped at an inn in a Westphalian village; they locked Kinkel in a room but he got the key to it by distracting the guard outside his door. He managed to lock the guard in and run out the back. As he sprinted down the stairs, through the kitchen and garden, then into the open fields ahead, the *gendarmes* mobilized and told the townspeople that Kinkel was one of the most dangerous criminals in the Rhineland; therefore, everyone, including the coachman, ran in pursuit, carrying lanterns and torches. Kinkel saw the lights and heard the shouting behind him; when he turned to look back, he ran headfirst into a log sticking out of a woodpile. He was dazed and possibly unconscious; the pursuers caught him, put him back in the coach, and took him to his tower in Spandau.

Kinkel was jailed in Spandau prison, which was built before 1876. Schurz meantime traveled back to Germany ostensibly to meet with "democratic committees". On August 1, 1850, he was in Cologne meeting with Johanna Kinkel. She had raised a substantial amount of money for her husband's "liberation." They agreed to send the money to a friend in Berlin so Schurz, unable to use a bank, would be able to draw on it as needed. Johanna had found a way to communicate the news of the escape plans to her husband by using the word "fugue" (*Fuge* in German), which is close to the Latin word *fuga* meaning "flight." Her musical training and background qualified the "artistic" letters to her husband that would go right by the censors without raising an alarm. Kinkel knew what was coming and he responded to her letter that he wished to talk more about "*fuga*" but she told him to be patient.

Schurz went to Berlin by rail from Cologne; quite by accident, he met his friend, Abraham Jacobi, on the train. They were seated in a compartment facing Professor Christian Lassen from the University of Bonn, who kept staring at them.[18] Schurz and Jacobi laughed and chatted as if they did not have a care in the world, fearing recognition in a town where there was still a warrant for Schurz's arrest. The professor did not recognize them. On August 11, 1850, they arrived in Berlin. The false passport and the alias worked smoothly for him, and he found two fraternity brothers, Müller and Rhodes, living at 26 Markgrafen Strasse to take him in.[19] He disguised himself as one of the students in the University quarters of the city but was still careful. He wanted to go to the theatre to see the famous actor Rachel (Elisabeth Felix) in Racine's *Thisbe*, when she was on tour in Berlin.[20] Despite his fear of recognition, he went anyway. Schurz's description of her performance reveals his artistic inner core and a love for theatre, language, and poetry that is not evident in his political writings. As in any experience of good theatre, he was transported despite the "dry words of Racine." He would see her again in Paris, and then in the United States where she was apparently weakened with the final throes of tuberculosis. He was about to enter a real-life dangerous drama of his own.

He went to a public bathhouse with his two friends, where he slipped and fell on the tiles; he was laid up in bed for two weeks suffering from a severe "contusion." He recovered and finally could go about his task of freeing Kinkel. Schurz found two doctors that had been in touch with Frau Kinkel; one was a student friend from Bonn, Dr. Tendering, and the other was Dr. Ferdinand Falkenthal. Both doctors were Democrats. They took Schurz to meet an innkeeper named Friedrich Kruger in Spandau, a member of the town council who offered his hotel as a center for the escape plans. Schurz commuted from Berlin to Spandau at night, trying hard not to arouse any suspicion.

They considered liberating Kinkel by force because, as revealed later in 1855, Frankenthal had a cache of weapons at his house.[21] They rejected this plan since the fort was filled with Prussian troops, and violence would not work as a rescue attempt. Kinkel, they felt, was not skilled enough with his hands to tunnel his way out, so they settled on trying to bribe the guards. After three failed attempts, Schurz decided to give the affair a rest, travel to Hamburg, meet with friends there, and carry on the "Democratic activities." After meeting Strodtmann and others, he traveled back to Berlin and this time stayed with Dr. Frankenthal on the Moabit canal. For cover, he carried a small surgical kit, trying to pass as a young medical student to those in the neighborhood who might be curious. He kept trying to find guards who could be bribed, but the risk was high if people started to ask questions or gossip about the inquiries.

Via unnamed friends, Schurz found a man named Georg Brune, a turnkey who had served as a non-commissioned officer in the Prussian Army and who now was trying to support a wife and family on a miserable salary. He was close to ten years older than Schurz, and after considering the "escape offer" for three days, he agreed to help. His initial plan was to wait until he had duty in the upper story of the tower and then he could escort Kinkel from his cell to the gate leading out of the fortress. He was assigned to this floor on November 5. After the escape, he would receive a sum of money accumulated by the German Democrats including a substantial amount from "personal admirers" of Kinkel including 2,000 thalers from Russian Baroness Brüning.[22] Schurz, following Johanna Kinkel's directions, went to collect the cash for the bribe from a mysterious female relative of Felix Mendelsohn-Bartholdy in Berlin. He received the packet from a meeting with a "lady in black" in an elegant parlor.

The next problem facing the "rescue" was the determination of an escape route from the fortress to where ever it was that was safe. The Swiss and French borders were too far away and they would have to cross hostile territory to get there. Schurz decided that England was the safest place; however, the Prussian Government would certainly watch closely the major harbors in Hamburg and Bremen. The chosen escape route to England was by way of Rostock and Warnemünde; it was carefully laid out, designed with way stops and waiting carriages. Brune asked Schurz to give the money to his family in case he should be caught; they then hatched an elaborate scheme based on a stolen key left behind by another guard. Schurz wrote of his exploits fifty years later, and other authors and newspapermen embellished them so thoroughly that it is difficult to separate the actual from the fantastic. Kinkel was probably imprisoned in the Julius Tower (Julius *Turm* possibly named from an earlier "*Judenturm*"), which was 30 meters (98 feet) tall and had been used as a keep since the fourteenth century. However, the elaborate plot to walk Kinkel downstairs from one of the lower floors failed.

A distraught Schurz did not know what to do. He considered enlisting in the army of Schleswig-Holstein to fight for their cause and leave the whole affair behind, but, instead, he retreated to his room and another sleepless night. He still believed that another opportunity might present itself but still tossed and turned over the possibilities. He later wrote:

> I have frequently in life had the experience that when we are struck by an especially heavy blow, we can do nothing better than present to our minds all, even the worst, possible features of trouble that may still be in store for us, and so in imagination drink the cup of bitterness down to the last drop; but then to turn our thoughts to the future and occupy them entirely with that which must be done to prevent further misfortune, to repair the damage and to replace what has been lost with something equally desirable.[23]

Fate interceded. When he saw the guard again, he found the man assigned to the upper floor was out sick the night of November 6, 1850, and Brune had volunteered to take his place; he could then, with the aid of a rope smuggled in around his waist, lower Kinkel down to a waiting carriage. They agreed to the plan; Schurz wrote that the drop from the third story could be 60 feet and he was afraid that some of the old tiles and rubble would fall to the street below and cause an alarm to be raised. He fortunately planned to have an iron-wheeled wagon to go by to disguise the noise.

Brune wrapped a rope around his waist and went to his post. The other guards were celebrating a birthday and Kruger offered to supply them with punch in his inn. All went as planned this time; there was a lookout on the four corners of the fortress and after the town night watchman passed, at the arranged hour, and on a signal of three perpendicular lantern flashes down a long rope came Kinkel. Schurz was overjoyed, but Kinkel had rubbed his hands raw on the rope coming down. True to Schurz's guess, the old shingles and mortar came rattling down with Kinkel; however, the assigned cart rumbled by, covering the noise as planned. Schurz and his rescued professor galloped off to Kruger's *Wirtshaus* to change Kinkel's clothing. As they entered the back door, they heard an old German folksong "*Wir sitzen so fröhlich beisammen*" being sung by the celebratory jailers from Spandau. Kinkel was ushered into a backroom, redressed in a black bearskin overcoat and a Prussian forester's cap the visor of which covered the top of his face. After bandaging Kinkel's chafed and bleeding hands, Kruger offered both men a toast direct from the same punch bowl used by the jailors and off they went by carriage through the Potsdam gate on the road to Hamburg.

Kinkel was effusive in his thanks, repeatedly hugging Schurz and declaring his disbelief at the success of his escape. They galloped through Oranienburg, Teschendorf, and Löwenberg; they stopped in Gransee to feed and water the horses before reaching the relative safety of Mecklenburg. They stopped again for the sake of the horses in Dannenwalde, and then in Fürstenburg to rest them yet again. They finally reached their destination of Strelitz where a fellow Democrat, city magistrate Carl Petermann, welcomed them.[24] His aid to these fugitives cost him his position as a local judge when he was caught after they left. He invited friends to meet the two of them and celebrated with wine and a good meal. They needed fresh horses because one of the faithful pair that brought them there died shortly after they reached the stables. Petermann brought a friend Moritz Wiggers of Rostock to help them move along to the ultimate destination of the harbor in Warnemünde.[25] They were taken in a wagon to the Hotel Wöhlert, where they registered under the aliases of *Herr* Kaiser (Kinkel) and *Herr* Hensel (Schurz); Hensel was the name of the original wagon driver.

Warnemünde is a small port and resort area on the Baltic Sea. Wiggers was sure that the fugitives would be safe there, protected by the local democratically sympathetic residents. Schurz wrote that he had never seen the sea before. Wiggers cared for them and found a place to stay until a ship could be found. In 1857, he wrote his account of the escape called *Gottfried Kinkel's Befreiung*, in which he describes his version of the miraculous rescue; however, there is some embellishment of the facts. Wiggers told of being awakened on Friday morning November 8, 1850:

"Great stranger, whoever you are, be merciful and do not wrest me from the arms of my god Morpheus," I exclaimed in a drowsy pathos, eyes wide and staring at the dark outlines of the unknown, which began to shake me impatiently and violently.

Two men approached me expectantly, both tall and slender, one taller than the other by some inches in height. The taller one, by reputation, was close to the forties. He wore a black overskirt and black pantaloons, and, like the younger one, glasses. His gray-flecked black hair was cut short. He had a high and bald forehead. The unshaven face showed the germs of a black full beard, the yellow-greenish color of the face indicated long dungeons. At first glance, I recognized the original of the picture I saw. There could be no one else but Gottfried Kinkel.

His real name was—Carl Schurz. His personality was less impressive than the Kinkels'. But the attentive observer did not fail to notice the firm character and the masculine determination which manifested in his marked youthful features and assured demeanor. The brown eyes flashed wisely and ironically out of the somewhat low-lying eye sockets. His long hair was dark blond.[26]

Wiggers' account, written seven years after the rescue, is reminiscent of German Romantic writing, and despite the language of an ardent admirer of Kinkel's, in the person of Wiggers, the danger of the whole operation bleeds through. Schurz and his charge were introduced by Wiggers to Ernst Brockelmann, a wealthy industrialist who owned four factories in Rostock, including an ironworks and a machine factory.[27] More importantly, he was a ship owner and his vessels crossed as far as the Arctic Ocean for seal fishing and wheat transport. Wiggers arranged transport to Brockelmann's home in Krummendorf, a suburb of Rostock, where Schurz and Kinkel were introduced to anyone that met them as two foreign merchants in this area who had been members of the old Hanseatic League. Warnemünde, on the coast, was an independent fishing community where politics and Prussian policing were not part of life. Schurz and Kinkel were relatively safe there. Brockelmann and Wiggers helped them find the safest route out of Germany. Denmark had been ruled out; the final choice was England via Scotland. They were to sail on a ship named the *Little Anna* on Sunday, November 17, 1850. They had to wait for the 40-ton cargo cruiser to be loaded with wheat, and while they did, they were wined, dined, and breakfasted in the true North German tradition of five daily meals. Schurz called them the "indispensable first, breakfast and second breakfast and sometimes third breakfast, and the noon repast, and the afternoon coffee with cake, and the suppers and a 'little something' before going to bed."[28] Later on in life, Schurz was a lover of fine meals and wine, and he appeared to be one of those people who burn through food with an indefatigable energy without gaining weight.

Despite his descriptions of wining, dining and *gemütlichkeit*, this was a dangerous time for both fugitives; Schurz's involvement had not yet made the newspapers but Kinkel's escape, in an earlier incarnation of sensational journalism, had. The Prussian Government, through the media, labeled him an escaped convict; some newspapers sighted Kinkel in different places at the same time including England, Zurich, and Paris. These reports could have been sensational accounts or sightings reported by allies to confuse the authorities. One pastor, Rudolf Dulon, a socialist agitator in Bremen, noted that Kinkel had already passed through his city and was on his way to England. In the meanwhile, while the two men were awaiting a "stranger" claiming to be farmer Hensel, their friend, who had driven them from Spandau to Strelitz. The danger of captivity was drawing nearer.

They sailed across the Baltic on very rough seas toward freedom. Kinkel got seasick as the ship tossed wildly on the rougher North Sea. Schurz loved his first exposure to the wild waves and at one point had himself tied to the mast to watch the course of the little vessel as it made its way roughly through the ocean waters. The stormy passage lasted ten days, but beautiful weather returned on the last for days as they headed to Newcastle. Schurz claimed that he and Kinkel read Homer's *Odyssey* (in the original Ancient Greek) aloud as they sailed up the rocky coast of Scotland to the port of Edinburgh.

When they landed on a Sunday, they found everything closed for the Sabbath. Passers-by were staring at them in their odd escape "costumes." They also came to the realization that between them, they only knew two words of English: "beefsteak" and "sherry," which even repeated over and over, the native Scots could not understand. They finally found a hotel in Leith and made their wants known with gestures. On the next day, they found a Mr. Charles McLaren of Counting House in Edinburgh, who spoke fluent German; they had letters from Ernst Brockelmann, which told of their situation and McLaren invited them to use his home as often and as long as they liked. After cleaning up and touring a bit, and after the obligatory dinner, they set off on the night train to London.

Schurz wrote: "At last all danger past, no more pursuit, a new life ahead!"[29] However, the trail of problems for those who helped Kinkel escape had not ended. Johanna Kinkel and her children were forced to leave Baden-Württemberg. Baroness von Brüning had to join the German emigres in London. Dr. Ferdinand Frankenthal was convicted in 1853 of collecting weapons for an arsenal in his home for the purpose of revolution. Newspaper accounts included "the dress" (meaning costume, though American papers reported him disguised as a woman) in which Kinkel escaped from Spandau was found at Falkenthal's house.[30] On June 29, 1855, Dr. Frankenthal was taken to Lichtenburg penitentiary to serve a term that had been delayed because of interrogation about Kinkel's escape.[31]

Georg Brune, the prison guard, served three years in prison for his part in the jailbreak; he probably knew that he would be caught because he was the sole jailer on duty when Kinkel climbed out the window to freedom. He made the request to have the money given to his family in case of his pending arrest. After his release, there was enough money for him and his family to move out of the Berlin area and live comfortably in his home in Soest, Westphalia where he became a janitor in an ironworks.

Friedrich Kruger, the innkeeper in Spandau who arranged for the guards' birthday party, was questioned, tried, and released because of a comical defense he made to the jury. He made a habit, he said, of not inquiring who his guests were since his experience with two unidentified men who arrived at his inn, one of which was His Royal Highness, the Prince of Prussia (later Emperor William I).

Poritz, Leddihn, and Hensel, all of whose first names have been lost, were tried and acquitted according to Schurz. *Herr* Liddihn (possibly Ewald) visited Schurz in 1888 in Berlin. Although Moritz Wiggers, the lawyer and notary from Rostock, was tried and acquitted for his aid in Kinkel's escape, he was retried and convicted in 1853 for "high treason in Rostock." Even though he was imprisoned for four years, in 1867, he was elected as a representative to the *Reichstag* of the North German Confederation, and, in 1871, to the German *Reichstag*. He served until 1881, while continuing to write historical works.

Ernst Brockelmann remained active in local politics and had a ship named after him in 1927 by the Ahrens shipping company. Captain Niemann, who guided the *Little Anna* through the rough waters taking the two fugitives to Scotland, died at the turn of the century at sea in a vessel named the *Uranus*.

Schurz was connected for the rest of his life to the miraculous prison break. The story was embellished with "detail" as it was retold through the years. One account depicted him disguised as an organ grinder with a monkey and Kinkel disguised as a woman. Karl Marx described the escape as a copycat version of Richard II's escape from a French tower. In the German version of his *Lebenserrinnerungen*, Schurz wrote:

> ... this story, whose subject matter in those days was very much talked about, and as frustrated as I am in recollection, and this brief experience of my youth, is of course, very sharply impressed on my memory, I believe that the narrative of this essential content and discussion of the described is truthful.
>
> I have already mentioned that at the beginning of the sixties Moritz Wiggers published in the Leipzig newspaper *Die Gartenlaube* a detailed narration of freeing and escape of Kinkel. But that hasn't ended the more or less fantastic legends that were told. On the contrary, for almost every year that has passed since then, there are various legends from German newspaper pages and letters that contain whimsically embellished stories and still from time to time I receive letters from unknown people telling me that their fathers told them that they had seen me somewhere at the time or even helped me with your liberation adventure.[32]

This passage was omitted from the English translation of the *Reminiscences*.

# Expatriates in London

The reality of a new life outside Germany was slowly beginning to affect Schurz; upon his arrival in London, Schurz and Kinkel were taken to the banking house of Hambro and Son, where they received money from an unidentified source. They saw the sights of London guided by a young man named Heinrich Verhuven. They saw the famous actor William Macready's Shakespearean farewell performances at Drury Lane in Covent Garden.[1] Although he knew the plots and could follow the play, Schurz put off learning English because of his admitted difficulty with the language.

After the sojourn to London, Schurz and Kinkel went to Paris. Kinkel only wanted to stay a short time and then return to London to be with his family, which he did after a tour of the museums and sights. Schurz found the faithful Strodtmann, now in the city, and joined him in a spacious room in a *Hotel Garni* in the Faubourg area of Montmartre. The arrangement worked for a while, but Strodtmann cooked smelly food and accidentally set Schurz's cloak on fire. After an agreement that their living arrangements were not working, they parted ways. Schurz went to 17 Quai Saint Michel, a "respectable" small hotel along the Seine. He resumed writing for German newspapers and found that as a "quasi-celebrity," he could earn 180 francs a month, of which he could keep eighty as a reserve for emergencies. He wanted to learn French and to enjoy the student life of the Left Bank, enjoying the writer's life in a room and dining on the Boulevard Saint-Germaine. He had achieved a level of independence for which he was very proud. He could visit the German exiles and the salon of Countess d'Agoult, Franz Liszt's common-law wife.[2] Once a week, the young musicians met in Schurz's salon for musical performances and entertainment. He was living the life of a student for the first time with no political connections or responsibilities. He found a French teacher with the improbable name of Madame Princesse de Beaufort, who was supposed to be from a family of old French nobility. She taught in her hotel room to make a living. Schurz paid two francs for his twice-weekly lessons and discovered his own way of learning the language. He would write on an interesting subject, and she would correct it until he reached the point of a perfect paper. He came to believe that expressing one's own thoughts, on paper, is the best way to learn a new language. He did not realize that his knowledge of Latin grammatical structure and constructions made it easier to learn the Romance language.

Living the "Bohemian" life, Schurz enjoyed intellectual companionship while studying French history and revolution. He attended the theatre and a masked ball during carnival season in 1851 at the opera. He was "shocked" by the dancing degenerating into the ordinary can-can and the "bestiality" of the patrons at the end of the evening. It took the militia to clear the wild crowd out of the doors. This annual event repulsed Schurz, with the men in evening dress and many of the women prostitutes, mingling with disguised upper-class women and the continual abandonment, drinking, and carousing until the very early hours of the next morning.[3] He concluded that the events of this kind represented "moral decay" and that it was a shameless display. The observation was written later in life, and the question arises: was Schurz a moralistic observer, or since he was drinking with his German friends, how much of a part did he take?

Schurz's recollection of a Parisian séance was printed in *The Annals of Physical Science* in 1906 and is in the Harry Houdini collection in the Library of Congress.[4] Houdini spent his life debunking psychics and duplicating their feats, but Schurz was unshaken in his belief in the paranormal. However, the wild parties and the séance were all a part of the artistic literary life of the St. Germaine student quarter of Paris, which Schurz was soon to leave. He planned a visit to the Kinkels' house in London, which was delayed by a stop with the Parisian police.

Schurz was walking with Mr. and Mrs. Reinhold Solger, German refugees, who migrated to America later in life, when a police agent arrested him and took him to the prefect of the police.[5] Schurz spent four days in a French prison cell without being charged. Finally, after two impassioned letters, written in "perfect" French to the Chief of Police, he was given an audience and told that he had to leave France. The reason given was the "wishes" of higher powers. After his release, he found that his apartment had been thoroughly searched but nothing was disturbed. Although the government had filed no charges nor found evidence of any political activity, it soon became apparent to Schurz that the preparations of Louis Napoleon for a *coup d'état* required that no activists related to a democratic government remain in the country, and in particular one as the now famous as Carl Schurz.

He arrived in London during the middle of June 1851, where Kinkel had secured rooms for him in the St. John's Wood area of London, in the Bloomsbury district, near Little Venice and Marylebone. Schurz began to give German lessons in this neighborhood. He did not as yet speak English, finding it "repugnant," and confessed that only in later life, with a full command of it, he learned to appreciate the "peculiar charm of its cadence." The Kinkels' thankfulness and the expression of it was an embarrassment to him, and only after they took his youngest sister Nettie (Antoinette, later Toni) to their household to study to be a teacher; after accepting the offer from Johanna of piano lessons on her newly purchased Érard grand piano, he was mollified.[6] The lessons, and practice on this instrument, made Schurz into the very accomplished pianist that he was. He and Johanna Kinkel were the only ones allowed to play this very expensive and sacred instrument. There was a practice piano for the children and the other students. The Kinkels also insisted that Schurz join their social circles; however, admittedly, his English was almost non-existent. German was very much in favor in London because of the arrival of Prince Albert. Schurz could get along on the slightest bit of English.

The refugee community in London was divided by nationality and political bent since the 1848 influx from Germany, France, Italy, Hungary, Poland, and Russia. The intellectual community regarded Kinkel, according to Schurz, as a poet by his opponents and not a "practical revolutionist." In a typical positioning of divergent philosophies, leaders of factions evolved from the expatriates. Arnold Ruge, a Hegelian, was the leader of one faction and Karl Marx and, to some extent, August Willich were the centers of others.[7] There were those also who ignored the conflicting groups and stayed neutral.

Kinkel was highly criticized by the "revolutionary" community for his attention to earning a living and staying with his family. Eventually, in a reaction to it, he conceived the plan of the "German National Loan," which would be monies collected from German Americans and others to be placed at the disposal of a central committee to disperse for revolutionary funding. He hoped to raise millions to finance a government takeover, which would pay back the supporters' investments. Kinkel decided to leave for America immediately to make a speaking tour and to raise the funds. Schurz, living in his house while he was gone, called the plan "striking illustrations of the self-deception" of the political exiles.[8]

Kinkel's efforts in America, even after a meeting with President Millard Fillmore, became more and more futile. Schurz wrote:

And it was really a fortunate circumstance that these revolutionary loans miscarried. Even with much larger sums hardly anything could have been done but to organize hopeless conspiracies and to lead numbers of patriotic persons into embarrassment and calamity without rendering any valuable service to the cause of liberty.[9]

Although, as Schurz put it, "the revolutionary fires burned out." Kinkel, in fear of being judged by the refugees as a suspicious person, kept working steadily on the task of funding a committee. Schurz, meanwhile, had been invited to meet the Italian revolutionary Giuseppe Mazzini, who was in hiding in London after several failed attempts at Italian revolutions. He wrote to Schurz and they met. At first, Schurz did not understand why the meeting had been arranged but soon found out that Mazzini was looking for money for aid in Northern Italy. Schurz kindly declined, saying he did not know the outcome of the German National Loan. He was also called into the presence of Lajos (Louis) Kossuth, the "father of Hungarian Patriotism" and this time it was quite a production; in October 1851, Schurz was summoned into the man's presence and introduced, and recognized as a hero. Kossuth was also looking for monetary support to bring independence to Hungary. Kinkel returned from his fundraising tour highly disappointed: "he had to confess to himself that the practical result of his mission was discouragingly trifling."[10]

As Schurz became acclimated to the London exiles community, and its mixed ethnicities and political fervor, he became more and more disenchanted with that lifestyle. The Kinkels were being pressured to take a very active part in the plans for the "coming revolution" while they were "struggling" to make a living and raise their four small children. The Kinkels, in 1851, were living at 1 Henstridge Villas in the exclusive neighborhood of St. John's Wood near Regents Park in London. The same property there today can be purchased for $2.5–3.5 million. Johanna had received money from "O," an unnamed source, allowing them to live there. Kinkel found tutoring work, and Johanna taught music; Schurz's sister continued to live with the Kinkels with a retinue of three servants (1851 London census). Johanna wrote in a letter that appeared in the *London Daily Telegraph*, to her friend Fanny Lewald.[11]

> For the instant I set my foot on the stairs the whole burden of work returns, together with the numerous demands of our unhappy exiled acquaintances. Have you an idea what it is to be looked upon as a sort of mother to all the emigrants? I can assure you that the office of overseer to public works is light in comparison.[12]

She continued to say that Kinkel's escape and their settlement in London put them into more debt with their friends than they thought that they could meet; however, they were able to pay the debt by using up their savings. Kinkel, the children, and Johanna all got influenza in the fall of 1851.

Carl Schurz recorded his meetings, during this period, with the exiled Baroness von Brüning, who, entirely absorbed in the exile society, was putting pressure on him as well as Kinkel to get the "revolution" going again. Although she was always pleasant and obliging during her social circles centered in her "salon," she constantly asked the question of "Do you really think that this will happen soon?" Her circle included many of the revolutionary luminaries including Count Oscar von Reichenbach from Silesia, August Willich, Alexander Schimmelfennig,

Friedrich Nietzsche, and Richard Wagner's writer friend Malwida von Meysenbug.[13] Schurz, at first the darling hero of the exiles, and Kinkel, who was making more money teaching were becoming disillusioned with the revolutionary zeal fostered by the inner circles. Karl Marx and the communists harshly criticized Johanna and Gottfried Kinkel for not serving the cause. When Louis Napoleon defeated French Republicans after a completed "bloody subjugation of Paris," Schurz reached a crisis point and the beginning of an epiphany. He could not think after his lack of sleep from getting reports of the French *coup d'état*, and the following exhausted deep slumber, so he walked into a foggy Hyde Park where he concluded:

> One thing to me seemed certain: all the efforts connected with the Revolution of 1848 were now hopeless; a period of decided and general reaction was bound to come, and whatever the future might bring of further developments in the direction of liberal movement must necessarily have a new starting point.[14]

He felt it futile to return to Germany and continue the intrigue there, which he called a "reckless and wicked game." His parents had been struggling to keep their house in Bonn and had to ask him for money. Schurz decided that he wanted to do "something really and truly valuable for the general good."[15] He decided to go to America.

Schurz was vague in his description of the first appearance of the ray of sunshine that changed his life. He met Margarethe Meyer while he was transacting "business" with another German exile Johannes Ronge, an expatriate, who founded the "New Catholics" and fled to London. He was married to Margarethe's sister Berthe. The Ronges founded a kindergarten on Tavistock Square near where Schurz lived. After he had finished with the "business," Ronge wanted him to meet his sister-in-law, Margarethe, who had just arrived from Hamburg on a visit and to help her sister. Schurz reported that an eighteen-year-old girl entered, "fine of stature, curly hair: Something childlike in her beautiful features and large dark beautiful eyes."[16]

# Marriage and America

In the nineteenth century, family matters and relationships were not discussed publicly or published in memoirs; therefore, Schurz wrote little of his courtship of Margarethe. They met in November 1851, they were engaged in February 1852, and they were married in July of the same year. She was eighteen years old; her mother died the same day that she gave birth. Her brother, Adolph Meyer, older by eleven years, raised her and her siblings after their father died. He was a wealthy factory owner in the Harburg area of Hamburg, carrying on the business started and run miraculously by his father, Heinrich Christian Meyer. "Stöckmeyer" (Stickmeyer) as he was known was a boy so poor that his family had to beg for food when they left Nesse, near Bremen, to go to Hamburg for a better life. He started making his fortune by peddling walking sticks on the streets of Hamburg. As he grew, the business became a large, profitable company that still operates in the Lüneberger Heide area of Germany. The Meyer factory made walking canes and later, with an agreement with Goodyear Tire and Rubber Company, manufactured combs.

When Carl Schurz asked for Margarethe's hand in marriage from her brother, Adolph Meyer, now the titular head of the family, a conflict arose. The issue concerned her sister, Berthe, the family's independent "wild child." She was an activist, championing childhood rights, women's education, and religious freedom. At age sixteen, she was forced into marriage with thirty-year-old Christian Traun, the manager of the family's booming manufacturing company in Hamburg. He had been the private secretary of Princess Augusta, in Hannover, who became the Duchess of Cambridge by an arranged marriage, when she was twenty years old to her second cousin aged forty-four.[1] Traun, perhaps thinking that an arranged marriage was a seal of good faith for business partners, entered the same arrangement when in 1835, at her father's behest; he married young Berthe Meyer. She wrote later:

> Our union was the wish of my unforgettable father who gave me to understand
> that the marriage would be agreed without my consent ... I was only sixteen

years old—brought up in a religion in which the highest virtue rested in toleration and suffering in the self-sacrifice of the innermost being.[2]

Traun was employed in the family factory in Hamburg; when his father-in-law, Heinrich Meyer, died, he became a partner. Berthe and Christian lived the respectable life of the wealthy merchant class in Hamburg. They had four children. In the late 1840s, as the loveless marriage began to crumble, Berthe became a militant feminist and the founding member of the Association of German Women and the Social Club of Hamburg Women for Equalizing Denominational differences (*Sozialen Verein Hamburger Frauen zur Ausgleichung konfessioneller Unterscheide*) for the reduction of discrimination against Jews. She was so committed to religious equality that she also founded The Association of Women and Girls in Support of German Catholics (*Verein von Frauen und Jungfrauen zur Unterstützung der Deutschkatholiken*) in 1846. She visited the educational radical Friedrich Froebel in Bad Liebenstein, where she met Johannes Ronge, with whom she founded a school for women: *Hochschule für das weibliche Geschlecht* in Hamburg. Her activities angered her husband because she was "ignoring her responsibilities by not entertaining his clients and ignoring the expected household duties of a respectable wife."

He accused her of being influenced by the "lamentable, eccentric and fanatical ideas which represent the angry spirit of our times."[3] Berthe left for London with her lover Ronge, taking her youngest children with her so that her husband could divorce her on grounds of desertion. She wrote passionately that she never loved him:

> Love cannot be a duty, but that it resides in the soul, and that we only value love where we find the essence of one's soul and are thus given the opportunity to find within ourselves the divine. For me this was impossible to achieve, because our characters and spiritual directions are so different.[4]

Although she married Ronge in 1851, her behavior and militant liberalism left a taint on the family and complicated the relationship of Carl Schurz and Margarethe. Berthe gave birth to Ronge's child, Marie, a scant two months after their marriage. In London, Ronge and Berthe opened the kindergarten on Tavistock Square where Carl first met Margarethe.

Divorce for any reason was a stigma attached to any German family in the nineteenth century and well into the early twentieth. Divorced women were seen not as the victims but as the perpetrators of a bad union. Children of these divided families often suffered being ostracized and mistreated. When Carl Schurz and Margarethe fell in love and decided to get married, her brother, Adolph, opposed the marriage for two probable reasons: one was money and the other Carl's possible inability to support his sister. Although it is not recorded, there may have been opposition to another sister attached to a revolutionary figure. Tales of "derring-do" preceded Schurz, and his antics—now famous and illegal—might prove to be an embarrassment to an already stigmatized family. Margarethe was only eighteen, and perhaps family plans for her marriage were in the works; however, Schurz wrote to her brother, Adolph, in April, including his life history and background, his ability to support her, and, most of all, to calm opposition to traveling to America. Although Adolph Meyer was opposed to the journey, Schurz wrote, "If I cannot be a free citizen of a free Germany, then I would at least be a citizen of free America."[5]

Adolph Meyer did give his approval. However, they had to postpone the wedding for two weeks because Carl contacted scarlet fever, and Margarethe was ill with chronic "weak lungs." Carl Schurz and Agathe Margarethe Meyer were married on July 6, in a civil ceremony, recorded in the St. Marylebone Register Office of the parish church. Sister Berthe was the maid of honor and Johannes Ronge the best man. A bride's dowry of £78,557 added to Schurz's income as a tutor more than sufficed to support them. In modern currency, the dowry was worth $1,500,000. The ceremony has been considered civil because she was Evangelical Lutheran and he was Roman Catholic; however, another possibility exists. Johannes Ronge, as the leader of the New German Catholics, may have performed an exchange of vows in this very famous church of Dickens and Browning. The newlyweds stayed in Hampstead part of London in a cottage until they were able to leave and sailed from Portsmouth England in August 1852, arriving in New York on September 17, turning their backs to the revolution and their fatherland.

The sailing ship *City of London,* considered safer than a steamship, took twenty-eight days to get to New York, where the Schurzes planned to stay at the Astor House. They found it full and found rooms at the Union Square Hotel on 14th Street that was then the theatre district of old New York, Schurz was impressed by the comparative wealth in the city. After settling into a "plainly furnished room," they went to dinner, and years later remembered it vividly.[6] The dining room was lined with black waiters in white jackets and gloves who rapidly served the dinner with showy flourishes. This may have been his first encounter with black men at close range; however, he was more concerned in his remembrance of their exaggerated style of serving off large silver trays and tureens than he was with race. The dining fashion was much different from the staid British and Continental waiters who were to appear invisible and quietly at hand.

Schurz's memories of his entrance into his new country are fragmented and often random since impressions of first moments are colored by later experiences and achievements later in life. The young couple's first order of business was to spend three days seeing the sights of the city. Neither one of them spoke any English, and they depended on the residents of *Kleinedeutschland* (Little Germany), the German-speaking community on the Lower East Side of New York, for help. They saw Barnum's Museum on the corner of Broadway and Ann Street opposite St.

Paul's Church. They did not go to the theaters because of the language barrier; soon after their arrival, a feeling of isolation and loneliness settled upon them.

Margarethe, ill again, was treated by an American doctor who lived in the hotel. Schurz was impressed by the kindness and offers of help that came from the residents. She was ill for two weeks, during which time Schurz explored the surrounding neighborhoods. As was his habit, he sought solitude to sort out his own plan of action in a new, seemingly strange and mysterious, republic. His first task was to learn English well, so he decided to use the method he had created for learning French of tedious translation and retranslation from German to English and then back again, while never failing to look up an unknown word. He felt he had no need for grammar and structure as that would come by itself as he used and wrote the language. He started by reading every single part of the *Philadelphia Ledger*, including the entertaining editorials: "Joys of Spring," "The Beauties of Friendship," and the "Blessings of a Virtuous Life". He read Oliver Goldsmith's *The Vicar of Wakefield* and the Romantic novels of Sir Walter Scott, Charles Dickens, and William Makepeace Thackeray. Along the way, he read Blackstone's *Commentaries* to begin to prepare for the bar examination. Schurz remembered this process fondly and recommended it to those learning English; however, those who might try it would need a near genius intelligence added to a severe academic discipline.

They decided to go to Philadelphia in October of 1852 because they were sure of a warm welcome by the large German community. They had German friends in Philadelphia, including Adolph Strodtmann, who now owned a small German bookshop, and Dr. Heinrich Tiedemann, a physician and the brother of Gustav executed as the Revolutionary Governor of Rastatt. Tiedemann established the Lankenau Hospital in Philadelphia, had a good practice, and was married to the daughter of fellow revolutionary Charlotte Hecker. Although the Schurzes were not planning to settle in Philadelphia, they thought it a good place to start looking for a home in the new country.

Margarethe, although expecting their first child, seemed happy; she feared dying in childbirth like her mother did. She wrote to her older sister: "For me Carl is father, lover, and husband. Those who knew him before are amazed because he seemed so little fitted for family life. He even got up seven times at night when necessary."[7]

They stayed in Philadelphia from 1852 until 1855, by which time the rest of the Schurz family arrived in the United States. Schurz had to find a way to make a living rather than depend on his wife's dowry. There may have been some money given to him for Kinkel's escape; the donations Kinkel collected in the U.S. were placed in varied bank accounts in Germany saved for use in the next "revolution."

Schurz's recollections and reminiscences, later in life, are random. One memory leads to another, and the story of his adjustment to the new country is shrouded by later opinions and pictorial literary memories. He learned English; however, how long did that take him? His list of books that he translated is a lengthy one. Meanwhile, May 3, 1853, as he was becoming accustomed to a new life, Margarethe gave birth to their first child, a daughter named Agathe after her maternal grandmother.

In 1853, Schurz entered a business venture with Charles Dumming, who was an importer, as his sign read, of "Musical Instruments, Fancy articles and Toys" on 201 Chestnut Street, between Sixth and Seventh Front Arcade. Dumming also repaired musical instruments and made canes to order. Schurz got his brother-in-law Adolph to invest in the business, which Schurz envisioned could expand to the wholesale market and include the Meyer canes. Unfortunately, Schurz was no executive, and the venture failed; during that winter, his parents and sisters arrived from Germany, and to fill his remaining leisure time, he began to write a book about recent history. Margarethe, who spoke more English than he did, helped him.

The summer of that year turned out to be brutally hot in Philadelphia, and the Schurzes, baby included, decided to get out of the city. They traveled to Cape May, New Jersey, joining wealthy Philadelphians finding respite from the heat at the seashore. They made friends with financier Jay Cooke and his family in Philadelphia, who extended summer invitations to their beach house in Cape May. Schurz said the Cookes were attracted by the "beauty, grace, and ingenious conversation of my wife, in her naïve German-English." This friendship lasted for many years, leading to a financial connection and advisement that helped the Schurz family during the Civil War. Schurz used the time in 1853 to study the political climate and governmental structure of his new country. He wrote to his friend, Malwida von Meysenburg.[8]

A democracy in full operation on a large scale,—the most contradictory tendencies and antagonistic movements openly at work side by side or against one another, enlightenment and stupid bigotry, good citizenship and lawlessness, benevolent and openhanded public spirit and rapacious greed, democracy and slavery, independent spirit and subserviency to party despotism and to predominant public opinion-all this in bewildering confusion ...[9]

He saw a complicated society governed by the people themselves, not outside power or agency. His examination of the American way of life included the Pennsylvania Germans and the Quakers, such as Lucretia Mott, a prominent abolitionist, women's rights activist, and social reformer.[10] He wrote to Gottfried Kinkel in April 1853 about a visit from August Willich, who, after his arrival in New York, visited Schurz in Philadelphia wanting to propose the use of the funds collected by Kinkel for little political clubs. Schurz thought this purposeless and told Kinkel that the time had come to quiet the revolutionary fires and to see if the American Government at some time in the future could center attention on the political difficulties of Germany. He really was telling Kinkel, politely, that it was time to give it up.

# Introduction to American Politics (Washington, 1854)

Schurz, still frantically studying English, was affable and slid easily into social situations. There was something about his demeanor that attracted people. He was famous in the German-American circles, achieving notoriety for his rescue of Kinkel, all of which got him letters of introduction to meet the "important" people who could open a doorway to the political arena. It is hard to imagine an immigrant, not yet fully able to speak English, finding his way into the hall of the United States Senate and visiting prominent public figures.

Personally, Schurz was intensely bothered by the slavery issue in an otherwise "free" country. When Senator Steven Douglas's Nebraska Bill, which overruled the Missouri Compromise, was passed, he wanted to see more. He wrote, "The slavery question with all its social, political and economic bearings, stirred me at once, and deeply. I could not resist the desire to go to Washington and witness the struggle in Congress." The family stayed in a Philadelphia boarding house near the Jefferson Medical College in Philadelphia, where Schurz met a "Mr. Vaughn," a family friend of Jefferson Davis', the senator from Mississippi and Secretary of War. Bolivar A. Vaughn was completing his medical degree at the college; his family in Mississippi was friendly with Davis. Vaughn gave Schurz a letter of introduction to the secretary.[1] With letters of introduction to Senator Richard Brodhead of Pennsylvania and Senator James Shields of Illinois, Schurz pocketed the three of them and journeyed to the nation's capital in the spring of 1854.

Schurz's first impression of the city was "dismal," and the Hotel National in which he stayed "dingy beyond description." He stopped first at the War Department to meet Jefferson Davis, who received him "graciously." Although still a bit cautious about his English, the conversation went well. Davis was non-committal about the Nebraska Bill, only "hoping for the best." Schurz found Davis elegant, well-spoken, and dignified, not like many of his colleagues at the time. This part of Schurz's memoir was written years after the Civil War, and, interestingly, the author did not denigrate the president of the Confederacy as many others did.

Schurz met Senator James Shields of Illinois, an "enthusiastic Irish Nationalist," and veteran of the Mexican War, who greeted his visitor warmly, and steered the conversation away from the pending controversial bill, saying only that he supported Steven Douglas, and wanted to hear of Schurz's German "adventures."[2] Shields was famous, or infamous, because he almost fought a duel in 1842 with Abraham Lincoln. The two men resolved their issue and lifelong friends.

Senator Richard Brodhead of Easton Pennsylvania was the third stop on the personal political tour. Schurz found him dull as well as a self-appointed spokesperson "for the magnificent resources of Pennsylvania" and for the Democratic Party to which "all adopted citizens belonged." Much to Schurz's dismay, he dodged any commentary on the slavery issue. He continued on his journey, having a meeting with Francis Grund, a Bohemian-born newspaper writer and moralist, the following day.[3] In this meeting, Schurz reached his first political epiphany, when he discovered, through Grund, the American "spoils system" of political payback and favoritism. The idealist in him hesitated to discover and to admit to his new country's "public plunder" between members of victorious parties that was a matter of course. When he asked about the salaries for these appointed positions, he found that they were low because of the "pickings." He was shocked when he learned that extra money could be added to the base salary, either legally by asking some recompense or illegally from the customer or client. Schurz's first reaction was to ask if the United States Congress was corrupt. Grund told him that there were few a crooks *per se*, but that many would close their eyes to shady political dealings and compensations.

Schurz pressed him further on the slavery issue. Grund dodged it by saying that he hoped that the Missouri compromise would keep slavery in the "background" for a long time; however, he said, the new Nebraska bill might cause a crisis. Therefore, Schurz decided to visit both houses of Congress himself. His first impression was of "bushy whiskered men, dressed in black, chewing a quid of tobacco and lounging about the halls of both houses." He felt that there were few men of dignified "presence and bearing," but the "majority struck me as rather easygoing and careless of appearance."[4] He was impressed, however, with the quality of the speeches, many of which were "vigorous, sober, and elegant in language."

Senator Stephen Douglas did not impress him. From the first time Schurz saw the diminutive, bulldog of a speaker, he disliked him. He felt that Douglas, although plain spoken and direct, was as follows:

> Utterly unsparing of the feelings of his opponents. He would nag and nettle them with disdainful words of challenge and insult them with such names as "dastards" and "traitors." Nothing could equal the contemptuous scorn, the insolent curl of his lip with which, in the debates to which I listened, he denounced the anti-slavery men in congress as the "Abolition confederates,"

and at a subsequent time, after the formation of the Republican party as "Black Republicans."[5]

Schurz described the alignment of the political figures on both sides of the slavery question. The lineup of the Northern opposition included Senator William H. Seward, then of New York, as a mysterious individual, with a "thin sallow face, the overhanging eyebrows, and muffled voice."[6, 7] He found him elegant, polite and a very good speaker. Thurlow Weed, Seward's "political manager" and companion was "astute skillful and indefatigable."[8] The stateliest figure in the Senate was Salmon P. Chase, the Senator from Ohio, who was "tall, broad shouldered and proudly erect" and a "picture of intelligence, strength, courage and dignity."[9, 10] Charles Sumner, the senator from Massachusetts, reminded Schurz of "some Englishmen of distinction," and gave the impression as a "gentleman of refinement and self-respect."[11, 12]

Chase authored a "manifesto" setting forth the true significance of the Nebraska Bill, which was subjected to the wrath and vituperation of the "Little Giant Douglas," the leader of the anti-slavery "champions." Schurz described Senator Andrew Butler of South Carolina as a man seemingly with "bubbling good nature and as possibly a jovial companion."[13] He was, however, a fierce defender of slavery who would "assume the air of a higher class, and in fluent and high-sounding phrase, to make the Northern man feel the superiority of the Cavalier over the Roundhead." It was this attitude, according to Schurz, that brought about the altercation with Sumner which "had such deplorable consequences," coming to a head in 1856 when Butler's cousin, South Carolinian Democrat Preston Brooks, nearly killed Senator Sumner on the Senate floor two days after his anti-slavery speech, "The Crime against Kansas," characterizing Butler as a "pimp for slavery."[14] Brooks came to Sumner's office and beat him violently with a cane.

Schurz described Senator Robert Augustus Toombs of Georgia, who became an organizer and Secretary of State for the Confederacy as a large boisterous man, certain of "the sanctity of slave property and of the higher civilization of the South."[15, 16] Schurz saw him as the very picture not of the Southern aristocrat, but of the overbearing and defiant Southern middle class allied with the "rich slaveholding aristocracy." Schurz found Virginia Senator James Murray Mason's, "utterances pompous and offensive."[17] To Schurz, Mason's, whose attitude reflected "over weening self-deceit; assertive in manner, and even more in language," portrayed the superiority of the Southern slave-holder over the Northern people.[18] Mason was the president *pro tempore* of the United States Senate.

After his visits and observations, and the Senate's passage of the Kansas Nebraska Bill by a 37–14 vote, Schurz returned to Philadelphia. Although he recorded his Senate impressions much later in his life in his *Reminiscences*, after his diary was burned in a fire in 1866, Schurz's vivid portrait of a divided Congress in a divided country reflects the attitudes, which fostered the Civil War. History sometimes portrays the combatants as faceless politicians without their superior attitude that propelled the conflict. Schurz saw the champions of the slave power as overbearing, dictatorial, and vehemently demanding a chance for unlimited expansion. He saw their actions as a threat to the country's freedom. This visit to Washington led Schurz to another epiphany that led to his future career.

> I saw the decisive contest rapidly approaching, and I felt an irresistible impulse to prepare myself for usefulness, however modest, in the impending crisis; and to that end, I pursued with increased assiduity my studies of the political history and social conditions of the Republic, and of the theory and practical workings of its institutions.[19]

Senator Shields reinforced this idea while entertaining Schurz, suggesting that he go into politics in a "new" state, predicting that he would be in halls of Congress before long.

While in Washington, Schurz wrote home to Margarethe on March 23, 1854, about his experiences and President Franklin Pierce, who he did not get to meet. Pierce was a man, he wrote, "who has an unfortunate trait of wishing to please everybody and consequently he has displeased all. He agrees with everyone who speaks to him and so says something different to each one."[20] Schurz solidified the two main issues in his own mind that were important motivations propelling him into his own career in the American political arena. As a true idealistic moralist, he despised slavery, but he was shocked to discover, as some had not, that slavery was a class issue. The Southern so-called "Aristocratic Gentlemen" farmers, well connected to the original founding fathers, looked down upon the working class and farmers of the North. They saw no reason to separate the lower class from the slaves, and no reason to abolish an institution well-conceived and administered by their forefathers. Schurz found them surly, sloppy, and sneering. The whole class concept that he had seen repeatedly in his revolutionary war-torn homeland resonated in the new one.

Schurz realized that the country had no coherent foreign policy. The reasons were complicated but the tangled mess of affairs and the weak pro-slavery President Pierce appeared to Schurz as the cause of the current chaos in the Government. He wrote, in German, to Gottfried Kinkel much later, on January 25, 1855:

> At this moment, all is at loose ends. Confusion and intrigue reign. The Nebraska question, the tariff question, the Pacific Railroad question, the Cuban question, the Sandwich Island question, the Nicaragua expedition—all these

things are mixed up in a wild jumble and public opinion is unable to arrive at a sane conclusion.[21]

Schurz was charismatic and outgoing, even with self-conceived poor English. He returned home after meeting Senators and lawmakers; he must have had "press" precede him to be as well received as he was. His idealism never flagged; he welcomed the idealism that accompanied the liberty and the ability to express an unpopular opinion without consequences. He saw an opportunity in the American West and decided to go there leaving his wife and child in Philadelphia. He hoped to convince her that the West was civilized and healthier for all of them. She, however, envisioned that part of the country filled with savages and wild men, so she needed some very hard convincing. Schurz had relatives in Wisconsin and some friends in Illinois and Missouri. In 1854, he went to the West.

# The American Journeys
# (1854–1856)

Schurz left, in September 1854 on a tour of the "West," leaving Margarethe and the baby in Philadelphia. In the modern world, the journey would be called "networking," which the affable and intellectual friendly Schurz did very well. He started his journey in Pittsburgh, traveling on to Cincinnati, Cleveland, Indianapolis, St. Louis, and Chicago. His account of his experiences assumes a picaresque quality, telling them in no particular order. In his *Reminiscences,* he cataloged the "great" Germans in the Midwest to help stand against the "nativists" who hated all foreigners and were just about to surface as the "Know Nothing Party."[1] It is unclear whether Carl Schurz met all of the prominent Missourians on his first visit, but the German-American community provided a network of abolitionists and Lincoln supporters that led to Schurz's political career. He wrote:

> The infusion of such ingredients gave to the German population of St. Louis and its vicinity a capacity for prompt, intelligent, and vigorous patriotic action which, when the great crisis of 1861 came, made the pro-slavery aristocrats, who had always contemptuously looked down upon the "Dutch" as semi-barbarians, stare with amazement and dismay at the sudden appearance of their hardly suspected power which struck such telling blows for Union and Liberty.[2]

He visited Friedrich Hecker, now living in a log cabin on a farm, degenerated from an elegant lawyer in Baden to an unkempt, raging Missouri farmer. After a simple farm meal and an evening of "Hecker rants," Schurz traveled to Chicago, where he spent an uneasy night in a shabby hotel seated in a chair because of the bedbugs in the room. He continued on his journey to Milwaukee, where the presence of the strong German element, and the "Forty Eighters" brought something like a wave of spring sunshine into that life."[3] He noted that because of the influx of his culture, it was called the "German Athens of America." Schurz went from Milwaukee to Watertown to visit his uncle, Jacob Jüssen, who had immigrated to Watertown in 1853 to join his son, Edmund, the first of the family to arrive in the Midwest in 1847. Edmund and the other cousins, Otto Jüssen and George Rey, were schoolmates of Schurz's at the Jesuit *Gymnasium* in Cologne. Edmund attended a political rally in Cologne where Carl was speaking. According to the family, he was punished with solitary confinement, on bread and water, in the school's "carcer" (jail). That action cost him admission to any other university or school, so he left for America with his uncle, George Rey.[4] Edmund became an attorney and after the sad death of his first wife, he married his cousin, Antoinette Schurz, Carl's sister, in 1856.

Schurz found Watertown, Wisconsin, attractive and seemingly a good place to settle down. The town (formerly known as Johnson's Falls) had a settlement of German immigrants, many of whom were Forty-Eighters. He even met a fellow student from the Congress at Eisenach—Emil Rothe, a journalist and cigar maker, who founded the *Weltburger* newspaper. Schurz resolved to settle in the Missouri Valley, and since his parents and sisters had arrived in Philadelphia, he purchased property in Watertown, deciding to delay a trip back to Europe for his wife's health and to bring the parents to his new town. He also transferred some "business interests" to Watertown. He planned to buy 96 acres of farmland, hoping to subdivide it and make a 12–15 percent profit. Schurz, like his father before him, according to his sister's later memoirs, was never a good businessperson.

Margarethe's health was failing again. She continually suffered from a respiratory issue—either asthma or a chronic obstructive pulmonary disorder that was either hereditary or could have been the result of industrial and residential air pollution. She grew up in Hamburg, where an early ecological activist wrote: "While in Hamburg you might believe the whole world to be covered with clouds, you just have to pass the city borders towards Bergedorf to find clear and bright sunshine."[5] The smoke from wood, coal, and peat stoves filled the residential areas, causing "smog;" the same was true of London, where, in the 1850s, "The biggest cause of death remained consumption and lung disease."[6] New York and Philadelphia had the same issues. Mid Century, medical science was not concerned about air pollution. Schurz's a trip to the Swiss Alps was thought to be a curative benefit; they could not go to Germany since there still was an outstanding warrant for his arrest. Schurz, however, convinced his wife to go to Europe for Agathe's health so as not to worry her about her own. Before they could leave, he brought his parents to Watertown. While there, he wrote letter after letter to his wife extolling the virtues of the Western "frontier," the beauty of the landscape, and friendly *gemütlichkeit* of the new German settlers in the community because she still thought it was populated by savages.

On April 21, 1855, the Schurz family returned aboard the *Washington* to the cultivated, civil climate of Bloomsbury once again, meeting the Kinkels and old friends Malwida von Meysenbug and Friedrich Althaus, who was busy helping Prince Albert catalog his collection of engravings. A trace of the old revolutionary fervor and energy returned there when visiting Hungarian revolutionary Lajos Kossuth and Italian political activist Giuseppe Mazzini. Schurz encountered Alexander Herzen, a predominant Russian socialist who was tutoring Malwida's daughters and got to hear about Russian problems.[7] They saw the famous "Swedish Nightingale" Jenny Lind's performance of selections from favorite Richard Wagner's operas.[8] The only trouble they encountered was with the Ronges over diamond brooch that was a family heirloom. Whether they accused Margarethe and Carl of taking it or it was the other way around is unclear. Ronge, the renegade Catholic, never liked Schurz for his "free-thinking" ways.

Margarethe's health did not improve in London; therefore, Schurz took her to the water cure clinic sanitarium in Malvern.[9] While she remained there for six months, he returned to the U.S. on July 6, 1855. He returned to England on December 17, 1855. They were invited to the Heinrich Meyer's Villa in Montreux, Switzerland, where Schurz hoped that the mountain air and the familiarity of the European surroundings would improve Margarethe's breathing and coughs.

Upon his return to Watertown, Schurz found his uncle, Jacob Jüssen, doing well in the liquor business, and his sisters, Anna and Antonie, running their own "high class millinery and dressmaking business." He purchased the farmland as planned. In August, Schurz, who loved to hunt, reconnected with Emil Rothe and had a successful trip while waiting for the finalization of his purchase. He wrote weekly, and dutifully, to his wife, each time advertising the beauty of the countryside and the happy social life. He mentioned the *gemütlichkeit* of the local *Saengerbund* and *Kegel Abend* (bowling night), which were held in the true German fashion. He told Margarethe that German was the predominant language, but like other American settlements, one could hear the different dialects of a whole country in one room. While in Watertown, Schurz made a side trip to Milwaukee. He told his wife of the wonderful musical performances there and of the cleanliness of the American farmhouses and housewives, which he found far superior to those in Germany. At this point in his life, Schurz was committed to being a "gentleman" farmer, focusing all his efforts on the success and maintenance of his investment.

Schurz's troubles with his long legs in later life began on October 15, 1856, when his horse stumbled and fell on his left leg, injuring his knee. He took two weeks to recover and while he was "laid up," he designed their new farmhouse. There is a curious passage in one letter referring to an incident Margarethe had with the Prussian police, which was ostensibly about the whereabouts of her husband; the letter (to Margarethe on November 5, 1855) indicated that she had been in Germany visiting her family, most likely in Hamburg. Her husband was so upset that he wrote on November 19, 1855: "The longing for you and our child is often so powerful in me that it costs me an effort of will not to leave everything in the lurch."[10] He was finally able to get back to Europe on December 17, 1855, where he met his family, at the Kinkels' in London.

In February 1856, they went by way of Paris and Dijon back to Heinrich Christian Meyer's Villa Maison-aux Bains, in Montreux, Switzerland, where the beauty of the landscape and the clear air healed the family:

> It seems to me that Margarethe's condition in general has improved; at least many of the more disagreeable symptoms have disappeared or have greatly moderated. It is my opinion that a pleasant residence in a healthful climate, her own permanent housekeeping in which all comforts can be looked after, a quiet country life without excitement, supported by strict regularity in diet and moderated treatment, would prove more beneficial to her than this uncertain search after anything that might be good and the continued uncertainty of existence which leaves us restless today over what might happen tomorrow. [11]

Margarethe's brother, Henry (Heinrich), was there with his young wife, Emilie, for health reasons. Schurz thought that the hours spent there with the extended family were among "the very happiest." Brother-in-law Henry was of "lively disposition," his sister-in-law "one of the finest and noblest of women," his wife was at the height of her loveliness, and his daughter was just beginning to talk. They spent a lot of time together planning their respective futures while reading aloud from the great English works of literature.[12] All good times seem to end sadly. The realization that it is the end of a wonderful time together brings tears of happiness and sadness. The Schurzes set sail on June 21, 1856, for home, this time in Wisconsin.

# Watertown, Wisconsin

Schurz wrote glowingly of his new home in Watertown to his friend Frederick Althaus, describing the layout and the warm glow of his family life in it.[1] He was happy that his wife's health had improved and that she was getting settled. His own business ventures were progressing smoothly; he was selling his farmland parcels and had been appointed a public notary with a partner Charles J. Palme. He took the office of advocate, in March, and was named to the board of The Mutual Life and Insurance Company of the State of Wisconsin. It was originally in Janesville and moved to Milwaukee in 1857 where it lists Carl Schurz as a trustee. S. S. Daggett, the president, was a fellow Mason. Schurz's relatives had been members of that organization in Germany, and Schurz was a member of Herman Lodge, No. 125, in Philadelphia. He planned to study law in 1857 and apply for admission to the bar.

He chose the small town because of the large German population; however, he soon found that his "*landsleute*" did not share his political beliefs. He became a liberal Republican because of his strong opposition to slavery. His position was not a popular one, and it did bring him some grief that he excluded carefully from his writings. His problem with acceptance was twofold: first were the Democratic leanings of his fellow expatriates who had followed that party because of the opposing Whig's abhorrence of foreign-born Americans, and because of an inherited class differentiation in the eyes of Schurz's Germans.

Schurz discovered three classes of his clannish compatriots in the Midwest. The first were the real farmers who migrated for land, the second were the "Latin Farmers" who farmed but knew nothing about agriculture, and the third were the educated intellectuals who were in business but looked down upon the agricultural community. Many of them were still devoted to the German ways and even wanted to "found a German State" where they could preserve their mother tongue and their German customs."[2] A convention to found such a state was held in Watertown in 1851, but it all ended in just talk. This attitude is prevalent in the modern era, when foreign-born citizens cluster together with no need to learn the language of the new country.

The other issue was slavery. Schurz and Kinkel were followers of the British abolitionist William Wilberforce, the leader of the movement to stop the slave trade.[3] He was instrumental in getting the Slave Trade Act of 1804 and the Slavery Abolition Act of 1833 passed, which ended slavery in the British Empire. German-immigrant Democrats in Watertown did not much care one way or the other if slavery was kept or abolished. Schurz, an active anti-slavery politician, was immediately labeled a "liberal Republican," or, more accurately, "*ein verdammte Republikaner*" who had no right to hold different political ideals than the current residents of the small town.

Carl Schurz's reputation as a "Godless free-thinker" was created in Watertown. According to Watertown historian William F. Whyte, July 4, 1852, fell on a Sunday, and in most cases, the people would celebrate it on Monday, July 5, but the German immigrants insisted on a Sunday celebration marked by a speech, in German, by Schurz's colleague Emil Rothe, whom he had met at a student gathering in Frankfurt. The next day, the Reverend Barth spoke in German, denouncing those at the Frankfurt Revolutionary Student Convention for hissing at the suggestion of an opening prayer; Schurz was tangentially guilty by association and was branded as a freethinker atheist. When Schurz first lived in Watertown, he was busy with by his land purchase and studies. He was elected an alderman of the 5th Ward in April 1857; in May, he resigned as commissioner of public improvements but continued to attend council meetings with Emil Rothe. His anti-slavery position stood in the way of political acceptance. He was admitted to the bar in 1858, entering a law partnership with Halbert Eleazer Paine on January 1, 1859.[4]

His time in Watertown became troublesome because his farmland was not selling and the approaching panic of 1857 caused it eventually to be lost to the bank (it was finally all sold in 1867), and his popularity in the town for his political leanings had waned. He was no longer the Romantic rescuing hero of German Revolutionary lore. In his book *A Political History of Wisconsin*, A. M. Thomson describes Schurz at the State Republican convention of 1857:

> As he advanced, the impression was not favorable. His tall lank form and long legs were heightened by his dress, which was seedy, threadbare and ill fitting. His coat sleeves and his trouser legs were much too short, and his Emersonian nose, adorned with the ever present gold bowed spectacles, gave him a novel and picturesque appearance.[5]

Carl Schurz had arrived in the midst of upheaval among the local Wisconsin Democratic Germans. Those rejecting the Whigs were not inclined to join the brand-new Republican Party, which supported the abolitionist's plank. He was as, A. M. Thomson put it, "a stranger in a strange land," but the negative impression did change. Finally, the conclusion was that as soon as he started to speak, the visual impression faded away and it was apparent that he was the most able man in the room.[6]

There were other matters at work promoting Schurz into the public German-American eye. Louis P. Harvey, owner of an engine manufacturing company in nearby Shopire, absorbed later by Fuller and Johnson, was a founder of the new Republican Party. He was credited for launching Carl Schurz's political career while he was a member of the State Legislature and governor of the state. He asked Schurz to speak in Jefferson, yet he protested he was too "shy" to speak, which appeared out of character for the loquacious immigrant. He did go, the appearance promoted his local popularity. Newspapers began to write about his miraculous rescue of Kinkel, based on writing by another Republican pioneer, Horace Rublee, the editor of the Wisconsin State Journal.

While her husband, Carl, was embarking on his political journey, Margarethe had given birth to their second child, Marianne, in March 1857. As little Agathe started to toddle, their mother invited neighboring cousins, Anna and Nannie Jüssen and Julia and Margaretta Miller, in to play with her. Ellen (Ella) B. Flavin, then aged ten, was asked to stop by on her way home from school to teach the girls English. After Marianne was born in March 1857, Ella was asked to tend to the baby; she grew to be the girls' governess (in modern terms, the *au pair*).[7] Margarethe's children's group in the Schurz home in Watertown, November 1856, was the first kindergarten in the United States.

In the same year, the Schurzes acquired a piano, which both of them played well. Margarethe and Carl sang with the *Gesangverein*; he had a very good tenor voice and Margarethe was a soprano. The children were taught music and colors, and they were instructed in the manner of Friederich Wilhelm Froebel. Margarethe's sister, Berthe, and her husband, Johannes Ronge, wrote *A Practical Guide to the English Kindergarten* for presentation at the 1854 International Exhibit of Educational Systems in London. Their concept was revolutionary in the academic community, where play and learning had not been linked together. Even in modern America, there are school districts that do not embrace the idea of a joyful preschool learning experience. The kindergarten (literally translated from German as "garden for children") embraces the idea that a child is expected to bloom after careful nurturing. A little boy named Franklin Blumenfeld joined the in-house school and then, when more children showed interest, the kindergarten was moved into its own building on North Second and Jones Street in Watertown.

Margarethe had to have more help with the two little ones when her husband traveled the campaign routes. His parents moved into the household during 1857. During this time, Schurz took up hunting with a passion, so much so that he was called the "Country Gentleman of Watertown." For the next four years, Schurz stumped, spoke, cajoled, and politicked in two languages across the Midwest. His stamina was extraordinary. He could safely leave his wife at home with the support of his parents and relatives in Watertown. Some townspeople resented this "newcomer." Democrats disliked his politics; the Know Nothing Party members hated foreigners; earlier German settlers hated the "green horns." There were some reports of Schurz being pelted with rotten eggs or being ridiculed for his manner of dress.

In 1857, maybe by design or accident, the Republican Party nominated Schurz for the lieutenant governorship of Wisconsin. He had almost attained citizenship, but there was no law requiring it for office. Therefore, he campaigned vigorously throughout the area, and even though the Republican candidate Alexander Randall won the governorship by a small margin; Schurz lost his office by 107 votes.[8] He still valued the experience as it propelled him forward as a voice of the German-born Republicans and one of a premier abolitionist. This was a year of adjustment for the fledgling politician Schurz, with so much of his life crammed into a short time; he had been transplanted from one society to another in a strange small-town Midwestern society, became a father, owned a farm, brought his parents along, finished up a law degree, and launched a speaking and political career. He was just twenty-six years old.

The year 1858 held "great developments," as Schurz put it; the country "was quivering with excitement."[9] The Dredd Scott decision had been handed down from the bench of the Supreme Court.[10] According to Schurz, "the pro-slavery interest had expected finally to settle the burning question in its favor, but it only served to shake the moral prestige of the judiciary, and to make the slavery question more than it had been before, a question of power."[11] It was also the year of the Lincoln–Douglas debates, which Schurz believed propelled Lincoln toward American fame.

Reflecting on the climate of the time, Schurz saw the slavery issue smoldering beneath the surface of the nation's conscience, with most people (particularly in the Northern area) dismissing slavery from their thoughts leaving a relatively calm appearance to daily and political life. Schurz blamed Stephen A. Douglas for "rousing the public mind from its temporary lethargy by proposing his Nebraska Bill which removed the States rights in regard to slavery." Douglas, the incumbent senator from Illinois, was facing a double-edged sword over the issue of Kansas and slavery. If he could capitulate to the Northern anti-slavery elements by supporting the Bill and at the same time repudiate the fraud by which Kansas had become a slave state, he would lose the Southern voters for his hopeful ascendance to the presidential office. The Kansas Act had been proposed by the minority (pro-slavery) without the approval of the vote of the people.

Carl Schurz never liked or tolerated the diminutive Stephen Douglas. Both Lincoln and Schurz dwarfed his height of 5 feet 1 or 4 inches. It was not his stature that Schurz found repugnant but his supercilious attitude and rude process in a debate. Douglas probably abhorred slavery privately. His public position in the 1859 election, and in the debates with Lincoln, was one of the individual state's sovereignty. The concept did not align with Schurz's strong moralistic posture, which "set forth the inherent incompatibility of slavery with free institutions of government, the inevitable far reaching conflicts which the existence of slavery in a democratic republic was bound to produce."[12] During the campaign of 1858, local politician Carl Schurz was asked to join the campaign of the Republican State committee. He was able, with everything fairly settled at home, to go into Illinois and give speeches, mostly in German, to the different constituencies. The hope was to convince his fellow expatriates to vote and convert to the Republican Party. He met Abraham Lincoln on October 12, 1858, on a train bound for Quincy, Illinois.

# 13

# Lincoln

They must have been an odd-looking pair when they met on a railroad car on the way to the sixth debate with Douglas. Lincoln was taller by inches than his German campaigner was; both men were not well dressed, both wrinkled and worn and both had different speech sounds and patterns, contrasting the high-pitched voice of Lincoln with the accented English of Schurz. Schurz describes Lincoln as he remembered that first meeting:

There he stood overtopping by several inches all those surrounding him. Although measuring something over six feet myself I had, standing quite near to him, to throw my head backward in order to look into his eyes. That swarthy face with its strong features, its deep furrows, and its benignant melancholy eyes, is now familiar to every American by number less [sic.] pictures.... On his head he wore a somewhat battered "stove-pipe" hat. His neck emerged, long and sinewy, from a white collar turned down over a thin black necktie. His lank, ungainly body was clad in a rusty black dress coat with sleeves that should have been longer; but his arms appeared so long that the sleeves of a "store" coat could hardly be expected to cover them all the way down to the wrists. His black trousers, too, permitted a very full view of his large feet. On his left arm he carried a gray woolen shawl, which evidently served him for an overcoat in chilly weather. His left hand held a cotton umbrella of the bulging kind, and, also, a black satchel that bore the marks of hard usage.[1]

Schurz's initial meeting with Lincoln was more positive and friendly than he could have anticipated:

He talked in so simple and familiar a strain, and his manner and homely phrase were so absolutely free from any semblance of self-consciousness or pretention of superiority, that I soon felt as if I had known him all my life and we had long been close friends.[2]

Schurz was charmed; his later description of the President was colored by a lasting and close friendship during which the two men shared much private laughter-filled moments as well as very sad and sorrowful times. When they arrived in Quincy, Illinois, brass bands, celebrations, and streams of people were there to greet the train. Schurz was curious as to the reaction of people to Lincoln and was concerned about his speaking abilities.

Lincoln was not a natural or trained speaker and did not, according to Schurz, possess the desirable qualities of an orator. "His voice was not musical, rather high keyed, and apt to turn into a shrill treble in moments of excitement; but it was not positively disagreeable." Himself a fledgling student of speech and oration in this day when people lined up and crowded in for a prominent orator, and when speeches were regularly published in the newspapers, Schurz noted:

> [Lincoln's] gesture was awkward. He swung his long arms sometimes in a very ungraceful manner. Now and then he would, to give particular emphasis to a point, bend his knees and body and with a sudden downward jerk, and then stood up again with a vehemence that raised him to his tiptoes and made him look much taller than he really was.[3]

Schurz's impression of Douglas was less favorable. He saw dishonesty, despite eastern polish, in contrast to Lincoln's honest "western" language and homespun humor. "As I looked at him, I detested him deeply; but my detestation was not free from an anxious dread as to what was to come," wrote Schurz. He was disappointed in the outcome of the election with Douglas going off to Congress, but he felt Lincoln had achieved a moral victory and was viewed as a potential leader by his constituents. This campaign, even though it did not propel either man into the Congress or legislature, was the start of Schurz and Lincoln's political prominence.

Schurz decided that when the campaign was over, he would settle down and practice law with his partner. However, his plans did not work out. His farm plan went to dust with the panic of 1857, and he lost money when the bank foreclosed. He was not alone in his failure financially, as the country faced hard times. Fortunately, he was guaranteed a legal income in Milwaukee, where a group wanted to retain him and his partner's services. He also made an agreement with the *Milwaukee Atlas,* a radical German weekly publication, to write for them on a regular basis. As he continued on the speaking path and was asked to speak in New England, Margarethe's health began to fail once again. Shortly after Christmas, he read in the newspapers of Johanna Kinkel's tragic death. She had fallen out of a window from her upper story of the house in Bloomsbury. Many thought she had committed suicide, but later accounts described her as falling because of a flu-like condition that caused her to lose her balance from a dizzy spell as she went to the window to ease her troubled breathing. Schurz was heartbroken and wanted to run to England to be with his friend Kinkel, but he could not leave.

To make the situation worse, vicious attacks were leveled at him as he became more prominent, and as German immigrants were leaving the Democratic Party. The *Wisconsin Free Democrat* published the following on Wednesday, January 12, 1859:

> The editor of the *Beaver Dam Democrat*, who discovered that Carl Schurz amassed a princely fortune in the service of the King of Prussia, has discovered that the father of our respected contemporary of the Sentinel was also a pliant tool of Kings. He is evidently exercised on the subject of kings. In the case of Schurz he has never made it appear clearly how it occurs that a gentleman who has served the king with such zeal as to have amassed a princely fortune in that service, should now be an exile from the presence of that King unable to set foot again in his native land without danger, When the informant of the editor, who ran the original saw on him, gets back, we shall doubtless have the rest of the story.

The *Wisconsin Free Democrat* on Wednesday, January 19, 1859, in an article on the "Offences of the Republican Party" referred to "Carl Schurz, who is almost deified by the party in this State appealed to the prejudices of his infidel countrymen against the Democratic Candidate because he was a 'professor' of the Christian religion."

When Schurz was branded an "infidel" and Prussian spy by the local Democratic press, Judge Mertz of Beaver Dam, accused of the slanderous remarks, denied them vehemently in a letter to the newspapers. One of the more tragic accusations appeared in the *Wisconsin Free Democrat* on March 16, 1859. "A late member of the Watertown *Volks Zeitung* charges Emil Rothe, editor of the *Weltburger*, with furnishing the Beaver Dam paper the article containing the villainous assaults on the character of Carl Schurz."[4] Although possibly hurt by the accusation, Schurz realized that his friend was a fellow Republican and innocent of these charges.

The slanderous remarks did not affect Schurz's fledgling popularity as a speaker. The *Milwaukee Sentinel* reported on January 7, 1859, when Schurz delivered a lecture at the Racine Wisconsin Young Men's Association: "Mr. S. stands higher as a lecturer, scholar and orator, than perhaps any man in the State, and in securing him the Lecture Committee did well for themselves and the Association." However, the brand of "infidel," "atheist," and "free-thinker" never left him and was used regularly in the Democratic Journalists.

The year 1859 became a banner year for Schurz as an orator, despite the antagonistic press. He began to speak primarily in English, spreading the political gospel of the Republican Party outside of Wisconsin. His first task of the year was to support Byron Paine, a lawyer who had defended Sherman Booth. One of the founders of the Republican Party, Booth had been in and out of courts and jails for his part in helping Joshua Glover, a runaway slave from Missouri, escape from jail in Racine, Wisconsin, by rallying a riot to get him released. Sherman Booth supported the repeal of the Fugitive Slave Act in Wisconsin in his paper, the *Wisconsin Free Democrat*. On March 23, 1859, at Albany Hall, Milwaukee, Schurz delivered a speech, "For States Rights and Byron Paine," defending his anti-slavery position and supporting his election to the Supreme Court Bench in Wisconsin.

> I will not speak here of slavery as a moral and political and economical [*sic.*] evil. I will stifle all my sympathies with the downtrodden and degraded. I will repress that feeling of indignation and burning shame which overcomes me when I hear the clanking of chains in this vaunted Republic of equal rights, and all my horror at the atrocities growing out of the inhuman system I will bury in silence. Neither do I intend here to claim any political and social privileges for the slave, or to assert the rights to which he may be entitled as a member of the human family. We have often been accused of meddling with affairs not our own, and forgetting those interests which concern us nearest, but now I will speak of our own rights, our own liberties, our own security, and unbiased by sympathies as well as prejudices I shall try to measure the depth of the chasm before which we are standing.[5]

The successful election of Byron Paine to the Wisconsin Supreme Court added to Schurz's reputation. He was invited to speak in Boston, on April 18, 1859, at Faneuil Hall. The occasion, hosted by Senator Henry Wilson and Edward L. Pierce, was ostensibly to celebrate Thomas Jefferson's birthday, which was not the real reason for the gathering. The Know Nothing Party had taken over the Massachusetts State Government and legislature during the years preceding 1859, to the point that it adopted an amendment to the State Constitution that would deny the right to vote until two years after citizenship was granted. This famous party billed as the "American" movement considered themselves "Nativists" and were summarily opposed to any foreign or Catholic immigration to the shores of the United States of America. They spread rumors of "Romanist" takeovers and of Pope Pius IX's opposition to democracy. The German and Irish Catholic immigrants bore the brunt of their wrath. The secret society was called "Know Nothings" because when asked about their party, they were required to reply, "I know nothing." The Democratic Party speakers, campaigners, and newspapers used the movement as an indication of the problems the country would face if the Republican "foreigners" would come into the office. Carl Schurz, a Catholic-born immigrant with newly acquired American citizenship, was sent into the very center of the Know Nothing Party in Massachusetts.

He made his first trip to Boston in April for the gathering followed by a trail of positive and negative publicity portraying him as a hero, rescuer, orator, spy, and some sort of German boogieman. His speech on States Rights had preceded him; many knew of his reputation, but to his shock, his reception was overwhelming. On April 14, he wrote to his wife that the dinner at the Parker House in Boston was one of the "most sumptuous affairs I ever attended." Schurz was wined and dined. Each course was served with a different wine. According to the *Boston Traveler* of Thursday, April 14, 1859, there were over 120 persons, including sixty or seventy of the most prominent Republicans in the state, present when the event started at 3 p.m. Schurz, the "German orator of Milwaukee," was seated next to Representative Henry Wilson at the "laden" round table surrounded by a "who's who" from literature and politics. Seated with him was Henry Wadsworth Longfellow, the poet; Edwin Percy Whipple, the literary critic; Oliver Wendell Holmes, the physician and poet; Governor Nathaniel Prentice Banks; Representatives Anson Burlingame; John Bassett Alley; John McKeown; Snow Williams; John S.C. Knowlton; Chief Justice of the Suffolk County Massachusetts Supreme Court Charles Allen; Charles Francis Adams Sr. (son of John Quincy Adams); attorney J. Q. Griffin, John Brown's lawyer and later governor of Massachusetts; John Albion Andrew, politician and Massachusetts legislator; George S. Boutwell, prominent lawyer and author; Edward L. Pierce and his brother, Henry Lillie Pierce, politician and chocolatier (Baker's Chocolate); abolitionist leader and legislator Francis William "Frank" Bird; Samuel Bowles, "brilliant" editor of the Springfield *Republican*; Senator John Parker Hale; Stephen Henry Phillips Attorney General of Massachusetts; and H. D. Parker, the owner of the Parker House and more anti-slavery leaders of Massachusetts.[6]

Carl Schurz's speech, "True Americanism," delivered the next day at Faneuil Hall, became one of the landmark speeches of American letters that has been quoted throughout the 150 years from its date of delivery in newspapers and magazines across America. The following very famous quote comes from this speech:

> Ideals are like stars; you will not succeed in touching them with your hands. But like the seafaring man on the desert of waters, you choose them as your guides, and following them you will reach your destiny.[7]

This speech was one of many he made that year, but it was the eloquence of a transplanted foreigner that resonated with the men seated in front of him that made the difference. He was to repeat this speech over the years but never again to an audience of the literary and political elite as he met in Boston. He stayed in the city for three days after his address and met Oliver Wendell Holmes, Ralph Waldo Emerson, the poet James Russell Lowell, and the naturalist Louis Agassiz. He met Charles Eliot Norton, a social activist considered by many the most cultured man in the United States; author, poet, and publisher James T. Fields; and Senator Charles Sumner. These men and the others from the dinner were a very close circle of the intelligentsia in Boston at the time; Carl Schurz fit right in. His speeches had a developed rhythm, which sounded poetic when delivered. Schurz was never afraid to use images or metaphors appealing to the emotions. He was so well-received that they took him to visit the famous poet John Greenleaf Whittier.

His political star was on the ascendant; however, slanderous and venomous accounts still appeared in the newspapers. Schurz was called a renegade German and an atheist who was on the attack against the "protestant ethic" of all that was good in America. The *Boston Liberator* reprinted an article from the *Boston Courier* on Friday, April 29, 1859, that denigrated Schurz for his activities in support of the repeal of the Fugitive Slave Act, which the "Know Nothings" regarded as a strike against the Constitution as set forth by the founding fathers:

> What a pity it is that ignorant constitutional charlatan, Daniel Webster, died before the sight of this political Gamaliel, Carl Schurz, at whose feet he would doubtless have been proud to sit, and taken easy lessons in constitutional construction! It is too late to reform his errors, but not too late for us. What a cause of gratitude it is for us that the great political geniuses of Germany, after having reared so symmetrical and lasting edifice of constitutional liberty in their own country, should condescend to visit us, benighted Western barbarians, to teach us how to interpret our own laws, construe our own constitutions, and govern our own citizens! Renouncing the political opinions of Washington, and the religious doctrines of the Puritans; putting ourselves under the guidance of Schurz in things temporal, and of Strauss in things spiritual-we shall secure all the blessings promised to the saints in this world, and the world to come.[8]

The writer linked Schurz to the controversial theologian David Friedrich Strauss, who believed and wrote that Jesus existed but was not divine. His controversial work *Das Leben Jesu, kritisch bearbeitet* was translated into English as *The Life of Jesus, Critically Examined in 1846* by author George Eliot (Mary Anne Evans), making its existence a rallying point for the traditional conservative Christian. The Earl of Shaftsbury called it "the most pestilential book ever vomited out of the jaws of Hell."[9]

These articles categorized Schurz as a militant atheist; the writer continued:

> Mr. Schurz, with his transcendental declamation about humanity and equality and the rights of man, is one of those superfluous blessings for which the most devout mind is not called upon to return thanks. He is as unseasonable as a fish dinner in a Catholic household the first day after Lent. His sphere of duty is that of the domestic missionary and not the foreign. Let him preach his gospel to the heathen at home, for we are more advanced Christians than they.[10]

The *Weekly Wisconsin Patriot* quoted the *Madison Patriot*:

> Schurz is a mere political adventurer, a soldier of fortune, who works for pay; he
> has exhausted his transcendental vagaries, which were capital in trade, for the
> benefit of the Republican Party in Wisconsin.[11]

Schurz realized his unfavorable position, knowing that all public figures have
to bear the brunt of opposing venom as a politician, and even more so as a
foreigner who was more likely to be attacked than a native. When he returned
home, he found Margarethe was upset with his new idea to seek the nomination
for governor of Wisconsin. She felt abandoned. His travel, lectures, and minimal
correspondence to her and his children isolated him from his family. She tried to
dissuade him from running for governor to no avail. They had been married for
seven years, and he wrote to her in August of his devotion and marital happiness
to soothe the waters. His daughters were two and six years old, and even though
they had their mother and a governess, they needed their father.

The need to replenish the family finances put Schurz on the road again in the
fall and winter of 1859, during which time the country was undergoing crisis
after crisis. The Southern states were threatening secession; John Brown, who
raided Harpers Ferry in October, was captured and executed. The House of
Representatives could not elect a speaker and the slavery issue was coming to
a head. Schurz, now receiving a $100.00 per speech, moved Margarethe, and
the children, from the cold Wisconsin north to the relative comfort of his friend
Dr. Henry Tiedemann in Philadelphia, where the doctor could keep an eye on
his wife's condition. Schurz traveled extensively through Minnesota, often
giving two speeches a day. Fortunately, during that time, lecturers were in great
demand, and those with some fame and notoriety were a draw. Eminent speakers
included Henry Ward Beecher, Ralph Waldo Emerson, Wendell Phillips, and
Charles Sumner. With news speeding by telegraph, Schurz's fame and ability were
broadcast widely and his speaking tours became profitable.

His speeches and travels ended at the start of the Republican convention
in May 1860 preceding the crucial presidential elections of that year. Schurz
was appointed to the resolutions committee, supporting anti-discrimination
legislation of foreigners and free homesteads for settlers. At the same time, he was
the head of the Wisconsin delegation.

He went into the convention supporting the Republican candidate William H.
Seward, an advocate of abolition, immigration, and Catholics. However, as the
convention progressed, it became obvious that Seward's connection with political
boss Thurlow Weed was a hindrance to his nomination. Although Seward had
173.5 votes (based on the state's allotted ballots) on the first ballot, Lincoln
gained on the second as Salmon B. Chase, and Simeon Cameron lost ground.
Schurz supported Lincoln on the second and third ballots, and when he was

nominated on the third one, Schurz was chosen to be a part of a committee that went to Illinois to give to Lincoln the official announcement of his nomination. Schurz noted that the commitment to the anti-slavery movement was growing stronger and stronger; men like Joshua R. Giddings of Ohio made abolition "the religion of his life."

After the nomination, Schurz was asked by the Republican National Committee to campaign primarily in the German communities and to do so in both languages. He had no trouble speaking in support of Lincoln and even wrote him a letter of apology for supporting Seward. His relationship with the future president began to grow; for some reason, Lincoln related to the German American community. Perhaps they shared the same viewpoint on the slavery issue or maybe Lincoln saw the support of many, many votes. He had purchased a printing press for a neighbor in Springfield, which became the foundation piece for the *Illinois Staats Anzeiger* (*Illinois State Advertiser*), a German-language newspaper. Dr. Hermann Theodor Canisius was the publisher and a Forty-Eighter. The condition of the purchase was that the paper would support Lincoln and the Republicans.

Carl Schurz began to speak for Lincoln's campaign in the summer of 1859. Travel and lodging were expensive and he needed party support. His enemies accused him of campaigning for profit and notoriety, but in reality, he needed the money. In spite of his finances, his stature grew larger and larger on the public stage and in the political arena. Republican papers in the Midwest proposed him for Governor. When he spoke, he was often greeted by the bands of the "Wide Awakes" formed spontaneously across the country. They were young men in paramilitary organizations excitedly demonstrating and drinking whenever and wherever they could. Some believe that they were the link between politics and the Civil War; perhaps they loved Carl Schurz because of his student activities with the *Burschenschaft*.

After the convention and nomination, Schurz felt a strong attachment to Lincoln the man. They were growing closer, sometimes at odds with each other, but more often comrades and colleagues who shared emotional moments. There were similarities and marked differences between these two men of such different backgrounds. They both came from farmland, but Schurz was more educated than Lincoln was. Both men loved theatre and music, but Schurz, with a fine voice and excellent piano skills, was a musician while Lincoln made fun of his own inability to sing or make music. Both men married a wealthy wife whose families did not approve of the marriages. Carl Schurz enjoyed his beer, wine, and cigars; Lincoln was a teetotaler and a non-smoker. They must have appeared, to many observers, as characters out of a comic opera—the tall German with the pince-nez glasses perched on his long nose, and the even taller presidential candidate with the tall stove pipe hat and perennial gray shawl led to cartoons and satirical attacks against both men.

Carl Schurz continued his campaign stumping for Lincoln in July of 1860 in Egypt, Illinois. The press, depending on the politics of the area where he was going, preceded him both favorably and negatively. The *Cedar Falls Gazette* named him as "one of Europe's best gifts to America." [12] On the other hand, the *Cleveland Plain Dealer* quoted by the *Weekly Champion and Press* reported:

Carl Squirts. This hair lipped renegade, who left his country for his country's good, has been furnished money and means by Black Republicans to the stump the country for Lincoln. He is a red Republican all but his heart that is black. [13]

Schurz's travel itinerary was exhausting and amazing. He covered many, many cities often sleeping on the train from town to town. There were two personal issues, however, that the now famous speaker and politician encountered: one was money and the other was the time spent away from his wife and family. Although his personal finances had suffered during the panic of 1857, his campaign speeches and other lectures were costly. Train travel from city to city cost approximately $1.30 each way if he was not in a sleeping car, and hotel rooms averaged $3 a night, including meals, which in modern currency is $35 a trip and $54 per night. Lincoln's campaign alone went over 21,000 miles. The Republican State Committees now paid him $200 per week more than twice his usual fee. His wife, despite the income, and despite her daily involvement with her kindergarten, wrote an angry letter to him in August that was waiting for him in Evansville. She accused him of paying too much attention to other women and keeping things from her. [14] He returned home in the fall, protesting his innocence, echoing that in his letters to her during that period.

The campaign during that hot summer was invigorating and exhausting. Schurz at times was too hoarse to speak more than once in a day, even though large crowds demanded a second speech to follow in either German or English. This was the day of the orator as an entertainer; people paid admission to hear a famed speaker speak and expected at least two hours. When a free speech was offered, crowds gathered and Schurz spoke to large assemblies of up to, according to the press, 25000 people. The orator, in the days before amplification and microphones, was expected to project his voice to the very last person in the last row. Proper training and breathing helped keep the vocal cords in condition to do this for two or three hours; however, Schurz was traveling, smoking, drinking, and often letting his emotions carry his speech with the end result of a hoarse, tired voice and strained vocal cords.

The other issue was the heat in that summer of 1860. Men kept their coats on when speaking from the lectern. In one instance, it was so hot that the moderator asked the ladies in the audience if it was all right for Schurz to remove his jacket; the ladies waved their handkerchiefs in approval and as he spoke, Schurz removed not only his jacket but his vest and tie too. At the beginning of the campaign, he wrote:

> The campaign was hardly opened when the whole North seemed to get into
> commotion. It looked as if people, especially in the smaller cities and towns
> and the country districts, had little else to do than to attend meetings, listen to
> speeches, march in processions, and carry torches after nightfall. "Wide Awake"
> companies with their glazed capes and caps, the prototypes of modern marching
> clubs of party organizations sprang up all over the land as if by magic. Brass
> bands, some of them very trying to the musical ears, seemed to grow out of the
> earth.[15]

One of the highlights of his tour was his dinner with Lincoln in Springfield,
Illinois. He ate with the family and then Lincoln accompanied him to his speech
clad in an old linen coat with sweat stains on the back, which Schurz likened to a
map of the two hemispheres. To his surprise, Lincoln refused to sit on the podium
after greeting many people in the crowd by their first names but instead sat in the
front row, nodding and smiling at Schurz whenever the audience applauded. The
tour was very successful. The newspaper *Trump of Fame Weekly* on Wednesday,
August 22, 1860, in Warren, Ohio, reprinted article from the *Milwaukee Sentinel*:

> The course of Carl Schurz through Illinois and Missouri has been marked by a
> complete [*sic*.] revolution in sentiment: and even here, in our own city we can
> name scores of prominent Germans who have come out boldly from the rank
> and file of Democracy and signed their names on the Republican Club book.

Schurz's political star was on the rise; he was becoming more and more well-
known even in the small Midwestern towns. The Democratic press, representing
the "Conservatives" of the day, attacked the image of both Lincoln and Schurz.
Lincoln was called a bumpkin and "Sagamore rail splitter."[16] Schurz was an
intruding foreigner who spoke in contempt of the Declaration of Independence,
a "Red Republican," a "Negro Worshipper," a "Teuton fugleman, (spokesman)"
and a "Prussian puppet." There was a report of Schurz holding a cabbage head
during a campaign speech that represented the intellect and brainpower of the
Democrats and Stephen Douglas. The negative sensational press had the opposite
effect and—combined with the continuing Republican reports about Germans
leaving the Democrats and joining the newly formed party, along with the stories
and the names of the men, including Schurz's brother-in-law (cousin) Edmund
Jüssen, joining the popular "Wide Awakes"—increased his popularity. The name
Carl Schurz started to appear in the news as a candidate for governor or senator.

Schurz's year of speeches was effective for turning the German vote to Lincoln.
His own fame increased. There now was a demand for the well-known, notorious
foreigner whose fame was spread by published versions of his "famous" speeches,
photographs, and etchings of him published for sale as souvenirs. The campaign

speeches, printed by his friend Thurlow Weed, were for sale, including those of Seward, Lincoln, and Schurz, who was in great demand.[17] His pay was now sufficient to start replenishing his accounts. In the fall of that year, Margarethe and the children moved to Philadelphia for the winter for health and companionship with the Tiedemanns, as the indefatigable Schurz started to travel once again. One reviewer described him in glowing Romantic terms:

> Whichever principality or power in the High places or the Low, of Vaterland, may claim Carl for its lawful born, he is really of that southern and noblest Teuton type which combines the impressibility, enthusiasm and expressiveness of the Latin blood with the concentration of will and the quiet intellectuality of the North. All this is seen in one person-slender, rather tall, with the professorial stoop and spectacles, the delicate refined hand, the Greek jaw, with nose translated from the Greek into pretty fair German, strong chin, angular, metaphysical eyebrow and expanding though retiring forehead. It also proved in his life and partially in his lecture.
>
> His delivery reminds one, though with favorable difference for himself, of the lecture in German universities; quite as forcibly as of the popular harangue. The voice is even, without slowness or monotony; on the cool intellectual key; not pure in tone (of course not for it is a German's); and unaccompanied by gesture. His pronunciation of the English is certainly admirable; the honest guttural Dutch being only now and then tripped up by some tricky labial.[18]

The press loved to compare classical scholars and philosophers to each other; the anti-slavery idealist Carl Schurz was being compared to great intellectual orators like Ralph Waldo Emerson, Horace Greeley, and William Jennings Bryan. These comparisons, the controversy of his campaign speeches and the negative media attached to them, his foreign birth, and widely distributed versions of his rescue of Kinkel produced a dashing and marketable persona.

# Ambassador to Spain

After the great victory, a very lonely and busy Carl Schurz traveled again before he was scheduled to be in Washington for the inauguration. As his travels carried him throughout the Midwest, he had to forego Christmas with his family. He wrote to his wife that they needed the money and that all would be better in the future. They would all be together soon. He arrived in Washington on March 1, 1861, in time to attend for Lincoln's inauguration. During January of that year, Kaiser Frederick William of Prussia died and was succeeded by his son, Wilhelm the First, who became King of Prussia and eventually of the German Federation. He immediately pardoned the "old" political prisoners who had been convicted or wanted because of the 1849 revolution. The only one omitted was Carl Schurz, whose offense was deemed "not political." He could not return then to Germany because he was still wanted for breaking Kinkel out of prison. Therefore, the anti-Schurz faction in the United States' media called him unfit for any further political appointments. He had made an enemy in William Seward, when he removed his allegiance in the presidential nomination to Abraham Lincoln. Schurz now viewed him as almost pro-slavery, an official who would allow the slavery issue to fade out while he was Secretary of State. Lincoln wanted to appoint Schurz to political office but ran into trouble when he proposed Schurz as ambassador to Sardinia; Seward blocked the nomination, and when the post to Portugal was suggested instead, it was again denied. Finally, after a visit to Lincoln by Schurz, the President overrode the veto of his secretary and Carl Schurz became the ambassador to Spain. His colleague, Cassius M. Clay, a prominent abolitionist, who was slated to go there, accepted the post to Russia instead.

The newspapers printed more than 460 articles about the conflicts caused by the appointments. Opponents headlined the "radical Red Republican foreigner being appointed," yet the Republican papers praised Schurz as an able executive. The threat, according to his deterrents, was that Schurz, as a former revolutionary, would propose and support rebellion in any foreign country in which he would hold office. The underlying theme was that the man was not really an abolitionist but was using the platform for personal gain. The brand of "racist" was placed on Schurz in a twenty-first-century article because in one letter to his wife, Schurz used the phrase "my darkey" when referring to a hotel servant.[1] The letter was in German, and the word did not have the same connotations it has today; it is possible that the translator substituted the word for "*Schwartze*," meaning "black". In Schurz's day, because of the Know Nothings, ethnic hatred was rampant. Based on his earlier writings and education, it is apparent that Schurz was not a "racist" in the modern sense of the word.

Despite the negative articles in the media, Schurz went to New York to book transportation for the family to Europe. Before he left, he had the opportunity to take his brother-in-law, Henry (Heinrich), to meet Abraham Lincoln and was shocked when they were invited to lunch with the President, who greeted them warmly with an informal handshake and asked all about Hamburg before he began a round of funny stories. Meyer, who was fluent in English, was very impressed. Heinrich was in the United States to obtain a license from B. F. Goodyear for the hard rubber patent and eventually started working at College Point, Long Island.[2]

The Schurz family stopped first in England to visit the American Minister Charles Francis Adams, son of John Quincy Adams, inquiring about conditions in Europe regarding the start of the Civil War in America; they traveled on to Paris to see Minister William Dayton, who was instrumental in keeping France from joining the Confederate states in the war. Margarethe and the children, anxious to visit the family in Hamburg, went on to Germany, while Schurz, who could not enter his native country, traveled by rail to Marseilles then by steamboat to Alicante, and then by rail again to Madrid. They decided that the climate of Northern Germany would benefit Margarethe's health; they would reunite after the steamy summer in Spain was over.

Schurz, with his salary of $12,000 a year, landed in Madrid and was met on his arrival by Secretary of the Legation Horatio J. Perry, the official clerk and advisor to the ambassador.[3] Schurz learned that he was expected to appear in court in "official dress," consisting of an embroidered dress coat, a cocked hat, and a court sword. His outfit, ordered in Paris, was not yet ready or sent on to Madrid. Perry was very agitated about this circumstance and hoped that the *Introductor de los Embajadores* would not take this lack of costume as an indication of disrespect.

Negotiations with the officials, including the Queen, resulted in allowing the newly appointed ambassador to appear in evening dress. Upon arrival at the court, Schurz discovered that he left the official introductory "Letter of Credence" back at the hotel. In the moment, Schurz took a piece of newspaper and put it in an official-looking envelope, while Perry convinced the Minister of Foreign Affairs to accept the real letter the next day, since the Queen was not going to read it anyway. All went well, until the guards outside the grand staircase in the palace would not allow them to enter improperly dressed; after much conversation, a guard went to fetch the *Introductor* who apologized profusely. The meeting went well; "the Queen appeared, a portly dame with a fat and unhandsome but good natured looking face."[4] He continued meeting the rest of the "Royals:" the "King" Don Francisco de Assisi and the Minister Don Saturnino Calderon Collantes.

After the diplomatic formalities were over, Schurz discussed, in diplomatic French, the delicate issue of slavery. Spain still had slaves; any mention of the abolitionist stance would not be welcome. Seward had foreseen the difficulty of sending anti-slavery men into the diplomatic core at that time, especially to Spain, which had holdings in the West Indies, near American soil. Carl Schurz had to successfully walk the diplomatic tightrope; he enjoyed his stay in a villa outside Madrid, but when the news of the Union defeat at Bull Run reached the foreign press, he had, he felt, a problem because European newspapers were sympathetic with the cause of the Southern Confederacy. *The London Times* was the most vocal.

Schurz believed that Lincoln had quieted his previously loud anti-slavery support. Seward had written to the president requesting that the "slavery issue be put out of sight."[5] He wanted to avoid Confederate allegiance with sympathetic foreign powers. The Europeans were going to war with Mexico; the question arose—how would the American government treat foreign ships?

The court, countryside, and politics of Spain had never been a happy marriage for Schurz; he was alone and alienated in the diplomatic ranks. Distant foreign war clouds rumbled when European warships sailed for the waters near Mexico and the United States. This "Mexican Business" was alarming to the Americas and it placed Schurz in the diplomatic center of negotiations. France, Britain, and Spain were trying to extract repayments of loans made to their creditors suspended. Napoleon III saw this as an opportunity to add influence and trade and to seize Mexico. The United States could only stand by since it was involved in the Civil War. Obviously, the fear in the Union was the possible intervention of the foreign powers on the side of the Confederacy. Schurz visited the Spanish officials, seeking assurance that Europeans would stay neutral. Finally, the Spanish government told Schurz that they would not recognize the Southern Confederation; after the turmoil settled, Schurz asked for a leave of absence to go home and see Lincoln.

He wrote to Seward expressing the opinion that "a manifestation of the anti-slavery tendency of our Civil War would be most apt to remove the danger of foreign recognition of the Southern Confederacy and of foreign interference in its favor."[6] Seward replied and Schurz described his answer as a "characteristic exhibition of Seward's command of vague and sonorous language when he wished to talk around the subject instead of directly at and upon it." He was not sure that his original dispatch ever got to Lincoln, and with the vague answer of being so busy with the Civil War effort he wanted to resign, but Secretary

Perry advised him not to do so. The feeling was that the desertion of his post would have a negative reaction on the part of the Spanish Government, and that it would be better to ask for a leave of absence and go home.

Schurz sent a letter to Lincoln, through Seward, asking to leave; however, the "Trent Affair" happened and caused an international incident when the United States man-of-war the *San Jacinto* stopped a British mail steamer and took two Confederate envoys (James Mason and John Sidell) as captives. There were rumors that England would send troops to Canada in reprisal and invade the north. Lincoln ultimately freed the men, who were on their way to England to get diplomatic recognition and possible financial and military support. Even after their release, they failed in their mission. Carl Schurz, meanwhile, was happy to receive his leave of absence from Lincoln; he learned that Margarethe needed to return home because one of the girls was ill. The major problem to overcome was a journey to Hamburg since he had not been cleared of his old revolutionary charges. He was able, however, to arrange the trip safely via Prussia through diplomatic channels.

# 15

# Emancipation

On January 1, 1862, Carl Schurz and his family sailed for home on the German ship the *Bavaria*. The trip turned into a nightmare because of rough seas for six days and what Schurz described as a "hurricane" off the coast of Newfoundland. Actually, it was a terrible Nor'easter, which left the ship, already battered by crosswinds, with a great deal of damage, illness, and fright. The trip was long, wearying and, with a family, certainly difficult. Upon landing, Schurz took the family directly to Washington D.C. to see William Seward about his earlier dispatch from Spain on the "slavery" issue; during the conversation, President Lincoln appeared and interrupted them. He excused Seward and talked directly to Schurz. Seward had not acknowledged that he received Schurz's document, but Lincoln and Schurz agreed that only the destruction of slavery would save the Union and would prevent foreign powers from taking sides and intruding into the American Civil War. They both decided that the best way to reach this end was to promote gradual emancipation, which had occurred in the Northern States earlier in the century.

Schurz proposed the emancipation of slaves first in the District of Columbia, followed by the confiscation and *ipso facto* emancipation of slaves belonging to people involved in the rebellion, offering fair compensation to loyal slave owners who would agree to a system of freeing their slaves. He found, however, that the same party divisions still existed. Republicans supported abolition while the Democrats had "resumed their old vocabulary of criticizing the abolitionists in power."[1] Schurz remembered that the National Emancipation Society was formed as a new movement; however, there were many organizations in place since the early part of the century. Lincoln commissioned Schurz to make an anti-slavery speech at Cooper Institute in New York on March 6, 1862, and at the same time, the government would enact the D.C. Emancipation Act while a gradual compensation act was presented to Congress.

On March 6, 1862, Carl Schurz, a thirty-three-year-old immigrant, stood at the front of the crowded main hall of the Cooper Institute in New York facing nearly 300 of New York and the East's avid anti-slavery faction. James Alexander Hamilton, Alexander's son and President Andrew Jackson's Secretary of State,

*Above left*: Carl Christian Schurz, born on March 2, 1829, Liblar, Germany, and died on May 14, 1906, New York City. (*Courtesy of the author*)

*Above right*: *Geburtsurkunde* (birth certificate) of Carl Christian Schurz. (*Courtesy of the Erftstadt Archives, Erftstadt, Germany*)

Carl Schurz memorial and Schloss Gracht, Liblar, Germany. (*Courtesy of the author*)

The town of Liblar in the twenty-first century. (*Courtesy of the author*)

Entrance way to Schloss Gracht, described by Carl Schurz in *Reminiscences*.
(*Courtesy of the author*)

*Above left*: Schurz memorial plaque on the wall of Schloss Gracht. (*Courtesy of the author*)

*Above right*: Dr. Franz Bartsch: Erftstadt/Liblar historian and archivist pointing to the grating Schurz described in front of the "family room" in Schloss Gracht. (*Courtesy of the author*)

The Metternich crest over the entrance to Schloss Gracht. (*Courtesy of the author*)

*Above left*: Wolf door handle—one of many family wolf symbols in Schloss Gracht. (*Courtesy of the author*)

*Above right*: Carl Schurz's birthplace: Schloss Gracht, Liblar, Germany.

*Above left*: Christian Schurz (1796–1896), Carl Schurz's father.

*Above right*: Marianne Jüssen (1798–1877), Carl Schurz's mother.

*Above left*:  Carl Schurz as a student at Bonn. (*Courtesy of Sabine Bishop-Klaus*)

*Above right*:  Carl Schurz as a university student.

*Above left*:  Gottfried Kinkel (1815–1882) and Johanna Mockel Kinkel (1810–1858).

*Above right*:  *Paulskirche*, Frankfurt am Main, before World War II.

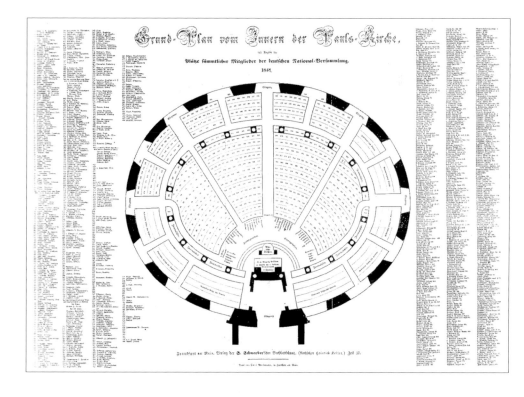

*Above*: Floor plan of *Paulskirche* at the time of the Frankfurt Convention in 1848.

*Left*: *Paulskirche*, Frankfurt am Main, in the twenty-first century. (*Courtesy of the author*)

An artist's conception of drawing of Frankfurt Parliament *Paulskirche*.

*Above left*: Memorial plaque for Carl Schurz on the outer wall of *Paulskirche* in Frankfurt am Main. (*Courtesy of the author*)

*Above right*: Carl Schurz's cousins: Sabine Bishop Klaus and her daughter, Katharina Klaus, in front of the plaque for "Uncle Schurz." (*Courtesy of the author*)

Modern interior of the meeting hall of *Paulskirche*, where Schurz saw the Frankfurt meeting. (*Courtesy of the author*)

Rastatt, Germany, in the nineteenth century. (*Courtesy of the author*)

Gottfried Kinkel and Carl Schurz.

*Above left*: Gottfried Kinkel "In Chains," a publicity drawing to raise money for his escape.

*Above right*: Widely circulated drawing of Kinkel's escape.

Kinkel and Schurz's escape route from Warnemünde, Germany.

*Above left*: Agathe Margarethe Meyer Schurz (1833–1876).

*Above right*: The Meyer (Stockmeyer) Family, *c.* 1846: Henry, Margarethe, Heinrich Christian Meyer (seated), and Adolph. (*Courtesy Sabine Bishop Klaus*)

Schloss Rastatt, Germany, where Carl Schurz was during the Revolution of 1849.

Schloss view, Rastatt. (*Courtesy of the author*)

*Above left*:  Last gate still standing in Rastatt. In 1849, the Prussians were guarding all of them, preventing escape. (*Courtesy of the author*)

*Above right*:  Rastatt market place where revolutionary soldiers were camped. (*Courtesy of the author*)

Carl Schurz's room in Rastatt during the 1849 Revolution. (*Courtesy of the author*)

The front of the "*Konditorei*" where Schurz stayed during the Revolution.
(*Courtesy of the author*)

Balcony in front of the "Old *Rathaus*" in Rastatt where revolutionaries spoke.
(*Courtesy of the author*)

*Above*: Schurz's ceiling in the *Schloss* in Rastatt. He wrote that he stared at it from a couch while deciding his fate. (*Courtesy of the author*)

*Left*: Memorial to the twenty-three men executed as revolutionaries in Rastatt, 1849. (*Courtesy of the author*)

Memorial marking Carl Schurz's escape through the drainage tunnel next to it. (*Courtesy of the author*)

Cover of Carl Schurz's escape drain. It is covered over because too many parties were held in it. (*Courtesy of the author*)

*Above left*:  Carl and Margarethe Meyer Schurz in America.

*Above right*:  Carl Schurz's "*carte de visite*." (*Courtesy of the author*)

The "Wide Awakes" and Lincoln's campaign, 1859.

*Above left*: Carl Schurz, 1860.

*Above right*: Mathew Brady's portrait of ambassador Carl Schurz.

*Above left*: "Abolitionists" before the Civil War. Carl Schurz addressed 300 of them at Cooper Institute in New York at Lincoln's request. (*Courtesy of the author*)

*Above right*: Major General Schurz, 11th Corps, Union Army.

Newspaper drawing of General Schurz in battle. (*Courtesy of the author*)

*Above left*: Defenders of the Union. (*Courtesy of the author*)

*Above right*: Agathe Schurz, aged eleven, in her yearbook photograph in 1864, at the Moravian Seminary for Young Ladies, Bethlehem, Pennsylvania. (*Courtesy of the Moravian Archives, Bethlehem Pennsylvania*)

*Above left*:  Senator Schurz.

*Above right*:  *Westliche Post*: Schurz's newspaper.

Fanny Chapman, sketch from her sketch book of Maine. (*From the collection of the Mercer Library of the Bucks County Historical Society*)

*Above*: Luchow's restaurant, a favorite of Schurz and Steinway. (*Courtesy of the author*)

*Left*: Agathe and Marianne Schurz, *c.* 1872. (*Courtesy of the author*)

Memorial at Margarethe Meyer Schurz's gravesite in "*Garten der Frauen*," Ohlsdorf Cemetery, Hamburg. (*Courtesy of the author*)

Villa Forsteck: artistic center of the Meyer family in Kiel; it is no longer standing as it was bombed during World War II.

The remains of Villa Forsteck in Kiel. (*Courtesy of Joachim "Yogi" Reppmann*)

*Above left*: Carl Schurz at rest. (*From the collection of the Mercer Library of the Bucks County Historical Society*)

*Above right*: Rutherford B. Hayes meets the "Indians" with Mary Lawrence Chapman and Fanny Chapman (on the left).

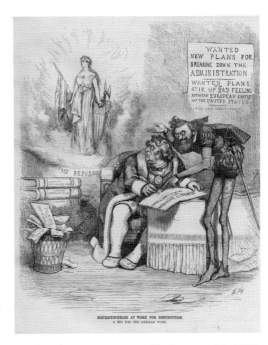

*Above left*: Political cartoon: "No More Outbreaks," *Harper's Weekly*, January 25, 1879, by Thomas Nast.

*Above right*: "Mephistopheles at Work for Destruction," *Harper's Weekly*, Saturday March 2, 1872, by Thomas Nast.

*Above left*: "Whose Funeral Is It?" *Harper's Weekly*, March 20, 1875, by Thomas Nast.

*Above right*: "Getting in Tune," *Harper's Weekly*, July 29, 1876, by Thomas Nast.

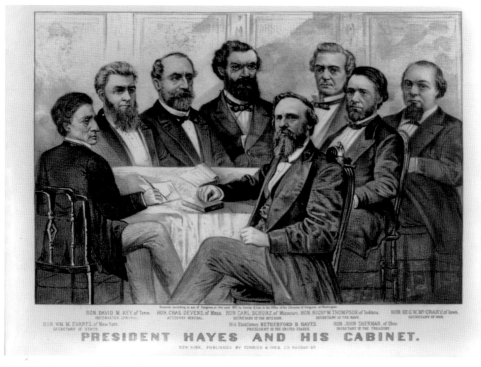

President Hayes and his cabinet: Currier and Ives Print, 1870.
(*Library of Congress Picture collection*)

*Above left*: Lillie de Hegermann Lindencrone, a.k.a. Mrs. Charles Moulton.

*Above right*: Fanny Chapman. (*From the collection of the Mercer Library of the Bucks County Historical Society*)

Dinner for Carl Schurz at Delmonico's.

November 9, 1888, Steuben dinner at the Liederkranz Club; Carl Schurz is on right with a cigar and beer mug.

*Above left*: Herbert Schurz at Harvard, 1896. (*Courtesy of the author*)

*Above middle*: Herbert Schurz at Harvard, 1897, was voted class "Ivy Orator."

*Above right*: Dr. Abraham Jacobi, Carl Schurz's best friend and medical pioneer.

The autograph of Carl Schurz, February 17, 1887. (*Courtesy of the author*)

Bolton Landing, New York, on Lake George—Carl Schurz's view.

Dedication of Carl Schurz monument in Morningside Park, May 10, 1913.

*Above left*: Carl Bitter's sculpted monument: Morningside Park, New York.

*Above right*: Carl Schurz's cousins at the Morningside Park monument of their 'Uncle Schurz:" Sabine Bishop-Klaus, Katharina Klaus, Sean Bishop, and Henrik Klaus. (*Courtesy of Sabine Bishop Klaus*)

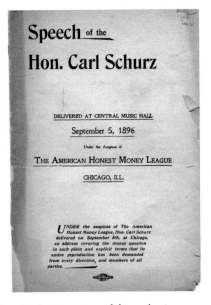

*Above left*: Carl Schurz memorial park, Bolton Landing, New York. (*Courtesy of the author*)

*Above right*: Published version of the speech of Hon. Carl Schurz, Sept 5, 1896, at "The Honest Money League."

**Kämpfer für Freiheit und Recht**

*F. Reuter · Blum · Gandhi*

### S c h u r z

Carl (* 1829 † 1906) wurde als deutscher Demokrat wegen seines unerschrockenen Eintretens für freiheitliche Ideen verfolgt und zur Emigration nach Nordamerika gezwungen. Dort nahm er als Befehlshaber am Sezessionskrieg teil und wurde später Innenminister der USA.

*Right*: Carl Schurz German trading card.

*Below*: First day cover: April 29, 1983, Germantown, Pennsylvania, Herman Masonic Lodge #125.

GERMANTOWN. PA
APR 29 1983
19144

Concord 1683 — German Immigration Tricentennial — USA 20c

FIRST DAY OF ISSUE

**CARL SCHURZ – FREEDOM FIGHTER**

As a young militant liberal in Germany, he fought for and lost those liberties which were a birthright in his adopted land. Here he found a home with which he could identify and where he could work for change without revolution. Herman Lodge #125 Phila. *Edsel*

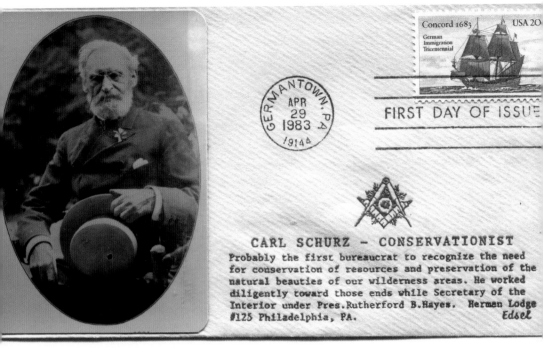

First day cover: April 29, 1983, Germantown, Pennsylvania, Herman Masonic Lodge #125.

First day cover: June 3, 1983, Watertown, Wisconsin.

First day cover: April 9, 2007, honoring ships named after generals.

*Above*: Carl Schurz Grill in Erftstadt/Liblar, Germany, in the twenty-first century. (*Courtesy of the author*)

*Below*: Shoulder insignia from the Carl Schurz *Kaserne*, Bremerhaven, Germany. (*Courtesy of the author*)

First day cover: June 3, 1983, Watertown, Wisconsin.

Carl Schurz's family grave in Sleepy Hollow Cemetery, Tarrytown, New York.
(*Courtesy of the author*)

was the moderator of the meeting. The poet William Cullen Bryant and the Honorable George Bancroft, who had established the U.S. Naval Academy, sat in the forefront along with every abolitionist clergyman and politician in the city. After preliminary speeches by ex-Governor Boutwell and Judge John Worth Edmonds, Schurz delivered his anti-slavery speech, "Reconciliation by Emancipation." While the meeting was in progress, Horace Greely delivered a message from Washington which read, according to Schurz:

> The United States ought to co-operate with any state which may adopt gradual abolishment of slavery, giving to each State pecuniary aid, to be used by such State, in its discretion, to compensate for the inconveniences, public and private, produced by such change of system.[2]

The assemblage was overjoyed; at the end of the meeting, everyone started singing the "Old Hundred" hymn. Although the meeting was successful, the resolution for the "gradual abolishment of slavery," passed March 6, 1862, did not get a single response from any of the slave-holding states. Lincoln issued the Emancipation Proclamation in June of that year. He had support not only from the Northern States in the Union but also from Manchester, England, where the working men of Lancaster refused to handle cotton picked by Southern slaves. The results in December 1862 were demonstrations, strikes, and hunger for the men who were out of work. In thankful reply, Lincoln sent food and goods in support of their effort.

When Schurz returned to Washington, he found Lincoln happy about the outcome of the speech, and the Emancipation Proclamation made public in September 1862. Lincoln was still sad and depressed about his son, Willie's, death. Schurz attended the funeral and was said to have consoled and wept with Lincoln while a distraught Mary was in bed for weeks and unable to mourn or attend her son's interment. Sadly, his account of this sad time was written years later after Schurz had also lost both a son and daughter to disease as Lincoln had.

The new concern for Schurz and his family was his entrance into the Civil War. After Lincoln asked him to return to his diplomatic post, Schurz and Margarethe had dinner with William Seward, who, despite his earlier objection to the original appointment, urged him to return to Spain. No mention of slavery arose in the course of conversation, which disturbed Schurz. After an appropriate wait, Schurz approached Lincoln again, who, after Schurz's rejection of a larger salary, and the relative safety of a foreign post, said, "Have you talked it over with that handsome dear wife of yours?" Lincoln met Margarethe several times and appeared to like her. Lincoln would only appoint Schurz to the military if Margarethe agreed; she apparently did after two personal visits to the White House to present her husband's case to the President who recommended Schurz's appointment as a General to the Senate. Civilian commanders were needed because many of the trained West Point Military had gone over to the Confederacy. General Schurz was off to war.

# 16

# General Schurz

Agathe Schurz turned nine years old that May, and her sister Marianne was just five. Papa had joined the Union Army. After his return to the U.S., Schurz had been ill twice and returned to see Dr. Tiedemann in Philadelphia. His ailments, never documented, seemed to occur intermittently; he suffered from headaches and, in May, stayed in his bed in Philadelphia for eight days.

The new general took a circuitous route through Pittsburgh and Wheeling, West Virginia, to get to his post in the Shenandoah Valley. The regular route to Harpers Ferry was flooded and impassable. He may have realized that the politics of command resembled those of the elected officials. He was caught in a crossfire of opposition for his every action. Like many educated Germans, the solution to learning about an occupation or a skill is to read as many books as possible on the subject. Schurz had read every classic on military tactics while he was stationed in Madrid, and he had set his mind on how to behave in command. He was indeed a moralist looking for logic and equality in the military system of his new country; however, he was not to find it.

The West Point military academy officers, who had remained with the Union, were not accepting of untrained or inexperienced officers. A commission in the newly formed volunteer army was not equal to the same rank in the regular army. A captain in the Union forces often became a private after the war in the regular army. Politically appointed officers were viewed very much in the same way that the "ninety day wonders" were seen during World War II. The career men resented Schurz, who was appointed by the President. The fact that he was a famous German revolutionary, abolitionist, and Liberal Republican refugee added to the prejudice. Democratic generals like McClellan had little use for the opposing party commanders. The Know Nothings in the Army adamantly and admittedly hated and denigrated the Germans and Irish in the ranks, who were considered clannish and odd in their behavior. The fact of the matter was that the German regiments spoke in their native language as many of them had not learned English. The Irish, too, particularly from the northeast mining areas, only spoke Gaelic. The other problem was alcohol consumption. The prohibitionist movement began in nineteenth-century America. President Lincoln did not drink at all; however, the Army issued whiskey rations to some and tried to monitor any alcohol from coming into camp and being consumed just before the battle. Germans were thought of as alcoholics, particularly after Revolutionary War legend of drunken Hessians at Trenton.

Schurz, however, had to face other problems. He was assigned to General John C. "The Pathfinder" Fremont's command in Harrisonburg, Virginia, after the Union Army's defeat at the hands of "Stonewall" Jackson at the Battle of Cross Keys. The general had an interesting background, one that was antithetical to the ideals of the strong moralist Schurz. The Columbus Ohio newspaper, *Crisis*, on Wednesday, June 11, 1862, reported:

> In July, 1861 General Fremont, surrounded by his personal and political favorites, gathering from the Atlantic seaboard and the coast of the Pacific, like vultures to their prey, assumed the command of the western department, with the rank of major general, and established his headquarters at the city of St. Louis. He at once proceeded to inaugurate a system in the purchase of military supplies.[1]

The article accuses him of misappropriation of government funds for an extravagant personal lifestyle funded with government money. He was a Mexican War veteran but appeared to have a lofty self-opinion and was purportedly arrogant and difficult to see when in the field. He was married to Senator Thomas Hart Benton's daughter, which gave him influence and an inflated concept of his own power.[2] Therefore, after much dissension, he was finally relieved of his Western Army command and given the command of the Mountain Department. Fremont was, however, popular with the German community therefore; Schurz's old German revolutionary compatriot General Louis Blenker and his German Division were transferred into the new department.

Given command of the Third Division of the XI Corps, Schurz inherited a largely German-speaking unit. This corps was in shambles, underpaid, and underfed. Morale was low and when the different divisions had been consolidated, there were officers and equipment missing. His division consisted of the two New York regiments, the 54th and 58th; two Pennsylvania regiments, the 74th and 75th; the 61st Ohio; 8th West Virginia; the Battery; 1st New York Light Artillery; and the 4th New York Cavalry. Included in the makeup of these units were friends and fellow Germans: Major Ernest F. Hoffmann, who had served as chief of staff for Garibaldi; Captain Karl Spraul from the Baden infantry; Schurz's wife's nephew, engineer Willy Westendarp; and Fritz Tiedemann. Franz Sigel, Schurz's friend from the revolution, eventually commanded the corps. Many soldiers who fought alongside Sigel spoke little or no English, and many of the officers became friendly with the new General Schurz.

Colonel Eugene A. Kozlay, the commander of the 54th New York Voluntary Infantry, wrote in his diary:

Near Strasburg [*sic.*]: June 23, 1862:

Genl Schurz is very diligent to see his troops. Every day 4 or 5 times he passes between our lines and asks questions appertaining to the necessaries of the men. Good movement how long it will last. Schurz made repeated visits to the men in his command promising to make the poor conditions of lack of personnel, food and equipment right. I have no orders yet to send recruiting officers to New York to recruit up the ranks of my regiment. But Genl Schurz says that it will be done in a few days. Genl Schurz it seems to me likes us very much, because he visits our camp mostly every day. Yesterday he was here twice. I understood this afternoon that perhaps in two or three days we will march away from this place, I have no orders yet to send recruiting officers to New York to recruit up the ranks of my regiment. But Genl Schurz says that it will be done in a few days. southward toward Stanton. June 27th Genl Schurz sent a telegram to Washington to appoint Sigel to the Command. I hope it will be done at once to restore piece. June 29th [*sic.*]

Sperryville July 13.

On the 11th we arrived at this little town. We are encamped on the easterly side of the town on the top of a small hill. Genl Schurz always praises my regiment. He makes us too many compliments. Why is this? What is in the wind? He said to day that my men marched through the town and on the road as the old Grenadiers and he thanked at least a dozen times for it. So did Krizianowsky. But to this later named gentleman cannot trust much. He is deceitful. He talks, but does and thinks otherwise. Another compliment. Genl Schurz has thanked again for the order which exists in my regiment. I should like to know what are these gentlemen ever driving at with their daily praise. I presume to give courage and good will to do it and their duty cheerfully every day. Superfluous. My men are the best in the division, and the regiment too. Here is at least order and good will. When we have taken up our arms in the Defence of the Union, we thought that the Republicans will not take into consideration the political distinction. But I am very much mistaken. If a man is even an ass or an ox, and belong to the Republican party, than he is made by Schurz and others a General. This is our experience in this Army Corps, and I have no doubt, it will be or it. In his early battles, he handled himself well.[3]

Schurz, trying his best to lead and command, faced political opposition from some of the "foreign" officers who objected to his prewar politics, and his connections. Kozlay wrote:

We have here Brigadiers who do not deserve to be Captain in the line, but they are Republicans, therefore must have the title. Such men are Steinwehr, Bohlen, Krizianowsky, Schurz and half a dozen others; and such brave soldiers as Gilsa, Bushbeck, Armsberg, Wratislaw—well they are left behind. No wonder that the Union forces are beaten mostly in every engagement with the enemy. It cannot be otherwise. We must loose when we have such leaders as these. Genls and hundreds others. Now I should lik [*sic*]. Armsberg says that under such asses as Schurz & Schenk he dont want to serve, he will wait till Stahel returns, and then hand in his resignation. In fact he is disgusted with such a war pursuit. Gilsa I presume will not return any more, because he has the same opinion about matters here.

July 14, General Schurz has every day some kind of compliments for myself and my Regiment. Why! What is his object? Very good policy to encourage us, but we know what we have to do without his praises and compliments. He nominated Krizianowsky to command a brigade, though he knows, or at least must have known, that he (Krizianowsky) never was a soldier, that he is not educated, in fact does not understand anything, and totally unfit for the position.

July 28th

Genl Schurz pays me visit, mostly every day. He says that my Camp is the prettiest and best ordered in the whole Army Corps. In fact he is right. No Camp here is as well ordered and beautiful as mine.[4]

Although Schurz was making inspection tours at the President's behest, he made no friends with his report to Lincoln about the abysmal conditions in these units. There was low morale and a lack of food and supplies. Lincoln responded positively. Schurz recommended German-born officers in his division and corps to fill in the missing adjutant and quartermaster to Lincoln; therefore, the charges of favoritism were leveled at him. Lincoln then ordered the consolidation of the forces under Generals Fremont, Banks, and McDowell into one army, now to be called the "Army in Virginia." Major General Pope, named the commanding officer of the Mountain Department, would remain under General Fremont, at which point Fremont balked at serving under a junior officer and promptly resigned his commission. Franz Sigel was his successor.

It was into this maelstrom of military confusion that Schurz went into battle. Oddly enough, his oratory skills prevailed when he presented a calm, confident face to the men serving under him. Captain Karl Maria Spraul, his adjutant, wrote in a letter to the *New-Yorker Bellatristisches Journal* on March 9, 1877, "His social intercourse with his fellow officers was most agreeable, and one of his friends was the French military adventurer Col. Gustave Paul Cluseret." His men liked him and he liked them; this led to his overwhelming difficulties when facing the remains of those lost on the battlefield. His first battle was Second Bull Run, which started in Grovetown, Virginia, on August 28, 1862; he faced the best of the Confederate command: Robert E. Lee, "Stonewall" Jackson, and James Longstreet. The battle, also called the Second Manassas, comprised of 125,000 soldiers within 35 miles of Washington, D.C. The rebel forces won the two-day conflict, losing 8,353 men while the defeated Union Army had 13,824 casualties. Schurz lost almost 20 percent of his units. The field was confusing, and horrifying; the Union Army outnumbered its enemy by 15,000 men (70,000 Union against 55,000 Confederates). Lack of communication and egocentric commands caused the loss. Longstreet ended the rout by sending 28,000 men on to the Union left flank. Schurz wrote:

> The old story of the war—to be repeated again and again—time and strength and blood uselessly frittered away by separate and disconnected efforts of this and that body of troops, when well-concerted action of all of them together might have achieved great and perhaps decisive results.[5]

Schurz, however, did well, drawing praise from the *New-York Tribune* and other officers. He had done his best in a losing cause, turning back retreating troops that General McDowell reported as running from the battle. Although no harm was done then to Schurz's reputation, it was here that the idea of the cowardly German or "Flying Dutchman" began. After the battle, Schurz returned to Washington to visit with Stanton and the President. Margarethe came down in early September to join him. Secretary of War Stanton, who was on good terms with Schurz, quizzed him about his opinions of the current generals, including McDowell, Pope, Fremont, and Hooker. Margarethe arrived for a short stay with her husband; far from the battlefield, they dined with James A. Garfield, who brought Salmon Chase's daughter to dinner and an impromptu piano and singing concert provided by the musical Schurzes.

This "timeout" from the battlefield was also a time of inter-army political upheaval in Washington; the generals were jockeying for position during the fall and winter of 1862–1863. Schurz impatiently wrote letters to Lincoln about what should be done in the war and with the Emancipation Proclamation. Lincoln did not take one letter well and wrote a stern reply to Schurz; however, they still liked and respected each other, ending their quarrel in front of a warming fireplace. It is hard to ascertain, even from correspondence and newspaper articles, which part of Schurz's persona made his contemporaries angry with him. He may have been prejudged as one of "those Germans," or perhaps it was his quick rise to prominence. Was he playing favorites with his German associates? Was he arrogant and egotistical? His wife wrote that when he was happy, he had the face of a small boy; the men in his company liked and respected him. The artistry and intellect that Schurz brought to his work was either removed or overlooked in the documents he left behind; however, the formal and stiff style of the mid-nineteenth-century correspondence and reports may also be the cause of misjudgment.

# "The Flying Dutchmen," Chancellorsville

Schurz was riding high, heading for a fall. The Democratic generals, including McClellan, were in some ways disloyal to Lincoln; to make it worse, Franz Sigel, with whom Schurz lived during these early war years, got embroiled in a controversy over a new command. Generals Schurz and Sigel visited General Burnside, who had replaced McClellan, suggesting that the Army of the Potomac sweep the Shenandoah Valley of rebels; Burnside decided not to and proceeded with the attack at Fredericksburg. Fortunately, Schurz's XI Corps was sent to Dumfries, Virginia, 20 miles away from Fredericksburg, where they could only hear the sounds of the ill-fated battle.

After the Union defeat at Fredericksburg, Schurz was able to return to Washington and his family for Christmas and New Year. Unfortunately, Margarethe was ill; to make it worse, both of the girls had whooping cough. He met with Lincoln about the Emancipation Proclamation, which had now become a political hot potato. Many Democrats felt that it was not necessary to make the freeing of the slaves a part of the battle for the Union. Republicans—Lincoln and Schurz included—believed that it was. Schurz, meanwhile, was trying, during that winter, to get a promotion to major general, which after much persistence he received giving him command of the XI Corps. His tenure there did not last long. After a bout with jaundice in early March, Schurz found the army reorganized yet again. "Fighting Joe" Hooker replaced Burnside; Sigel resigned and because of the changes, Schurz was returned to the Third Division, this time under the command of Oliver Otis Howard, known as O. O. Howard or often as "Uh Oh" Howard. Schurz's rapid rise to the post of major general, coupled with the change in command, intensified the conflict within it. Howard was a West Point-educated puritanical evangelical Christian and a teetotaler who did not allow his men to use "swear" words. He was a hero, having lost his right arm at Fair Oaks almost a year earlier. An avid abolitionist, he found his "faith" later in life and had considered a career in the Ministry. After the war, he founded

Howard University for African Americans. Howard, however, replaced Franz Sigel as the Germans' general and the men of the XI did not like him. One officer was "caught" speaking German, which the Howard thought was "cursing" and punished him for his offense.

The XI Corps was lined up at Chancellorsville facing south and Lee's troops; Hooker's plan was to stay on the defensive, and Schurz was placed on the end of the line (west) as he wrote "hanging in air" on the extreme right. General Daniel Sickles, the only "political" general in command of a Corps, talked Hooker into chasing Lee's forces, which he believed were retreating. Hooker agreed, and Sickles engaged the enemy at Catharine Furnace with 18,000 men; he was effectively cut off from the body of the Army, leaving a large gap between Schurz's command and the rest of the forces. The Confederate artillery took this position on May 2, 1863, bombarding the Union's front.

Schurz realized his poor position, but Hooker and the upper echelons of command were convinced that the rebels were retreating. Jackson had split their forces, marching at night around the field to outflank the right of the line, which was Carl Schurz's division. This famous night march of 18,000 men appeared to all of the Generals at the higher levels of the Union command as a retreat of the Confederate forces. No matter how many times Schurz sent messages or reported the troop movement, the answer was always the same: "the Rebels are retreating." The new Major General Carl Schurz was commanding 5,000 men on the right flank, unprotected, with a dense wood on his right. He first heard the clanking of equipment in the forest and reported it; however, the answer was the same. Then, the rabbits and deer came running out of the forest, as he could hear the eerie rebel yells; he sent word again, which was ignored. When he finally realized that overwhelming forces were on his right, he commanded a "wheel" to face his troops toward the onslaught. The "wheel" was recorded as one of the best, quickest, and most effective in the war; however, it did no good. One brigade attempted to hold off the charging Confederates as Schurz called a retreat. His forces ran toward the Union ranks, but there was a huge gap left by Sickles. To make it more disconcerting, General Hooker was knocked unconscious by a cannonball over his head, hitting a post at his observation point. Therefore, he could not observe the retreat. One contemporary historian, Thomas P. Kettell, an American political economist and magazine editor, wrote of the battle:

> On the morning of the 2nd, a force of the enemy approached by the plank road from Fredericksburg, and attacked the Fifth Corps. The battery of Knapp opened upon them and caused them to return. In the afternoon, they again approached in force, when Geary's division of Slocum's Twelfth Corps was sent into the woods to flank the advance. They encountered sharp fire, and Kane's brigade broke in disorder, throwing the whole column into confusion. The retiring troops were drawn to the right of the road, in order that the artillery

might play upon the advancing enemy. This it did with such effect, that he soon retired. This seems to have been a feint, however since, during the night the enemy had cut a road through the woods which covered the right front of Howard, at Wilderness Church, fifteen miles, southwest of Fredericksburg, and while the attack was going on in front, wagons were moving to the left of the enemy, and it was assumed that he was in retreat. To ascertain the state of affairs, a reconnaissance by General Sickles' Corps was made, resulting in the capture of some troops, who stated the wagons were ordinance following General Jackson and staff. General Sickles then advanced in the hope of cutting the enemy in two, but at five o'clock, in the afternoon, while the movement was in progress, a terrible crash of musketry announced Jackson's appearance in force on the extreme right, where was Schurz's Division of the Eleventh Corps. With wild yells, the Confederates rushed on in overwhelming numbers, and the Germans, overborne, broke and fled in helpless confusion.[1]

Darwin Cody of Hubert Dilger's battery "eyewitness" of the retreat wrote: "Gen. Hooker soon ordered the 12th Corps to kill every man that run in the 11th. I saw a number of officers and privates shot trying to break through the guard. It served them right."[2]

Later contemporary accounts, including that of Horace Greely, never mention the XI Corps' retreat. Carl Schurz bore the mark of a coward for the rest of his career; the retreat was uncovered and used repeatedly by the press. After this battle, Schurz tried and tried to get his side of the story told. He was denied requested hearings. His letter and dispatch to Hooker mysteriously disappeared from the official record. When a board of review was called to evaluate the loss, Schurz was not allowed to testify or even attend. He spent years trying to get exonerated from the blame placed upon him because of this retreat. The political infighting behind closed doors generated heat and excessive verbiage, fault-finding, and finger-pointing. The result was that Hooker was replaced by Meade as the army marched to Gettysburg.

The Germans were subjected to the wrath of the remaining Know Nothings and anti-Germans. The non-German men who fought with the XI Corps blamed the "Dutch" soldiers for the retreat. They encouraged the hatred measured at the "foreigners," which was underscored by the press; the report of the retreat reached the New York newspapers within hours, blaming the "cowardly Germans" for the defeat. The *New York Evangelist* reprinted *The New York Times* article of May 4, 1863, on Thursday, May 7, 1863:

D. H. Hill's division, numbering in all forty thousand men, had precipitated themselves on Howard's corps, forming on our extreme right wing. This corps is composed of the divisions of Schurz, Steinwehr and Diven, and consists in great part of German troops. Without waiting for a single volley from the rebels, this corps disgracefully abandoned their position behind their breastworks, and commenced coming, panic stricken, down the road toward headquarters. Our right was thus completely turned, and the rebels in the fair way of doubling us up.

The article goes on to call the Germans "cowardly rascals." It omits the fact that while the XI was decimated by the overwhelming force of the Confederates, Schurz, unsuccessfully, tried to rally the remaining men from all of the Divisions by leading three or four charges at the enemy. The troops were, however, now named the "flying Dutchmen" by the press and the Anglo-American soldiers although General Howard wrote in his report.

> I am deeply pained to find you subjected to such false and malicious attacks.... I saw you just as the battle commenced; you hastened from me to your post. I next saw you rallying the troops near the rifle pits upon the ground occupied by our corps. After this you were with me, forming a new line. The newspapers depending of battle near Berry's line. I do not believe that you could have done more than you did on this trying occasion.[3]

The newspapers, depending on the slant and political viewpoint of the editors, neglected the real tragedy of the battle; of the 154,734 men on the field (97,382 Union and 57,352 Confederates), the total estimated casualties were 17,304 Union soldiers and 13,460 Confederates. The losses included General Thomas "Stonewall" Jackson, who was accidentally killed by his own troops.

Other writers blamed Hooker for the loss, suggesting that he was drinking during the battle; however, at 9. a.m., the porch post on which he was leaning was struck by a cannonball that knocked him senseless. He probably suffered a severe concussion, but he when he awoke, he climbed on his horse and rode into battle; he was unable to function as he should. Schurz defended Hooker by saying: "General Hooker's mind seemed, during those days, in a remarkably torpid condition … I have never been able to understand, except upon the theory that his mind simply failed to draw simple conclusions from obvious facts."[4]

Schurz and his fellow Germans were obviously upset. He wrote:

> We procured whatever newspapers we could obtain-papers from New York, Washington, Philadelphia, Cincinnati, Chicago, Milwaukee—the same story everywhere. We sought to get at the talk of officers and men in other corps in the army—the verdict of the condemnation and contempt seemed to be universal.[5]

Schurz followed with a report dated May 12, 1863, describing in detail the events of the battle: "My division has been made responsible for the defeat of the Eleventh Corps, and the Eleventh Corps for the defeat of the Campaign."[6]

He asked to have it published and sent to the newspapers, but Hooker refused. He tried further, asking Secretary Stanton for a court of inquiry, but that too was denied as no charges were ever brought against any single person. A book written for the Military History Society of Massachusetts by Colonel Theodore Ayrault Dodge on the Chancellorsville campaign written in 1881 finally exonerated General Schurz:

> Schurz's report is very clear and good. This is partly attributable to the avalanche of abuse precipitated upon his division by the press, which called forth his detailed explanation, and an official request for permission to publish his report. There existed a general understanding that Schurz held the extreme right; and the newspapermen, to all appearance, took pleasure in holding a German responsible, in their early letters, for the origin of the panic. This error, together with the fact of his having discussed the situation during the day with Gen. Howard, and of his having remained of the opinion that an attack on our right was probable, accounts for the care exhibited in his statements. That he did harbor such fears is proved by his having, of his own motion, after the attack of three o'clock, placed the Fifty-Eighth New York, Eighty-Second Ohio, and Twenty-Sixth Wisconsin Volunteers, near Hawkins's farm, in the north part of the Dowdall clearing, and facing west. Still Schurz's report is only a careful summary of facts otherwise substantiated. He deals no more in his own opinions than a division commander has a right to do. Schurz states that he strongly advised that the entire corps should take up the Buschbeck line, not considering the woods a reliable *point d'appui*. For they were thick enough to screen the maneuvering of the enemy, but not, as the event showed, to prevent his marching through them to the attack.[7]

Colonel Dodge blamed the whole debacle on General Hooker partly for retaining his war records:

> But he retained in his personal possession many of the records of the Army of the Potomac covering the period of his command, and it is only since his death that these records have been in part recovered by the Secretary of War. Some are still missing, but they probably contain no important matter not fully given elsewhere. This report, based on military records, says about the "flight of the flying Dutchmen": "It has been called the German Corps This is not quite exact. Of nearly thirteen thousand men in the corps only forty-five hundred were Germans."[8]

Post-war newspaper articles in the Anti-German and Democratic press attacked Schurz, including the connection of the pre-war abolitionist movement and Schurz's later involvement in the "Negro" question to the runaway troops at

Chancellorsville. An article in the *New York Herald* on Wednesday, October 12, 1864 (p. 5), blames his absorption with "the Negro" in the worst possible racist terms as the reason for his retreat at Chancellorsville.

The Republican side dished up a wordy speech of General Schurz, the hero of the runaway troops at Chancellorsville under Hooker. "The speech was as a regular tirade about the Negro." It continues to accuse Schurz of being all absorbed with black people. It states in strongly racist terms that he sleeps with them, eats with them, dreams of them, and is colored all over like them and then it blames his "skedaddled loss at Chancellorsville on his obsession with the race.[9]

The negative press from the beginning of the war until the years after its end increased Schurz's stature and, after the ordeal of Chancellorsville, the replacement of General Hooker with General Meade, and after a brief visit from Margarethe, Schurz moved on to Gettysburg when the news of Lee's advance had reached headquarters.

# Gettysburg

The Battle of Gettysburg has been visited, analyzed, and dissected over many of the years following its end. Speculation continues even today about the efficiency of the Eleventh Corps. Schurz arrived with his division before noon on July 1, 1862. General O. O. Howard replaced General Reynolds, who had been killed and had been in command of the Union forces on the field. This appointment made Schurz acting commander of the XI Corps. Howard, however, kept one-third of the corps behind on Cemetery Hill; this action weakened Schurz's corps to about 4,000 men who were now facing 20,000 Confederate troops. Schurz ordered Barlow's division to refuse his right, which would protect against a flank attack. After finding its position, Barlow decided to move his 2,100 men towards the hill now known as Barlow's Knoll. The depleted XI had an unprotected flank again. This movement was General Barlow's blunder, ensuring the defeat of the XI Corps.

General Francis Barlow later claimed that the defeat was the fault of those "Damn Dutch" who ran away again. Confederate reports of the hard fighting of the Eleventh indicated a necessary retreat. Francis Barlow was a Boston lawyer, who hated the "German" immigrants, often beating exhausted men with the side of his sword to keep them moving; he had arrested Brigade Commander Leopold Von Gilsa for allowing his thirsty men to get water.

Barlow was not the only fault of the retreat; the men were exhausted from rapid marching, and effective communication was not good in any Civil War campaign. Mistakes and misjudgment were part of the mechanism of this horrendously fought war and, therefore, it was very easy to use the "foreigners" as a scapegoat. Schurz did the best he could by withdrawing his men to higher ground on Cemetery Hill, continuing even after his horse took a bullet through the ridge of his neck. Ironically, the "retreat" placed the XI Corps, and what was left of the other divisions, in a better place for the third day of the battle.

On the second day of the battle, however, a weeping Schurz held the hand of his mortally wounded friend and comrade from the Rastatt Castle, Colonel Franz

Mahler of the 75th Pennsylvania Infantry. The third day of the battle brought the famous victory at Gettysburg and the Eleventh Corps stood up under the onslaught of Cemetery Hill; Schurz viewed the battle amid waving flags, singing men, bands playing, and the wounded and the dying. When the battle ended, he was able to send a telegram to Ottilie Schimmelfennig, reporting her husband luckily safe after he had thought lost, dead, or captured.

While the Confederate forces were overrunning Gettysburg, General Alexander Schimmelfennig, clad in a cavalry man's coat that hid his insignia, and after receiving a blow on the head from a rebel soldier, played dead, escaping capture by hiding for three days in farmer Gracher's pigpen. Schurz welcomed him gladly and served him a breakfast of much-needed food.

Schimmelfennig's survival in the "hog pen" only contributed to the "flying Dutchman" rumor, adding to the melee and miscommunication with Barlow's troops to reinforce the slur of cowardice. Sadly, Schimmelfennig was suffering from chronic dysentery and tuberculosis; in the last year of the war, he had to return home. Schurz begged Grant to allow the sick general to remain in the service in order to collect a pension, to which Grant agreed and then forgot, eventually mustering Alexander Schimmelfennig out on August 25, 1865. He died suddenly in front of his wife at age forty-one. Schurz had lost another friend from two wars.

# The End of the War

After Gettysburg and the continuance of the Army politicians, Schurz's military career spiraled downward; the Eleventh Corps was sent to the Shenandoah Valley and comparative inactivity. He pardoned a young deserter using his friendship with Lincoln to help the hapless lad, who had been conned into desertion by older men, avoid the firing squad. The memory of the execution of friends in Rastatt and the situation reflected Schurz's sense of humanity and morality, which did nothing to endear him to the harsher and brutal commanders. In September, he was sick yet again, this time with "camp fever" (a general term for fever, nausea, and diarrhea). Schurz returned to Bethlehem, Pennsylvania, with his family and recovered quickly. After returning to the war, this time to the Tennessee Valley, he continued to butt heads with Hooker now a disgruntled general looking to blame others for his shortcomings. Schurz's XI Corps reached Bridgeport, Alabama, to help open the "Cracker Line." After General William Rosencrans' defeat at the Battle of Chickamauga, Ulysses S. Grant, now in charge of the Army, pushed to open a supply line to feed the starving Union troops. Schurz's unit was at the Battle of Wauhatchie in October. As Hooker and Howard were engaged at Lookout Mountain and Missionary Ridge, and after the return of the presses' condemnation of the German soldier, Carl Schurz felt sure that he would be killed at Citigo Creek, near Orchard Knob. He carried his fear on to the battlefield, but when a shell exploded under his horse; once he realized that he was not hurt his apprehension left him. He had even been thinking of writing another wartime farewell letter, which many soldiers carried in their uniform into battle so that loved ones could be notified of their death.

The troops were sent to Chattanooga, where Schurz met and liked William Tecumseh Sherman. They were moved again back to Lookout Mountain; winter nights there were long, cold, and boring. To pass the time, Schurz read Herbert Spencer's *Social Studies* played cards (Skat) with his old colleague, Colonel Hecker, and became ill again with fever over the New Year period.

January brought difficult times, when Hooker filed his official report on Wauhatchie. Schurz was attacked for not obeying a support order; this time, he got the hearing he wanted. He won the case but it was the end of his military career. In February, still ill with diarrhea, he took leave and requested a new command from Lincoln. The command of the Eleventh and Twelfth Corps was given to Hooker and Howard, and they did not want Schurz on any terms, so he was eventually assigned to an instructional camp in Nashville.

Resigned to his fate behind the lines, Schurz did his duties well; however, he was never able to lose the label of a "despised foreigner" while in the service. The "American" command found it easy to despise the "foreign element." Simon Cameron, the first Secretary of War and a former Know Nothing, believed "all men are created equal, except negroes, and foreigners and Catholics." He originally wanted no non-English speaking soldiers in the Union Army; when questioned by Lincoln, he agreed that if these soldiers were accepted, all orders had to be given in English. Complex political situations and this belief had him removed from the post and replaced by Secretary Edwin Stanton.

The anti-foreign feelings in the military of this time were not all based on ethnic prejudice and assumption; part of the negative treatment was caused unwittingly by their own behavior. The German-trained military soldiers considered themselves, in many cases, superior to the political appointees and West Point graduates. Some of the officer's corps came from "German nobility;" for example, the Third New Jersey Cavalry had twelve German barons as officers.[1] Some of these men were arrogant and rude. The foreign troops— including Italian, Polish, Irish, and German—were clannish and many did not care to, or were not able to, learn English. American soldiers felt shunned and were worried about these other men talking about them. Their choice of food was odd; they drank beer and whiskey, which offended the more puritanical types. Schurz, who had run from an awful political situation, always believed and repeated often that one takes the best of the fatherland and combines it with the best of the new land; however, he was often alone in that kind of thinking. In his own way, he irritated the higher command with his demand of being heard and for his connection to Lincoln. He was also a Republican and many of the higher generals, including McClellan, were Democrats who were fighting for the preservation of the Union and were not totally in support of the Emancipation Proclamation.

He was sent to New York to speak at a "War Meeting," Despite the earlier negative newspaper accounts, he was cheered at the meeting on March 9, 1864, in Tammany Hall in New York. He was to speak with General Hancock; and General Meagher. The March 9, 1864, *Philadelphia Enquirer*'s headline read: "Great meeting at Tammany Hall-Speeches by Generals Hancock, Meagher and Schurz and Hon. James T. Brady." The article that followed reported that Gen. Carl Schurz was cheered and when the applause died down, he said:

The cause in "which we are engaged is very apt to abolish all the reelings of party enthusiasm, to join those entertaining the most different political feelings together, unite all patriotic and loyal hearts, and make all lovers of their country work hand in hand for one great object (Cheers)".[2]

Schurz asked Lincoln if he could leave the Army and campaign for him, but the answer was no. Therefore, Schurz planned to continue in whatever position was given to him until the end of the war. In August 1864, Lincoln (who endured a contentious and difficult nomination process) called Schurz (who was on leave in Bethlehem) to the White House to offer him a command in Rosencrans' inactive department. Schurz turned it down, agreeing to make campaign speeches for Lincoln in the fall with the condition that he could return to the Army after the election. The election allowed soldiers in the field to cast absentee ballots; accusations of manipulation of the vote flew on both sides, with Lincoln the winner in the end.

Schurz could not accept a new assignment immediately after the election because Margarethe was expecting their third child. He had to return first to New York, and then with his family to Bethlehem, Pennsylvania, to wait for the new baby. Margarethe had a difficult time; she suffered from both *prepartum* and *postpartum* depression and premonitions of death; ten-year-old Agathe was in school at the Moravian Seminary for Young Ladies in Bethlehem. It was more convenient for the Schurz family to be nearby for the birth of the baby. Emma Savannah, named after the victory in the South, was born on December 30, 1864.

Schurz wanted to return to Washington to seek a new commission; however, during that period, even as a general, he had to request permission from the War Department, and after he got it, his trip turned out to be futile since Stanton and Lincoln wanted him to wait for Grant's return, which did not happen. However, while he was there, on January 31, 1865, the House of Representatives, with Schurz in the gallery, passed the Thirteenth Amendment, abolishing slavery. Everyone in the room celebrated loudly, yelling and hugging. Schurz quietly wept. He was overcome with emotion after all the tension of the speeches, including negative bitterness directed at him and the war itself. He wrote to his wife on February 1, 1865: "In such moments one feels that he has his reward for laboring in the interest of great ideas even though in other respects one has ever so much to quarrel about his fate."[3]

His fate at the end of the war was yet to be determined; he got permission to visit Grant at City Point, where the general assigned him to recruit for the "Veteran's Corps" (February 27, 1865). These units were created from the old "Invalid Corps," now renamed and also known as Hancock's Corps. The idea was to recruit soldiers who had finished their term of enlistment into a "back up" unit so that more fit soldiers could be released to fight. He toured the Midwest in the spring of 1865 on a recruiting mission. While he was on the road, on March 8,

1865, he was named, by an Act of Congress, to a corporation group of 100 men for the National Military and Naval Asylum for relief of totally disabled officers and the men of the volunteer forces of the United States. The act was passed on the same day as the establishment of a bureau for freedmen and refugees. The newspapers listed 100 men on the corporation committee, including prominent generals: Schurz, Grant, Sigel, Sherman, Butler, Meade, Hooker, Burnside, and Howard; prominent politicians: Andrew Johnson, Salmon P. Chase, Edwin Stanton, and Hannibal Hamlin; and the rich and famous: Henry Ward Beecher, Horace Greely, Oliver Wendell Holmes, Jay Cooke, and William H. Astor.[4]

In March, Schurz returned to Washington after an unsuccessful recruiting mission. Hancock was returning to his old command; therefore, Schurz was looking to be placed back in one of his own; from the capital, he went to City Point Virginia, where he met Lincoln and his wife. Schurz agreed to a command in 20th Corps under General William Tecumseh Sherman, and further agreed to accompany Mary Lincoln back to Washington, traveling on the steamer *Monchansett* arriving at 11 a.m. in Washington. He wrote to Margarethe:

> The first lady was overwhelmingly charming to me; she chided me for not visiting her, overpowered me with invitations and finally had me driven to my hotel in her own state carriage. I learned more state secrets in a few hours than I could otherwise in a year. I wish I could tell them to you. She is an astounding person.[5]

After a journey to the South, landing in New Bern, via Norfolk and Roanoke, and after the fall of Richmond, Schurz was assigned as General Slocum's chief of staff; although some thought Schurz was unhappy with this assignment, his outlook was positive, knowing the war was nearing its end. He was in Raleigh, North Carolina, when he heard the news of Lincoln's assassination. It was a terrible time for all involved. Schurz was finally able, on April 18, to write to his wife in Bethlehem, Pennsylvania:

> I should have written yesterday if I had been able to shake off the gloom that has settled on me since the arrival of the news of the murder of Lincoln. A thunderclap from the blue sky could not have struck us more unexpectedly and frightfully. Our good, good Lincoln! Even now, whenever my thoughts drift to some other object and then return to this terrible event, I am obliged to ask myself whether it really can be true. The murderer who did this killed the best friend of the South.[6]

His letter crossed with Margarethe's, written in German, consoling her husband by describing a memorial service in Bethlehem. She and her children, dressed in black, processed to the cemetery to hear a eulogy delivered by her doctor,

Frederick Flickhardt, who had lost both his sons in the war; they then processed back to the Episcopal Church for music and weeping. She wrote:

> Now you know all, and I see you sitting silent and alone, and thinking, thinking, thinking! All that Lincoln has ever said to you, the little struggles you had with each other, and the joyous hours, all must come back to you, and make you alternately glad and sorrowful.[7]

The armistice with Confederate General Johnston arrived with the news of Lincoln's death; within a week and a half, Schurz was in Washington, mustering out of the service. The war had affected him greatly; he had seen much of death, destruction, and political infighting on two continents. Many years later, he wrote:

> I must confess that my war experience has destroyed some youthful illusions as to the romantic aspect of bravery or heroism in battle. If I were to venture a definition, I should say that true bravery or heroism consists of conscious self-sacrifice for the benefit of others or in the performance of duty…. My experience taught me that there is no vice, no cowardice, that may not sometimes be found in the same person, together with that physical courage and fighting spirit which may make that man a hero in battle, and that there is no virtue, no degree of moral heroism, no spirit of noblest self-sacrifice, which may not sometimes be found in a person unnerved by the sight of blood, or otherwise incapable of meeting an adversary sword in hand.[8]

Although he could go home from a desolate capital, Schurz stayed to watch the muster-out parade and to greet old comrades. For him, all wars were over, battle flags stored, and a time for healing was needed. Citizen Schurz returned home to Bethlehem to join his family.

# Years of Turmoil

The years following the Civil War were filled with political unrest, race rioting, and arguments. These were troubled years on both a personal, political, and national level, so much so that author Claude Bowers named it the "Tragic Era."[1] Carl Schurz, just as his adopted nation, was at a crossroads. He needed to make a living. He could live for a while on the money that financier Jay Cooke had supplied on a monthly basis to Margarethe from his general's salary and the balance that was invested for him. His legal career had dissolved and although he had a few offers from different newspapers to write for them, he felt that a political venture in the German immigrant-laden state of Missouri would be possible. He started his venture by going to see President Johnson, who although apparently cordial and engaging, also appeared to be a consummate politician bent on ruffling as few feathers as possible. Unfortunately, Schurz had to return home to Bethlehem. Margarethe was suffering again from "rheumatic attacks" after the birth of the baby. Earlier asthmatic issues or a part of an arthritic condition that surfaced more severely after birth may have precipitated these. She wanted to return to Germany with the three girls. This trip had to wait, Schurz believed, until his affairs were settled and Margarethe was healthy enough to travel. Frederick Flickhardt, her doctor in Bethlehem, was a prominent physician and obstetric specialist, so it was possibly best for her to remain in Pennsylvania. Agathe, nicknamed Hans and later "Handie," was in mid-semester at school; eight-year-old Marianne, nicknamed "Pussie" was being homeschooled; the baby, Emma, was a year and a half. Margarethe had a governess and maids to help with care, cooking, and cleaning, but she continued to be handicapped with illness; Schurz, torn between home and his future career, did not fully trust the administration in Washington.

Although the president treated him amiably and with respect, Schurz did not like him; he found his drinking habits abhorrent. He believed that Johnson was drunk the night Lincoln was shot and drunk again at his inauguration. After writing and then visiting the President, Schurz voiced his desire to be part of a trial for Jefferson

Davis; he disagreed with Johnson's action providing a full amnesty declaration for the people of North Carolina directed only at white male property owners. Schurz favored an appointed overseer to restructure the Union. After the correspondence, President Johnson called Schurz back to the White House; on his way, he stopped in Philadelphia to visit Heinrich Tiedemann. He attended a "spirit writing" séance conducted by fifteen-year-old Charlotta Tiedemann, who was "gifted" with the ability to write messages from the "other side." Schurz tested her by asking for the spirit of Schiller to recite one of his verses, which the girl wrote correctly. Schurz then called on the spirit of Lincoln, who "told him" he would be sent on a mission by Johnson into the South, and that he would be a senator of the United States. When he arrived in Washington, he found that the prophecy came to be true; President Johnson wanted to send him into the Southern states to examine "the Negro Question." It is not clear whether that was just his way of getting rid of Schurz as an annoyance or if he was afraid of the "radical" Germans that Schurz represented. The post-Civil War statesmen were well-known and vocal in their appearances, speeches, and quotes. By this time, Schurz was very well-known, and his association with the late President gave him even more credibility. His friendship with Radical Republicans Charles Sumner, Thaddeus Stevens, and leaders Stanton and Seward placed him in the spotlight of the political area as the representative of the foreign factor with a loud anti-slavery voice. He knew that if the Southern Conservatives were to have their way with the "reconciliation," racial strife would continue.

Schurz volunteered to make the trip, hoping to help the country, which he believed was still reeling with post-war divisions complicated by Lincoln's untimely death. He boarded the steamer *Argo* to go to Hilton Head, but by now, he started to run out of money. The Secretary of War arranged for a travel reimbursement for Schurz for travel and lodging in the South at the same rate as a War Department clerk. Schurz decided to supplement this income as a correspondent for the *Boston Daily Advertiser* to be paid for five letters reporting on the South that would not bear his name (a common practice during this period). Schurz went first throughout South Carolina and then Georgia; he toured from Mississippi through Louisiana to St. Louis and then finally to Natchez, Mississippi. He met the same resistance everywhere he went. The black man was in constant danger; there seemed to be no way that the attitudes encouraged and cultivated for 250 years were to be changed. Schurz believed that ownership of land was the key to reconciliation along with the vote and education. However, he reported in one of his articles in the *Boston Daily Advertiser*: "Letters from the South No.1. The Sea Islands and Free Labor," of a conversation with a former rebel officer who replied to the question about working contracts for the freed slaves for his large plantation now that the emancipation was a law and a sure thing:

I know that is the intention. But I tell you I know the nigger. I know him, sir. He isn't fit for freedom, sir. President Johnson is a Southern man, and he knows the nigger too, sir. He knows him as well as I do, sir. He knows that the nigger must be made to work somehow. You can't make a contract with any of them. They do not know what a contract is. They won't keep a contract.[2]

Other newspapers reprinted these articles attributing them to Schurz; President Johnson got the news of the writings and took him to task for them. There was even a rumor that he would be recalled to Washington. Amid the political infighting, Schurz had not been aware that his stance on reconstruction was totally opposite to that of the President. The Southern turmoil continued; there was violence, poverty, lynching, and many of both races were in fear for their lives. Schurz persisted on his journey, despite very difficult travel conditions and violent opposition to his "Northern Radical Presence." He and an accompanying Army officer often found roads nearly impassable. They traveled at night to avoid the heat of the day had to send one man forward with a candle to light the way lest they ruin the wagons or even worse cripple a horse.

Schurz returned to Washington to see the President, and on the first day of his visit, he was told that the President was too busy to see him. He went back the next day and was kept waiting for about an hour; when he was finally admitted, the President was in a sullen mood and gave him no greeting. The newspapers during those years wrote daily articles recording the Presidential visitors; therefore, Schurz had to be seen. He told Johnson that he had more material in his possession on the "Negro issue." The President asked only about his health and, finally, Schurz offered to write a report on his findings; Johnson told him that there was no need to go to the trouble. He replied that he thought a document of this kind was his duty. He got no answer and in stiff silence bowed himself out.

Although he realized that Johnson wanted to, and did try to, suppress this document; he wrote it anyway. Ironically, Schurz's writings on the conditions in the South became one of his most famous, *Report on the Condition of the South* is still being reprinted in the twenty-first century.[3, 4]

On December 18, 1865, President Johnson wrote an introductory letter to the Senate, which stated, in part:

In "that portion of the Union lately in rebellion," the aspect of affairs is more promising than, in view of all the circumstances, could well have been expected. The people throughout the entire south evince a laudable desire to renew their allegiance to the government, and to repair the devastations of war by a prompt and cheerful return to peaceful pursuits. An abiding faith is entertained that their actions will conform to their professions, and that, in acknowledging the supremacy of the Constitution and the laws of the United States, their loyalty will be unreservedly given to the government, whose leniency they cannot fail to appreciate, and whose fostering care will soon restore them to a condition of prosperity.[5]

The reports reached the Senate on December 19, 1865. General Grant's was brief and praised the President's actions. Schurz's focused on the existing post-war conditions in the South, and he described, with no political prejudice on what he saw. He related both sides of the "Negro" question, and his report differed widely from Johnson's:

Aside from the assumption that the negro will not work without physical compulsion, there appears to be another popular notion prevalent in the south, which stands as no less serious an obstacle in the way of a successful solution of the problem. It is that the negro exists for the special object of raising cotton, rice and sugar for the whites, and that it is illegitimate for him to indulge, like other people, in the pursuit of his own happiness in his own way. Although it is admitted that he has ceased to be the property of a master, it is not admitted that he has a right to become his own master.

A belief, conviction, or prejudice, or whatever you may call it, so widely spread and apparently so deeply rooted as this, that the negro will not work without physical compulsion, is certainly calculated to have a very serious influence upon the conduct of the people entertaining it. It naturally produced a desire to preserve slavery in its original form as much and as long as possible—and you may, perhaps, remember the admission made by one of the provisional governors, over two months after the close of the war, that the people of his State still indulged in a lingering hope slavery might yet be preserved—or to introduce into the new system that element of physical compulsion which would make the negro work.[6]

He included his outlook on the Southern attitude toward freedmen:

While the southern white fought against the Union, the negro did all he could to aid it; while the southern white sees in the national government his conqueror, the negro sees in it his protector; while the white owes to the national debt his defeat, the negro owes to it his deliverance; while the white considers himself robbed and ruined by the emancipation of the slaves, the negro finds in it the assurance of future prosperity and happiness. In all the important issues, the Negro would be led by natural impulse to forward the ends of the government, and by making his influence, as part of the voting body, tell upon the legislation of the States, and render the interference of the national authority less necessary.

As the most difficult of the pending questions are intimately connected with the status of the Negro in southern society, it is obvious that a correct solution can be more easily obtained if he has a voice in the matter. In the right to vote he would find the best permanent protection against oppressive class-legislation, as well as against individual persecution. The relations between the white and black races, even if improved by the gradual wearing off of the present animosities, are likely to remain long under the troubling influence of prejudice.[7]

Ever the intellectual moralist, Schurz saw no difference between the white and black race; his close friend and colleague, Dr. Heinrich Tiedemann contributed in part to his beliefs. In 1836, Tiedemann's father, Dr. Friedrich Tiedemann, a professor of Anatomy and Physiology at the University of Heidelberg presented a paper, in English, to the Royal Society of London "On the Brain of the Negro, Compared with That of the Europeans and the Orang-Outang."[8]

This article, carefully documented, refuted the early century concept that the "Negro" was inferior in every intellectual way to the European. The "Orang-Outang" was used as a "control" in a comparative, charted study of the size and capacity of three different kinds of brains. He concluded that there is no difference between the races, and that any negative characteristics of Negroes were caused by slavery.

> The moral character and disposition of those Negroes who are not degenerated and ruined by slavery is in general very good. They are naturally affectionate, and ardently attached to their children, parents, friends, and countrymen. Their feelings of honesty, humanity, generosity, and gratitude are very acute. Their dispositions and manners are gentle, benevolent, and amiable.... The intellectual faculties of the Negroes do not in general seem to be inferior to those of the European and other races. Such of them as are not bodily and morally de-graded by slavery and oppression, have a pleasing and open expression of countenance, and are of a gay and cheerful turn. They exhibit proofs of good natural capacity, good sense, wit, and penetration. The truth of this statement is most fully confirmed by the accounts given by credible travelers.[9]

The Schurzes avidly discussed the issue of slavery with the Tiedemanns in Philadelphia and therefore knew of Dr. Tiedemann's conclusions. This early-nineteenth-century report repudiated the South American concept of inferiority and influenced Schurz's opinion of the Negro. He had interviewed people in the South about newly fashioned state laws and about his recommendation for education, voting, and the right to acquisition of property for freedmen. The former slave was not yet a citizen and that too had to be rectified. In retrospect, Schurz's voice was prophetic. If the reconstruction period did not change, the attitudes and equal rights there would be trouble and it would take years to reach even a modicum of equality for all men.

National newspapers covered the Senate reports extensively, emphasizing the President's "whitewashing" of the Southern situation. The *New York Herald* using Schurz's "poor military record" and Grant's success as a basis of comparison belittled Schurz. The *New-York Tribune* printed Schurz's entire report on Saturday, December 23, 1865, that and all 100,000 copies of it printed and distributed, promoted Schurz's fame, even though the President of the United States told a senator, "The only mistake I made yet was to send Schurz to the South."

# The Political Journey to Congress

On a trip to St. Louis, Schurz met with prominent Republican Benjamin Gratz Brown, Governor Thomas Fletcher, and German journalist George Hillgaertner (editor of the *Illinois Staats Zeitung*).[1,2,3] His visit and their meeting convinced Schurz to settle in St. Louis; however, the editor of the *New-York Tribune*, Sidney Howard Gay, offered him the position of Washington correspondent.[4] It was a fortunate opportunity because Carl Schurz, who had considered settling in St. Louis, remained in Washington. Margarethe would not join him because either she did not want him to buy a house there or she wanted to stay in Bethlehem. He was staying with Marquis de Chambrun, the French representative and friend of the Lincolns' in Washington.[5] However, he agreed to come home for Christmas. After the holidays, Zachariah Chandler, who invested $100,000 to establish the new *Detroit Post* offered Schurz the job of editor.[6] He accepted; after a visit to Bethlehem, via New York City, he moved to Detroit, planning to bring his family there later. The journey was disastrous because all of his personal papers and memorabilia were lost to a fire in a railroad station there. After he was finally settled, the newspaper began to lose money and his farm debt in Watertown became pressing.

Schurz was never happy in a routine job behind a desk; he would be found in the newspaper office, smoking his constant cigar long into the night. He remained separated from Margarethe and the children; he could not bring them with him since the Michigan heat was too much for her breathing problems, so Schurz arranged for her to go to his relatives in Watertown.

The whole country was heating up with violence and controversy. President Johnson was fighting with the Congress; on May 2, 1866, there were reports of fires and riots in Memphis in the Negro quarters with four white people and fifteen black people killed; political race riots occurred in New Orleans on July 30. In the melee, some of Schurz's acquaintances were killed or wounded; therefore, a continually unhappy, lonely, and depressed Carl Schurz was determined to take on the politics of Andrew Johnson and help defeat him in the next Presidential election.

Schurz started back to politics by attending the 1866 Republican convention in Philadelphia, which was called only to remove the Democratic Johnson supporters from Congress. Schurz addressed the assemblage, declaring that Lincoln would not have allowed the injustice towards black people and that the Fourteenth Amendment was not enough. The crowd cheered him loudly. Carl Schurz returned to the campaign trail, this time for Schuyler Colfax and James M. Ashley, both "Radical Republicans" and abolitionists.[7, 8] During the same period, President Johnson, accompanied by U. S. Grant and General George Armstrong Custer, made a "swing around the circle tour" to campaign for his congressional supporters. It was ill-fated when Johnson compared himself to Jesus as the nation's savior, and when a platform filled with the listeners in Johnstown, Pennsylvania, collapsed, sending 500 people into the dry bed of a drained canal, causing injuries and deaths, while the President left the scene; he was criticized at length by the press. Schurz said Johnson's speech in Cleveland on September 7, 1866, was "delivered in a drunken condition" in which he said:

> It has been said that my blood was to be shed. Let me say to those who are still willing to sacrifice my life, if you want a victim, and my country requires it, erect your altar to it, and take out the individual who now addresses you and lay him upon your altar, and the blood that now courses his veins and warms his existence shall be poured out as a last libation to freedom.[9]

After the Johnson debacle, he was able to speak against him and for his impeachment, using the overwhelmingly negative reactions to these events as material; his objections were well-received.[10] He wrote at night and spoke by day. However, his finances were continually shaky during this period; his farm in Watertown had been foreclosed, forcing his aging parents to move in with his sister, Anna, and her husband, August Schiffer (a grocer), in Monee, Illinois. Christian and "Mary" Schurz were in their early seventies and needed care. Margarethe and the children stayed in Detroit while their father toured the Midwest. The *Detroit Post* began to fail financially; fortunately, while touring St. Louis and Missouri, Schurz was approached by Dr. Emil Preetorius, who offered him an interest in the successful *Westliche Post*.[11] Theodore Olshausen was selling his share and returning to Germany.[12] His lawyer James Taussig raised $10,000 from prominent Germans in St. Louis in under twenty-four hours. This money was used to make Schurz one of the co-owners; more importantly, he could pay it back out of the paper's profits, and the steady income allowed him to move to St. Louis. He was able to pay off this debt within the next two years; however, unexpected dark clouds fell over his family.

Emma ("Emmy") Savannah, aged three, was deathly ill. Schurz was called home from his campaign orations in Connecticut because his little girl was dying. There had so much family tragedy; Margarethe's mother died giving birth to her and Schurz had lost his beloved brother, Herbert. It was now the Schurz family's time of mourning. There is no mention of the child's death in Schurz's *Reminiscences*; the toddler was buried in the Elmwood Cemetery in Detroit in a plot owned by the "Copper King," Simon Mandelbaum, near his family's one-year-old son, Henry Walker Mandelbaum.

Margarethe's health grew worse because of the trauma, as well as the pollution and disease in Detroit. Somehow, she managed the move to St. Louis but continued to worsen. The Schurzes decided it would be better for her to return to Germany and for the girls to continue their education there.

Schurz settled into a lonely life, staying in Emil Preetorius's apartment, carrying the burden of many worries about his family so far away and the increasingly lengthy separations. He was embarrassed by his financial situation and particularly his failed investment in the face of his rich in-laws; however, a partial solution presented itself when Margarethe's late father left an additional inheritance of land, helping the situation greatly. The Schurzes lived well, with servants and governesses even throughout the crises; they were now able to send Margarethe and the children to Wiesbaden, where she could visit the "*Kurhaus*" (cure house) and take the famous baths as a treatment for rheumatic and orthopedic disorders.

Although his political and journalistic career was advancing, Schurz promised to visit his family during Christmas. Another page had been turned and the moralistic revolutionary general was embarking in a voyage in a new direction. He was just thirty-six years old. He traveled through the St. Louis area, determined to become a spokesperson for the large German community. He had been elected the commander of the GAR—the Civil War veterans' "Grand Army of the Republic," who were viewed as a post-war "Radical" group. It was under attack because of the ideals of restitution of and punishment of the South and for the support of black suffrage. As the commander, Schurz was in charge of a reception for General Phillip Sheridan to St. Louis.[13] Some 4,200 veterans marched in the Grand Army line, which stretched for 2 miles, carrying banners that read in part, "The Phil of Radicalism a tough cure for rebels." This rally was one of the first to demonstrate the veteran's opposition to President Johnson's policies. This event, organized in part by Preetorius, placed Schurz in a position as the face of Missouri Germans. At the end of the day, the two "Generals" went to see a production of *Der Freisch*ütz.[14] Schurz towered over "Little Phil" Sheridan, who was almost 5 feet 1 inch, in front of a German opera in the Midwest. His importance in the city was increasing, even to the point that he was offered a chance to run for Congress but decided to wait for a better opportunity.

Schurz planned to travel back to Germany for Christmas; he wrote to George Bancroft, the American Minister in Berlin, to find out if the Prussian Government had any objections to his visit. He asked Bancroft to deliver the answer to

Bremerhaven, and if there were objections, he could travel to England and meet his family there. Meanwhile, Schurz visited his family in Watertown (his uncle and cousin); he then continued on to Chicago to visit his sister, Anna (Schiffer). She was involved in the burgeoning spiritualist movement of the mid-nineteenth-century, based on the belief that the spirits of the dead could deliver positive messages to the living. Schurz attended a séance with Anna and there, Emmy seemed to appear. Intellectually he could see that the whole process might be false; however, he was totally overcome with grief. It made him miss his family even more.

On his way from Chicago, to leave from the port of New York, Schurz stopped in Washington D.C. to see how he stood politically. Rumors were flying about the possible impeachment proceedings of President Johnson. On December 2, 1867, naturalized American citizen Carl Schurz received an American passport and on the seventh of that month, he was on the *USS America* headed for Bremerhaven. When he arrived in the port, he found a letter from Minister Bancroft reporting that not only would the Prussian Government allow his visit but also that he would be welcome.

When Schurz reached his family in Wiesbaden, a police officer who turned out to be an old university acquaintance visited him offering his service and hoping, he would visit Berlin to "see many things there which would probably please an old Forty-Eighter."[15] In January 1868, after Christmas with his family, Schurz was bound for Berlin. He had written to Lothar Bucher, a fellow refugee to London, who was now an aide to Chancellor Otto von Bismarck, asking to see him again. Surprisingly, he responded saying that would Schurz like to meet with the chancellor, who had expressed a desire to meet him. The arranged visit was not as Schurz expected.

The Chancellor, Count Otto Von Bismarck, later the Iron Duke, welcomed Schurz with open arms, Rhenish wine, and a Havana cigar; they talked well past midnight and the Count invited Schurz for dinner the next evening with a group of honored jurists. The irony of the situation was that the Prussian Government had never pardoned Schurz for his "crime" of freeing Kinkel. Bismarck knew all about the incident and regretted, only, that he did not have the time to go with Schurz to visit Spandau and hear the whole story on site.

The following evening began awkwardly as if the invited guests, who were preparing a new legal code for the North German Federation, were uncomfortable talking to a former "revolutionary;" however, after all settled down, the evening went well. As Schurz was preparing to leave, Bismarck invited him to remain with him. When they sat down over a bottle of Apollinaris water, Schurz answered the Chancellor's seemingly endless questions about world affairs and the comparison of German and American politics. Bismarck was between wars—first the Austrian conflict earlier and a currently impending Franco-Prussian War. He asked Schurz about the Civil War and his political standing in America. This meeting became famous. The American press carried rumors about reasons for his visit, but the only effect was to continue to elevate Schurz's stature in the German community.

Schurz returned to Wiesbaden, and then via Frankfurt returned to Kiel and Hamburg alone to visit his wife's relatives; Margarethe was still not well enough to go with him. The Meyers had built Villa Forsteck in Kiel, as a "country" estate and a family arts center. After a short stay, he returned to Hamburg, boarded ship the *Germanic*, and arrived back in New York on March 21, 1868, assured by Margarethe's now wealthy brother, Heinrich Meyer, that there would be no more financial worries.

He was happy to be home; Bismarck had offered him a political spot in Germany, but Schurz declared America was his true home. He wrote to his wife "how fresh and hearty life is here." He stopped in New York at the Fifth Avenue Hotel, where he met Marshall Jewell, the governor of Connecticut, who asked him to go to his home state and make some campaign speeches for him there. When done, Schurz was off to Washington for the impeachment trial of President Johnson. He was between jobs; his position with the *Detroit Press* was, on March 20, 1867, turned over to William A. Howard, a former member of Congress and "late" postmaster.

Schurz traveled back to St. Louis to the *Westliche Post* and a private office with all the amenities. The paper had just hired Jewish-Hungarian immigrant Joseph Pulitzer as a reporter. Emil Preetorius had arranged for Schurz to be a delegate to the upcoming Republican convention in Chicago. Schurz left for the convention and was elected as temporary chairman and made the keynote speech; the convention nominated General Grant for President with Schuyler Colfax as his running mate.

Once he returned to St. Louis, Schurz willingly began the campaign trail once again. He was now one of Missouri's state electors and had a louder and more prominent voice in the German community. The combined rigors and stress of thirty-three speeches in a few months was taking its toll. Carl Schurz continually missed his family. He was crushed when Margarethe told him that her health would not allow her to return until after the winter. He had rented an apartment for the family in St. Louis and, at one low point, thought of applying for a diplomatic post in Europe. Schurz's memoirs and biographies do not include very much of his personal feelings at that time; however, the loss of a child (even during a period that had a 50 percent infant mortality rate) must have been hard to bear. He must have felt, even with the increasing public acclaim and success, very alone and isolated in an alien world.

Schurz hoped against hope that his new political life and his future stability would enable the return of Margarethe and the family. He had to walk a careful line through the ethnic politics in the state of Missouri and the opposing factions. It was a political situation no different from the modern ones, with infighting, conflict, poor or false press releases, and the general pursuit for power. Schurz, however, took a clear path; his credentials were impeccable, and by combining the moderate and conservative Republican stance, his compatriots supported him fully. The state senate had to replace Senator John B. Henderson on the ballot, even though he had co-authored the Thirteenth Amendment, voted for the acquittal of President Johnson at the impeachment trial and had virtually left the party ranks. Schurz began to work very hard at gaining and accepting the nomination for the senate replacement.

Schurz asked Preetorius to keep his name out of the papers in regards to the Senate seat. He campaigned vigorously throughout Missouri for it, well aware that as a resident, a revolutionary, a Civil War veteran and a German-born citizen, he would come under fire. He was instrumental in forming the Twentieth Century Club political club:

> The meetings were held Saturday afternoons continuing into the evenings. Carl Schurz, as a rule presided. Perhaps no other coterie in the history of this city exercised for a like period such influence upon political affairs.... The Twentieth Century Club inaugurated the movement, which made Schurz United States Senator.[16]

By January 1868, Carl Schurz had become the face and voice of the German American Community in Missouri. He overcame criticism of his religious beliefs, his trip to Europe, and his lack of practical political knowledge. Finally, on January 11 and 12, he debated opponents Senator Charles D. Drake and Senator John B, Henderson; the speeches lasted two days in Jefferson City. Drake made a drastic error when he attacked the German community at large for not supporting him. This was a mistake, and Schurz jumped on it using the many Germans in the Civil War as an example of loyal Americans. Drake left town rapidly and Schurz became the honored senator from Missouri.

He was not the first foreign-born senator in the Congress but was certainly the first German one; therefore, he became known as the "German Senator." He was invited to parades affairs and dinners as that "German Senator." The large German-American community in New York invited him to a banquet at Delmonico's, while he was staying with his friend, Dr. Abraham Jacobi, now a prominent medical pioneer in New York. On the night before the dinner, a delegation from the German Republican committee visited to hail him as the "representative of the German element." Although he knew Jacobi from Germany, they now became closer friends for the rest of their lives.

# Senator Schurz

President Ulysses S. Grant was inaugurated on March 4, 1868. To Carl Schurz, this moment coincided with his swearing-in for what he considered his highest achievement. The new senator wrote:

Now I had actually reached the most exalted public position to which my boldest dreams of ambition had hardly dared to aspire. I was still a young man, just forty. Little more than sixteen years had elapsed since I had landed on these shores, a homeless waif saved from the wreck of a revolutionary war in Europe. And here I was now a member of the highest law making body of the greatest republics.[1]

He made quite an impression on the assembled senators, as the *Missouri Daily Democrat* of April 15, 1869, reported:

There is Carl Schurz seated not far from poor, old, quaky Brownlow, and daintily clad in the glistening new broadcloth in which he took the oath on inauguration day. Manners are one of Schurz's special qualifications; he possesses them in the highest degree; and graces the Senate Chamber admirably. His face, spectacles abolished, would be a little of the old cavalier type; and it is rich in expression and mobile as his mind. He can do more than any other man in our government to rouse the Germans in America from their political apathy, and push them forward to their true place ... the clerk had to stop pronouncing his name Shirtz.[2]

He made an impression in the political arena and became the congressional representative and voice of the German communities in the Senate. When he first arrived in America, the number of political favors that he observed in government shook him; however, he was now besieged with requests for appointments, help, and political favor. Veterans, office-seekers, prospective immigrants, and even fellow expatriate Germans wanted favors and support. He was known as "the Dutch Senator" and was criticized if he did not help and criticized even more when he did. Most of the attacks came because of his connection with Felix Coste, who was appointed surveyor of the port of St. Louis, as and with his brother-in-law, Edmund Jüssen's appointment to the income tax office; the opposition immediately cried nepotism.

His personal life was a continual problem as Margarethe and the children were still in Germany. He had wanted her in Washington for the swearing-in ceremony. He offered her a place in Washington D.C. instead of St. Louis, knowing she did not like it there. She insisted, however, that an American winter would be detrimental to her health, and she that wanted to remain in the hot baths in Wiesbaden. She wrote to friends how much she missed him but stayed in the home country. Carl Schurz was very unhappy that she could not share his success. He was a model husband, he claimed, because of his busy life. However, this was the beginning of the "Gilded Age" and Washington was afloat with dinners, parties, and with flirtations offered to him at every turn. He wrote to Margarethe that during this long separation, how long could he resist before giving in to them?

During the summer of 1869, the new senator traveled to California as a member of the Senate Republican committee, visiting Sacramento and San Francisco. He was greeted with cannonades, bands, and cheers from the German Americans in the far West. Margarethe and the children were in Switzerland for the summer and decided to return home that fall. Schurz had written to her about the social life in Washington and the prominent place that she would have as a senator's wife. For the Schurz family, this was the dawn of their life in the "upper crust." Margarethe, sixteen-year-old Agathe, and twelve-year-old Marianne would become part of the glittering, diplomatic, political world of nineteenth-century Washington. They arrived in New York on November 9, 1869, on the ship *Westphalia,* from the port of Le Havre, France. They were delayed because Margarethe took ill again; however, they finally got to the capital, where there was a large social circle of political friends and a large German population. The Schurzes entertained on Saturday evenings with musicales in their parlor; the whole family took part. "Handie" (Agathe) was a popular young woman. This was a happy and fruitful time for them.

The political seas never stay calm for long; Carl Schurz was caught between the nationalists, who accused him of loving everything and anything "German" and the German Americans who accused him of loving things "too American." His political career in the Senate did not start on a good note, and his travels through the vagaries and scandals of the Grant administration were numerous. The trials and tribulations of this administration are well-documented, and Senator Schurz was caught up in them on a grand scale. He went into the senate with his ideals intact, including nineteenth-century liberalism, clean government, low taxes, and "hard "money." He also carried with him his suffrage ideas for all men in conjunction with their personal freedom. The nineteenth-century industrial growth and its changes were complex and very new; Schurz had trouble dealing with them and their effects over the rest of his life. Critics forgot that he was raised on a farm in small-town Germany, and despite the veneer of an unfinished university education, he was a small-town boy on a large, international stage. Schurz's genius was attached to his accomplishments, but because of his lanky, bearded appearance and slight accent, he could easily be made the butt of jokes. However, his skill at speaking was his greatest gift and could not be satirized.

Shortly after his arrival in Washington, Schurz went to visit President Grant, looking for his share of political "patronage." He was able to secure a few appointments but was not very successful. Old friend Franz Sigel was refused a position, and only by repeating his visits was Schurz able to get some appointments. He hated the system. Office seekers besieged him. Even though he was, at this time, on good terms with Grant and his wife, dining with them at the White House, there was a rift developing between the generals.

Schurz decided to make Civil Service Reform a mission based on the German versions of attainment and promotion. His first speech, on March 19, 1869, was about the suspension of the Tenure in Office Act. It did not go well, and on the day after it, he was placed on the Senate Committee on Retrenchment, where he was able in a small way to take on Civil Service Reform. He returned to St. Louis that summer and started work on the destruction of the patronage system; he was helped by the appointment of General John A. McDonald, an old army buddy of General Grant's, as supervisor of the internal revenue in the district of St. Louis. In 1875, McDonald was discovered as part of the infamous tax evasive Whiskey Ring, which was connected to the administration. Schurz introduced a bill of Civil Service Reform, which also limited the power of political appointments. The bill failed, but it marked the start of the disintegration of his relationship with Grant. He kept Sumner on his side, hoping to get on the Senate Committee on Foreign Relations, which he achieved, after a messy correspondence on the old Civil War *Alabama* dispute and the death of Senator William P. Fessenden (a senator from Maine). This appointment also led to a major conflict with the President over the annexation of the Republic of Santo Domingo. A treaty had been negotiated with dictator Buenaventura Baez; however, Schurz felt, as did others, that the tropical country with a history of unrest would not be an asset to America nor could the population easily assimilate. Schurz's position against annexation, sent to the German press, was entirely opposite of Grant's. The bill was defeated on June 30, 1869; Grant was so angry that the payback for this action was a statement from the President calling Schurz, "an infidel and atheist who had been a rebel in his own country, as much a rebel as Jefferson Davis."[3] Eventually, all of Schurz's appointees, including Edmund Jüssen, lost their jobs on Grant's orders.

Somewhere in the course of that first year in Congress, Schurz softened his attitude toward radical Reconstruction and became more moderate. Although he supported the Fifteenth Amendment, he began to lean towards the sovereignty of the individual Southern states. In the summer of 1870, he returned to St. Louis for the gubernatorial election. The party politics were very involved in a fight between the Liberals and Conservatives. The Radical Republican candidate was Joseph W. McClurg, who left the mainstream Republican Party; Schurz was considered a liberal who helped found a new branch of Republicans, joining others in nominating Benjamin Gratz Brown as an alternate candidate for governor. Schurz campaigned throughout Missouri that summer, but it was to no avail. Even accusations of "Nativism" leveled at former Union officer McClurg did not entirely win over the German vote; however, Brown was elected governor, defeating the incumbent McClurg. The Democrats won the state legislative seats, marking the beginning of Schurz's political downfall.

His troubles extended to his home front. Margarethe stubbornly refused to leave Washington for St. Louis, which she hated. She was sick during the early days of a pregnancy; she was due sometime in February of the following year. She wanted Carl home. The separations in this marriage continued to be long and arduous; therefore, after the election, Schurz returned to Washington, with a stop in New York. He went to make a courtesy call to the President in the White House, but Grant would not see him, He never saw Schurz again until he was close to death in 1885.

Schurz spoke brilliantly in that session of Congress of 1870; he introduced a resolution to remove all disqualifications and disabilities of former rebels as soon as possible. He also called for Civil Service Reform again, and in January 1871, a Civil Service Commission was formed with Schurz's friend George William Curtis (the editor of *Harper's Magazine*) at its head. The committee turned out to be a "rubber-toothed" organization, apparently agreeing to any action connected to Grant and the powerful politicians in the Senate. Schurz continued that year to speak once again against the Santo Domingo annexation, the use of arms without congressional assent, the President's foreign policy, and a settlement with Britain of the *Alabama* affair. These speeches and stances did not win him any political popularity. He drew fire on his speech against the Ku Klux Klan Act— that despite the need to remove the Klan, he felt the use of government military would override the right of each state to govern itself.

On February 28, 1871, the Schurzes welcomed Carl Lincoln into the family. Margarethe's health and the difficult pregnancy had been a burden; however, the arrival of a male heir and the restored health of the mother eased the situation. The year marked the beginning of Schurz's attempt to break away from the Republican Party and to oppose the re-election of Grant. His remarks did not land well, particularly on regional ears and special interest groups. He was blunt, forceful, and sarcastic.[4]

That year in Congress, Schurz's eloquent use of language, coupled with his very distinctive appearance, provided great material for his critics. Opposition editorials were venomous. Pioneer cartoonist German-born Thomas Nast drew over sixty cartoons that included Schurz during his congressional service. Each one characterized Schurz as a bespectacled, gawky, funny-looking cartoon caricature; the drawings' theme is one of animosity. Nast was a very close friend of General Grant and often dined with the family; therefore, he sided with the President in his opposition to Schurz. Although he is more famous for his creation of the image of Santa Claus (as the modern world now knows him) and the Republican elephant, his political drawings in *Harper's Weekly* brought him fame as "the father of the modern cartoon." In 1871, he took on the Boss William Tweed Ring in New York. Local legend in New Jersey believes that Nast and his family were forced to move out of New York to Morristown to escape the danger of the Tweed Ring. The cartoon titled "A Group of vultures Waiting for the Storm to Blow Over—Let Us Prey" dated September 23, 1871, from *Harper's Weekly* shows Tweed's head on a vulture with Schurz peering over his shoulder.

That summer, the *Westliche Post* wrote to Schurz, suggesting he give up his senate seat to write more frequently for the paper; however, he negotiated with the paper, allowing him to keep his seat and his job. He continually tried to help heal the rifts in the Republican Party but to no avail. Grant attacked again saying Sumner and Schurz have "acted worse than any two men."[5]

The Democratic Party reveled at the discord and made things worse for the reformers. During the summer of 1871, Schurz went on the campaign trail again, only this time he was addressing the German population, hoping to get support for the Liberal Republicans. These pursuits only caused the newspapers that supported Grant to attack Schurz repeatedly. He returned home, this time to Bethlehem, to the relative comfort of the German community, there to be with his with the baby and his family.

Schurz was under the attack of the Republican press, led by *The New York Times* and the caustic cartoons by Thomas Nast. The venom was directed at every part of Schurz's career. The accusations of the past mounted to the point that he was labeled a "racist" because he did not support the congressional Southern Amnesty bills to which de-segregation conditions had been added. The vote was to be for all or nothing, and Schurz opposed it on the grounds of it allowing former, uneducated slaves to hold office while experienced Southern leaders were excluded from them because of the war. He never was able to live down, or escape from, the allegations leveled at him. The final, culminating one called Schurz a "Jesuit." His problem was one that surfaced repeatedly; those he thought were on his side deserted or sometimes gave him lip service. Schurz was a great speaker, but not a great politician. He was standing up to an existing political machine trying to remove his party's incumbent president from office in next election.

His plan was to lead a break from the Republican Party starting in January 1872 at the Jefferson City, Missouri convention. The platform included Civil

Service Reform, Southern reconciliation, and local self-government. It was hammered out and offered to those who thought the same for a "National Convention" in Cincinnati in May. Schurz's objective was to bring all the splinter factions with opposing views over each issue together and to remove Grant from office. This was not an easy path to follow; each possible candidate had shortcomings. Carl Schurz suffered personally, as Thomas Nast began a salvo of cartoons that went so far as to compare Schurz to the Devil—"Mephistopheles at work for Destruction," which appeared in *Harper's Weekly*. At the same time, an arms issue arose with the sale of rifles to the French during their war with Germany.

On February 20, 1872, Schurz addressed the Senate, demanding investigation of the sale of government surplus rifles to E. Remington and Sons in New York, who had a contract with the French Government. He had received a petition in the winter of 1870–71 from immigrant Germans complaining that American weapons were killing their "brothers and sisters." This speech, three hours long, crowded the senate, which passed a resolution allowing women to listen from the cloakroom; James Garfield wrote in his diary that Senator Carl Schurz had "made the most brilliant speech of his life."

Schurz prepared for a National Liberal Party Convention in Cincinnati, by campaigning and speaking with the hope that some Democrats would leave their party for this new one. He started at Cooper Institute in New York where a cheering crowd greeted him. His fellow Germans were worried about a Teutonic voice telling Americans and Nativists how they should act. After verbal jousting and jostling, two candidates emerged from the much-awaited May 1872 convention. Schurz's former employer, Horace Greeley, the publisher of the *New-York Tribune*, was nominated for president, although his temperance stance would upset the German vote. The vice-presidential candidate, Missouri Governor Benjamin Gratz Brown, was a controversial figure due to his post-war politics. The nominees so upset Schurz that after the voting, in the evening, during a gathering at Judge John Stallo's house where his colleagues were drowning their sorrows in wine, he did not say a word but sat down at the piano and played Chopin's "Funeral March."

His personal life, at this time, was not going well. He had been invited to attend *Sängerfest* (Song Festival) in St. Louis, and he had hoped that Margarethe would come with him, but she refused to go to St. Louis, which she still hated. He took her mid-spring in 1872 to the ship in New York where she boarded and returned to Hamburg with the children and their governess. This period of their relationship, apparently stormy, reflects Schurz's concern for his wife's health. His career had placed him into national prominence; whether it was good or negative, it was still keeping his name in the news. Over 4,000 articles about him, tracking his progress, appeared in the national newspapers in 1872. Margarethe's apparently mysterious lung issues never appeared in any correspondence; more than likely, her daughters removed them. Apparently, she was more comfortable in Germany.

Schurz started campaigning, alone, for the new party on July 22, 1872, in Temple Hall in St. Louis. He was well-received by both the audience and the press. However, his visit to North Carolina to talk about the doctrine of reconciliation brought every possible skeleton out of the closet that opponents could find. Crowds in Illinois, Indiana, and Ohio greeted him warmly; however, the press again accused him of being a traitor to the Union, a carpetbagger, a real estate scammer, and an overly ambitious Teutonic foreigner. Thomas Nast continued the attack depicting Schurz as Richard III, a racist, and a supporter of the Ku Klux Klan. Despite all his efforts in this campaign to unseat the incumbent president, the German-American community was divided equally for both candidates; it was hard to defeat a war hero of Grant's stature.

During the two years following the election, it was easier for Schurz to lead a liberal movement in the Republican Party; the Grant administration was continually under scrutiny for scandal and corruption. There was the breach of the treaty with the Lakota Tribe that incited a war to get access to gold found on their land, followed by the John Sanborn bribery tax scandal in 1874. In 1875, Department of Interior Secretary Columbus Delano was accused of taking bribes in exchange for fraudulent land grants. Attorney General George H. Williams was accused of receiving a bribe not to prosecute the Pratt and Boyd Company; the Whiskey Ring scandal indicting corrupt government officials was also exposed.

Schurz wanted to repair his relations with the German community; therefore, he returned to the "*Vaterland*" in April 1873, telling the *Westliche Post* that he had to see to his wife's inheritance. When there, he toured through Alsace Lorraine, visiting his hometown of Liblar as well as Munich. He finally joined Margarethe and the children in their apartment in Wiesbaden. His trip, like many social events and tours of the time, was closely followed by the American newspapers, and he hoped they would impress the compatriots back home. Margarethe had just inherited 1 million thalers from her family, which continued to help the financial situation. Schurz, however, grew restless and ill; he most likely suffered from migraine headaches, and his constant attachment to his cigars may have been a large part of the problem. The family (minus daughter Marianne, who stayed in Germany for school) returned in October.

They settled into the Capitol; the baby, Carl Lincoln, was a joy and twenty-year-old Agathe was the "*belle*" of local society events. The newspapers wrote of the Schurz family in Washington:

> But Missouri, with her eighteen hundred thousand people whose houses are as good and attractive as anybody's, is represented at the national capital by a single household: and four hundred thousand Missouri girls are represented by one. The representative home is that of Carl Schurz, and the representative

young lady is his eldest daughter. Now, I am prepared to maintain in the face of this seeming disparity that Missouri is still well represented socially, for the cheer of Carl Schurz' home, with its unaffected German hospitality, could represent the hearthstones of a nation, and Miss Schurz, with her modest, unassuming beauty and her charming unhackneyed culture, could well represent the young ladyhood of a continent. And for the part of Madame Schurz, there is no computing the scope of matronly grace dignity and attractiveness that would find in her an inadequate exponent.[6]

Schurz, with his home life more settled, began to attack the solutions to the Panic of 1873 and the government's financial policy. He spoke repeatedly on sound money policies, only once again to see defeat with the passing of the "inflation bill." However, Grant vetoed it and, for one short time, Schurz agreed with him. Unexpectedly, personal tragedy occurred when his friend and colleague Charles Sumner had an attack of angina pectoris, went home, and had a heart attack. His last words before he died were to Schurz, who then helped make funeral arrangements for his friend, traveling to Massachusetts to be a pallbearer at the funeral; he wrote to Preetorius, "Nobody knows what I have lost. He was my only friend here and a real friend. In him I have lost a piece of my existence which cannot be replaced." He spoke brilliantly at Sumner's funeral, expressing his friend's last wish: the passage of a civil rights bill.

23

# Losses

All was not well in Missouri; despite his best campaign efforts, Schurz lost the 1874 election to Francis Cockrell, the Democratic candidate and former Confederate general; his days in the Senate were ending. His campaign had been a lonely one; a jealous Margarethe had refused to join him, still loathing St. Louis and Missouri. He continued after his loss to speak in the Senate for the liberal Republican cause, standing for states' rights and noninterference by the government. He was at odds with his future, but with the urging of friends, he went on another lecture tour espousing his liberal cause. Margarethe stayed home with the baby, while he was toasted and celebrated in St. Louis. He returned to New York to accompany the family back to Europe, but before he left the city, he was feted and treated to a large dinner followed by another one at Delmonico's. After these accolades, Schurz decided to renew his political career.

Once in Germany, the family visited Margarethe's brother, Heinrich Adolph Meyer, at Villa Forsteck in Kiel. This house had become a center for the literary and musical lights in Germany at the time. Writers Theodor Fontane, Fanny Lewald, Klaus Groth, Charitas Bischoff, her mother, botanist Amalie Dietrich, composer Johannes Brahms, Julius Stockhausen, and pioneer concert pianist and musician Clara Schumann all visited at one time or another. The beautiful villa welcomed the Schurz family. Margarethe felt at home with her brother's family. While on the continent, Schurz traveled to Berlin, meeting with prominent scientists and historians. He went on to London, where he met liberal radicals John Bright and Sir Charles Dilke, also paying a visit to Parliament to hear Disraeli speak. Schurz then returned to Germany to take Margarethe for a rest cure in Switzerland; his stay was interrupted when he was called back to the States to help the Liberals and the reform candidate for President Rutherford B. Hayes.

Schurz left his family in September went on the campaign trail for someone else once again. His reputation in the German-American community had again been bolstered by his connections in Europe. His job was to turn voters to Hayes in Ohio and to convince the German Liberal Democrats to support the Republican candidate. Hayes was elected; the event marked the beginning of a good political association and friendship for Schurz with the new president.

Schurz moved his family and the servants to a townhouse at 40 West 32nd Street, New York. He began writing again; his new goal was to try to gather fellow Liberals into a group for a conference and ultimately avoid a poor political situation in the upcoming election of 1876. He joined his independent cohorts—Henry Cabot Lodge, Charles Francis Adams, Samuel Bowles, and Horace White—in a unified effort to propose alternative candidates to oppose presidential candidate James G. Blaine, the senator from Maine. Schurz felt that Blaine was as corrupt as the Grant administration because of suspected awards of railroad charters and illegal transactions with the Little Rock and Fort Smith Railroad bonds. Rutherford B. Hayes initially did not seek the nomination but received it as a compromise candidate. Several incumbent government scandals of that year were Secretary of War William Belknap's crooked connections to the French arms sale and his extortion money at Fort Sill, Secretary of the Navy George Robeson's alleged embezzlement, and Grant's private secretary, Orville Babcock, framing of a private citizen for uncovering corrupt Washington contractors. All of them helped to support a contrasting "clean government" platform for Hayes.

Schurz had started a speaking tour in upstate New York when his life took two tragic turns. He had to go quickly to Monee, Illinois, in February 1876 because his seventy-nine-year-old father was very ill. He raced to see him, and when he arrived, he was assured that his father was recovering. Margarethe, nearing the end of a very uncomfortable pregnancy, needed him home to stay with her because she was ill. She was confined for several months, too weak to climb the stairs; therefore, when his father died on February 17, 1876, he could not attend the funeral. Margarethe gave birth to Herbert Schurz on March 5, attended by Dr. Abraham Jacobi. Ten days later, despite all expert medical attention, Margarethe Meyer Schurz died of "child-bed fever" (puerperal fever, an infection) at the age of forty-one, leaving four children. Her heartbroken husband wrote to his friend, Francis William Bird: "For grief like this there is no consolation. It must be lived out. The loss of the wife of one's youth is unlike any other bereavement. It is the loss of the best part of one's life."[1, 2] The forty-seven-year-old widowed father prepared for her funeral. A private service was held in the house with Reverend Octavius Frothingham, a radial Unitarian minister presiding; the Liederkranz German Club's chorus sang two dirges that were followed a eulogy by the Reverend:

> To those who had known Mrs. Schurz no words of his or anyone else were necessary. The close of her life had been as happy and cheerful as had been her life when in health, and while those around her were striving to keep back their

tears, she believed that she was growing stronger and was thinking of the happy occasions in the future. Mrs. Schurz was no formalist; she was adverse [*sic.*] to all publicity, careless of show, and preferred quiet and seclusion. She came to the New World from the Old, but the former did not seem strange to her. She retained her old friends and gathered new around her. She enjoyed the freshness, the vitality, and the newness of the New World. She loved a republican life. Alike to her seemed the quiet life in a Western City or the busy life of Washington; she was always the same. The outside world saw a graceful cheerful person, full of noble sentiment, generous and sympathizing; but the inside world only know what a true and cordial heart and spirit she had. All who came in contact with her loved and respected her.[3]

The small group of relatives and friends—including Judge Palmer, Oswald Ottendorfer, William Steinway, and others—filed by the rosewood casket, covered with flowers from friends and her servants in Washington, to say a last goodbye. *The New York Times'* obituary listed Green Wood Cemetery in Brooklyn as her place of interment; however, the *New-York Tribune* reported Woodlawn Cemetery in the Bronx. Her coffin was shipped to St. Johannis Eppendorf Lutheran Church in Hamburg, for burial in the Meyer family plot. It was moved to the giant Ohlsdorf Cemetery in Hamburg, and although the grave no longer exists, a memorial stone and a description of her achievements are in a shrine in the Garden of Women (*Garten der Frauen*) there.

Carl Schurz's separations from his wife and family had been lengthy and painful; twenty-three-year-old Agathe took over the care of her little brothers and the household. He continued to work hard on the presidential campaign and on planning, with the help of Henry Cabot Lodge and Brooks Adams, an independent conference of selected Liberals to meet in New York on May 15 at the Fifth Avenue Hotel. The theme of the gathering was to convince the powerful men who would be delegates at the National conventions to support reform in the government. Ever the idealist, Schurz brought 250 of them together in New York. The list of attendees read like a nineteenth-century *Who's Who*. President Woolsey of Yale was the chair. Henry Cabot Lodge called the meeting to order; Theodore Roosevelt Sr., John Jay, William Cullen Bryant, Edward Salomon, Dr. Abraham Jacobi, Cyrus W. Field, Peter Cooper, and many prominent citizens were seated in the large banquet room. Schurz presented "An Address to the People," which attacked all current government corruptions and called for reform. The assemblage voted and pledged to support any nominees who were honest men but no one man in particular. Both parties placed men on the ballot that could potentially be supported by the reformers. Democrat Samuel J. Tilden had exposed the Tweed Ring. The Republican candidate Ohioan Rutherford B. Hayes became Schurz's choice.

Schurz and the Executive Committee of the Fifth Avenue Hotel Conference sent a letter to Hayes, urging him to publicly support Civil Service Reform and hard money. He followed it with another letter reminding Hayes of the need for the German-American vote. The two former Civil War generals finally met and became friends. Hayes realized the importance of the German vote and sent Schurz out to get it. The Teutonic population could as easily have supported Tilden as it could have Hayes. Much like the days of Lincoln, and in the same manner, Schurz was stumping throughout the Midwest. His efforts paid off, and after a wildly contested election, Hayes was declared president. Schurz moved his family to St. Louis taking his widowed Mother along. For his service, President Hayes offered Carl Schurz a cabinet post as either the postmaster general or Secretary of the Interior. The interior position with all of its inherent problems of Civil Service Reform, the negative effects of the withdrawal of troops from Southern states, Indian affairs, and conservation of natural resources presented insurmountable problems; however, Schurz chose this position over becoming postmaster. On February 13, 1877, before he could gather the family to move to Washington, his mother died. After a year of family tragedy, Schurz moved to Washington to face the biggest challenges of his political career.

# Secretary Schurz

President Hayes and his cabinet, Carl Schurz in particular, were facing difficult times; however, they attacked each problem in turn. The first was the Southern issue. The U.S. Army was occupying the Southern states and Hayes wanted to build up Republican strength in the South, even at the risk of a disastrous result for the Negroes. Schurz believed that they could be joining both parties helping the freedmen and ending racial divisions in political alignment. When Hayes did withdraw all the troops, Schurz believed the "pacification" of the South was a complete success. He did not realize the depth of the animosity between the races; when Hayes appointed Frederick Douglas as marshal of the District of Columbia, both men thought that could help solve the issue. What they could not see was that a swipe of a legislative hand would not remove mistreatment, misunderstanding, and negative state's legislation that would encourage the retention of racial injustice for years to come.

The civil service issue and reform seemed easy enough; the cabinet appointed a committee with Schurz to create civil service rules. They decided that only the applicants of the lowest grade had to pass a standard examination and then promotions that followed could only be from within. Schurz discovered that his Department of the Interior was one of the most corrupt and graft-ridden in the government. He set about "cleaning house" by seeking out his staff members for input, and then setting up rules of operation, including hiring and firing practices, purchase orders and competitive bidding for projects. Although these reforms sounded practical and sensible, they caused a violently negative reaction. The press led the charge, writing vicious attacks, implying that Schurz charged excessive amounts for his political speeches. Meanwhile, Hayes was not able to avoid political repayment appointments; therefore, Schurz's reform continued to be limited and open to the criticism that he was constantly inspecting departmental efficiency reports.

The political climate in Washington continued to be contentious; every officer's operations were open to public criticism. For example, Schurz's project to preserve the National Forests met with the criticism mainly from Blaine: "What does a foreigner know about American forests?" He continued by accusing Schurz of "trying to introduce German methods into free America in total disregard of the needs of frontiersman for firewood."[1] A proposed conservation bill was defeated in the Senate, allowing developers and industrialists to continue to denude the forests in the West.

The timber issue, including the removal of Native Americans from their homeland for lumber, crossed over to the "Bureau of Indian Affairs," which up until 1849 was run by the military. The Department of the Interior inherited it and its nest of corruption. The military wanted the Bureau back under its command, and with Indian agents stationed far from the government's seat, corruption and embezzlement were easy. In short, Schurz received a mess.

At first, the practice of resettling tribes did not bother him. One Indian nation after another was removed from their land. The long perilous journeys to reservations ended with the loss of life and tragic results. After the 1,000-mile chase, Chief Joseph and the Nez Perce were captured and returned to a reservation in unsuitable climate in the North. The Northern Cheyenne were forced to their reservation, decimating their population. Schurz took the blame and the negative press for this, until he reconsidered his position and, with the support of philanthropist William Welsh of Philadelphia and General Pope, started to make the effort to clean up the bureau.

The task was immense and complicated that became a losing situation for the beleaguered Schurz; whatever action he chose would be viewed as the wrong path by many of his opponents and his supporters. There were two sides to the "Indian" question. One was that the "only good Indian was a dead Indian," and the other side insisted on liberal terms and an overblown so-called "humanitarian" treatment. Schurz thought that fair dealing with the Native Americans was the answer; however, he was too far distant from the settlements or reservations that the wheels of his reform turned too slowly. He decided that, before anything could be accomplished, he had to reorganize the whole bureau. He enlisted the help of the current Indian commissioner, John Q. Smith, to go on an inspection tour and to report on conditions, communication, finances, suitability of land, and schooling. Schurz believed the Native American had to be assimilated into the society of whites. Consequently, he approved the foundation of Indian Schools at Hampton Institute, Virginia, Forest Grove, Oregon, and Carlisle Barracks, Pennsylvania. Unfortunately, the educational goal was to remove "native traits," including tribal names and "Indian" identity. Schurz, an immigrant who adapted to a new society, did not realize that the process of education was a reverse integration. The tribes were in America first and could see no sense in adopting "the white man's ways." Schurz established a board to examine the Bureau's finances, and Smith resigned because the inquiry found financial discrepancies in his records, including bribery and extortion. After new appointments and general "housekeeping," Schurz remained under attack from every side. The War Department, led by William Tecumseh Sherman, wanted to take the Bureau back. In December 1878, Schurz testified before a Congressional Committee and was able to keep the Bureau under his aegis. He had never before interfered with the army's handling of Native American hostility; however, in the fall of 1879, he did. There was a Ute uprising in Colorado where the local agent, Nathan C. Meeker, was murdered and his wife and daughters were taken prisoner. This time, Secretary Schurz intervened, and a treaty was signed, allowing the Utes compensation and retention of a small portion of a reservation. This agreement was accomplished despite the white settlers and military efforts for violent revenge and retribution. Chief Ouray, who died during the negotiations, so respected Schurz, or "Four Eyes" as he called him, that he left him his deerskin jacket, pants, powder horn, and tobacco pouch.

In September 1879, Carl Schurz decided to visit the Indian lands. He took Edwin P. Hanna, his private secretary; Count August von Donoff, the secretary of the German Legation in Washington; John M. Carson, correspondent of *The New York Times* in Washington; Henri Gaullier, a New York merchant; to the Indian International Fair in Muskogee Indian Territory (now Oklahoma).[2] The *Cincinnati Daily Gazette* of Wednesday, October 1, 1879, described the event:

AMONG THE INDIANS: Secretary Schurz's Tour Among the Indian Tribes and Agencies.

Muskogee, I.T. ... Leaving Wichita, Kansas, Thursday Morning the Secretary and his party, in charge of Indian Agent Miles, of the Osages, and Whitman of the Poncas, proceeded by carriages to the Kaw Agency where they arrived that evening. A council was held with the Kaws on Thursday. On Friday, the party reached the Ponca Agency, where councils were held with the Poncas and the Nez Perces, and the Pawnee Agency was reached Saturday, where an inspection of the Pawnees was made. The Sac and Fox's' Agency was reached Sunday; Okmuigee on Monday and Muskogee this evening.

Indian Agent Enfes, of the Upton Agency has made ample preparations to preserve good order at the fair. The Fair Association has a force of twenty police and twelve Indian police have been recruited, under the new law, to do the scalping of gamblers or whiskey men who may come to try our climate. There is a very large attendance of the Plains Indians and, the entries are much greater than ever before, particularly on the part of the wild tribes. Representatives from twenty-five tribes are present and will be addressed by Secretary Schurz tomorrow. John Shorb, Agent for the Sac and Fox; L.J. Miles, Agent of the Cheyennes, and P.R. Hunt, Agent of the Kiowas were with the Secretary.

The *New Haven Register* of August 5, 1879, reported the event inferring scalping: "Carl Schurz will visit Indian country himself. Carl has an attractive head of hair."

On this trip, Chief Crazy Horse of the Oglala Sioux presented Schurz with a tomahawk and war shirt. He put it on Schurz, declaring "He *Oglala*." One major problem he inherited was the Ponca tribe on the Dakota–Nebraska line. In 1868, a government treaty with the Sioux gave the Ponca's land to these enemies. They were removed from their homes and marched to a virtual desert in Oklahoma; many died along the way. There were reports of military brutality, such as children being picked up by their braids and tossed into wagons. The new land was flat, arid, and unsuitable. Chief Standing Bear, carrying a sack with his grandchild's bones, visited Schurz in Washington, demanding they return to their native lands. They had been duped by earlier agents and their forced move was violent, resulting in the title of the Ponca Trail of Tears. Schurz was powerless and could not help them; however, Thomas H. Tibbles, a Methodist abolitionist, intervened and brought the plight of the Ponca's to national attention through speeches and the press.[3] Schurz brought the case to Congress but was continually rejected or ignored. When the Chief and his people left the reservation to return home on their own, they were arrested. Schurz was blamed for the order; finally, Tibbles, after speaking in April 1879, brought the case to the District Court of Nebraska: *Standing Bear v. Crook*. The court interpreter was Susette La Flesche (*Inshata Theuumba*: Bright Eyes) who later married the widowed Tibble. Up to this time, Indians were legally non-persons—neither American citizens or recognized as a people or nationality. Judge Elmer S. Dundy ruled "an Indian is a person" and granted a writ of *habeas corpus*, freeing the Poncas from prison.

Carl Schurz bore the brunt of the attack about this situation; he was pictured as heartless and a persecutor of these innocent people. After a massive protest rally in Boston and a gubernatorial public castigation, Hayes's cabinet discussed the question and the President said that Schurz "had been shamefully treated." He called a special commission to settle the matter, which invited the Ponca chiefs to Washington, who said they were satisfied with the arrangements that had been made. Congress made a $165,000 financial retribution to the tribe. During this process, Schurz's foreign birth was made the target for retaliation; Senator Henry L. Dawes, who later proposed an act to end tribal government and control of communal lands, wrote: "From the Pequot War to our days there never was an Indian unjustly killed in this country until a German-born American citizen became Secretary of the Interior."[4]

Unfortunately, and probably admittedly, Schurz mishandled the inherited affair; Standing Bear never forgave him, and this one failure has overshadowed all of his other positive policies. The irony of these criticisms was that they conflicted with "Foreigner" Schurz's Romantic nature, which immortalized and admired the "noble Savage." James Fenimore Cooper's books were translated into German as early as 1826, and in the later part of the century, Karl May's Native American Novels became a rage in Germany.[5] Therefore, the idea that Schurz denigrated Native Americans was probably false. The problem lay in Schurz's difficulties with diplomatic language. He believed that he had every right to criticize that which he felt wrong, which left him open for negative press and continual satire.

Schurz was instrumental, however, in creating the extensive census of 1880, which, under the supervision of General Francis A. Walker, became a model for future population analyses. Schurz had a close enough relationship with the President to give advice on labor affairs and hard money policy. In 1878, he went on a speaking tour to encourage the German vote for the Republican candidates, but it was largely unsuccessful because the Democrats won in both houses of Congress.

Schurz's political life in Washington may have been stormy but his personal and family life was not. He had rented a townhouse at 1719 H Street in Washington, where he lived with Agathe, age twenty-seven; Marianne, age twenty-three; Carl (Carli) Lincoln, age nine; Herbert age four; and servants Agnes Baron, Catherine Donohue, Kate Tracy, and Mary Fogarty (all Irish). The *Washington Letter* described the family life in an article reprinted in the *Lowell Daily Citizen and News* on Wednesday, December 5, 1877:

> Secretary Schurz is keeping house; but the young ladies, not yet out of mourning for their mother, will not indulge in any great gayety. The Misses Schurz are not specimens of the buxom Teutonic beauty. They are very fragile and refined, with complexions of transparent purity, fine regular features, and fair hair. Miss Agathe, the eldest, takes care of the baby boy her mother left, and is devoted to the beautiful child, now running about the house, and talking in baby phrase. For this baby, whom she took when only a few days old from her dying mother's arms, she has given up everything with an abandon beautiful in a young girl. The other young daughter, Puss, has charge of little Carl, an active boy of 8 or 10. So beautifully pure do these fair girls live, the two grown sisters caring for little brothers, and receiving from their father the attentions almost as a lover in public or at home, that it brings up the ideal home affection, which has almost died out except in novels. *Washington Letter.*[6]

This family situation did not prevent Agathe and Marianne from being a part of the active Washington social scene that was covered closely by the society columns. As an eligible widower father, Schurz was linked with Evart's daughter, Betty, by the press because he was seen dancing with her. Agathe, on the other hand, in 1878, was "missed from society lately. She had been "detained home by the illness of her little brother Carl."[7] Agathe attended a charity ball at the White House Blue Room on February 27 of the same year with her father and sister. The account noted, "Miss Agathe Schurz wore black silk with insertions of black velvet embossed with white. Her sister wore an exquisite white brocade."[8] Agathe was still in black and in apparent mourning for her mother. By March 8, she wore the same dress. Almost a year later, on February 22, 1879, she was spotted wearing a "striking looking dress of white silk, trimmed with bands of black jet set on perpendicularly."[9] In spring 1879, Agathe attended "cookery school" with the President's wife, among others; she had become part of presidential life in the Capitol. She attended the opening of the National Fair in October 1879 with the chief executive and, at times, substituted for his wife at White House receptions while the First Lady was away.

Schurz was leading a "double life," always a hard worker when he was not at his desk at night; he was part of the Washington social whirl. Evening musicales were part of the local entertainment. President Hayes was a frequent visitor at the Schurz home, and the Secretary often entertained at the piano in the White House. One night, Thomas Alva Edison appeared and recorded the musicians with Mrs. Hayes and Schurz as the soloists.

The President took Schurz on trips, enjoying his company as the two somehow formed a friendship past the political relationship. They visited Harvard and James Madison's home in Virginia. The Schurz girls loved the attention, particularly the balls, fancy dresses, and the newspaper social coverage that their status brought.

In 1880, Hayes had decided not to run for the next term. This prompted many candidates to run to the political arena. Schurz had originally supported Blaine, but finally, after vacillating, Schurz supported James Garfield; after writing him a letter of his usual advice, he went on the campaign trail to garner the usual German-American vote. He was wrestling with the Ponca affair during this period, but in spite of all the rumors of his appointment in the next cabinet or of running for office, Carl Schurz decided, after eight years in public service, he decided to leave the Capitol and seek another career.

# Fanny Chapman

Carl Schurz weighed his options in 1881. He could return to St. Louis and take up the *Westliche Post* full time or do lecture tours to supplement his income. His best friend was Dr. Jacobi in New York; if he lived near him, he could return to writing full time. However, the one overwhelming factor that kept him in the east and near Pennsylvania was Fanny Chapman.

They met in Washington during the musicales and swirl of society. Fanny was traveling the world with her sister, Elizabeth Chapman Lawrence, one of high society's wealthy widows. The Chapman sisters were the daughters of the Honorable Henry Chapman, a state senator for Pennsylvania who resided in Doylestown, and Nancy Findlay Shunk Chapman, whose grandfather, William Findlay, was the governor of Pennsylvania and a United States senator. It was an old Pennsylvania family and when daughter Elizabeth married Timothy Bigelow Lawrence, she was whisked off to London as her new husband was the *attaché* to his diplomat father there. They were invited to all the musicales and events at the time, the high point being Queen Victoria and Prince Albert's wedding. She encountered literary lights Charles Dickens and William Makepeace Thackeray. She eventually toured most of Europe often with sister, Fanny, by her side.

Sadly, in 1869, Bigelow, after returning from Florence where he was the American consulate to Italy, suddenly fell ill of a brain abscess and died. He was forty-one years old. Elizabeth inherited over $1 million and Fanny was left an income of $5,000 per year for life. After a grand tour of Europe, Elizabeth Chapman Lawrence rented a townhouse on I Street, Washington D.C., for herself and Fanny. Her decision to settle there in 1875 coincided with one of the most exciting years for socialites. Elizabeth brought her niece, Lela, to live with them as a companion for Fanny, who was very close to her in age. The very pretty Fanny was the belle of many a celebration; one night, she attended the German ambassador's ball and danced with the Danish ambassador, Hegermann. The Chapman sisters held court at home and notables passed through the doors on I Street. James Blaine was seen frequently; whether he was thought of as a "close" friend of Elizabeth's or more is a rumored mystery. When and where Carl Schurz became part of this circle is not documented. He was in Washington when Elizabeth arrived with her entourage, but his relationship with her did not appear to blossom until 1879, after his wife's death.

The intellectual community was important to him; literary and international visitors often graced the large house on H Street, as well as the one of the Chapman Lawrences. The author Henry Adams lived nearby and was a frequent guest. Through the diplomatic community and musical affairs, Schurz met Lillie de Hegermann-Lindencrone, the wife of the Danish minister to the United States. The evening musicales attracted her because of her remarkable, trained singing voice and her acquaintance with composers Richard Wagner, Franz Liszt, Charles Gounod, and Gioachino Rossini. The newspaper coverage of the political squabbles in this era in Washington did not cover the musical accomplishments of Carl Schurz. Music was always a part of his life and Lillie (born Greenough) became a great influence and companion.

When she was seventeen, her mother took her to London for voice lessons from Manuel Garcia, who had trained Jennie Lind and Mathilde Marchesi. Lillie married Charles Moulton, the son of a very wealthy American Banker. The couple chatted with many of the nobility in Europe and was a particular favorite at the Court of Napoleon III. After Charles died, she married Johan Henrik de Hegermann-Lindencrone, the Danish Minister then in Washington, where in the diplomatic circles in which they traveled, she met and befriended Elizabeth Chapman Lawrence and her beautiful, intelligent sister Frances, known as "Fanny."

Lillie wrote two books in her later life. Her memoirs, *The Sunny Side of Diplomatic Life: 1875–1912*, included a letter to her mother written in Washington in February 1879, describing the social life with Fanny and Elizabeth Chapman and Carl Schurz:

Washington February 1879

Dear Mother, Monsieur Schlözer is one of the colleagues whom we like best. I wish you knew him! I do not know of anything more delightful than to see him and Carl Schurz together. They are not unlike in character; they are both witty, refined, always seeing the beautiful in everything, almost boyish in their enthusiasm, and clever *cela va sans dire* to their fingertips. They bring each other out, and they both appear at their best, which is saying a great deal. We consider that we are fortunate to number them among our *intimes*.

Would it interest you to know how these *intimes* amuse themselves? Life is so simple in Washington, and there are so few distractions outside of society, that we only have our social pleasures to take the place of theaters and public entertainments. It is unlike Paris and other capitals in this respect.

... We have organized a club which we call "The National Rational International Dining Club". To which belong Mrs. Bigelow Lawrence, her sister Miss Chapman, Mr. de Schlözer. Carl Schurz, Aristarchi Bey (the Turkish Minister) Count Dönhoff (Secretary to the German Legation) and ourselves. I am the President, Mrs. Lawrence the vice president, Schurz, the treasurer, Schlözer the sergeant at arms, and Johan has the most difficult—and (as Mr. Schurz calls it) the "onerous"—duty of recognizing and calling attention to the jokes, which his conscientious attempts to seize he often loses entirely.

The "rational" part is the menu. We are allowed one soup, one roast, one vegetable, and dessert and two wines, one of which according to the regulations, must be good. A stuffed goose from the Smithsonian Institution serves as a *milieu de table* and is sent, on the day of the dinner, to the person who gives it.

We always have music. Schurz and Schlözer play the piano alternately and I do the singing. I must say that a more appreciative audience than our co-diners cannot be imagined.[1]

She goes on to tell how Schurz, as the treasurer, carried the club's laws and by-laws in his coat pocket. At a particularly dull dinner party, which included other members of the society, he would pull this large document, impressed with a "huge official-looking seal," from his pocket and peruse it seriously as if there was great government importance attached to it. The N.R.I. members at the table had a hard time staying serious, while uninitiated guests were asking about what important matter the papers contained. Schurz would seriously put the paper back in his coat, and then wink at his cohorts.[2,3]

Lillie's letter told her mother about Schurz:

Mr. Schurz is now Secretary of the Interior, and a great personage. When one thinks that he hardly knew a word of our language when he came to this country (a young man of twenty) and that now he is one of our first orators, one cannot help but admire him because he has entirely identified himself with the politics of our country he has risen to the high position which he now holds. You said, when you heard him deliver that oration at Harvard College, that you were astonished that any foreigner could have complete control of the language. He is integrity itself, with a great mind free from all guile, and is filled with the enthusiasm and vivacity of youth.[4]

Lillie and Elizabeth described a side of Carl Schurz that is rarely seen in other accounts. Thomas Nast drew him as a funny looking cartoon character. The newspapers gave either an idealized portrait or one of scorn and derision. Carl Schurz, in the true Victorian fashion of the day, never let his sense of humor or his artistic nature show publicly. Another humorous incident occurred when the Native Americans visited Washington D.C.; Lillie described a meeting with the

Nez Perce Indians and Chief Joseph that she and the Chapman sisters wanted to attend. The interpreter (Indian agent) wanted the tribesmen to dress suitably for the occasion; however, when he heard that there would be women present, he purchased striped shirts to cover their bare chests, or so he thought. The Nez Perce arrived carrying tomahawks and wearing the shirts over their trousers. They were not happy with Schurz's refusal of their proposal to return to their own lands after much blood had been shed over the issue. When Schurz refused their offer, Lillie wrote:

> Mrs. Lawrence who saw everything in a rosy light thought that they looked noble. I, who am prosaic to my fingertips, thought they looked conceited, brutal and obstinate. They all sat with their tomahawks laid by the side of their chairs. The chief was not insensible to the beauty of Miss Chapman, and sat behind his outspread fingers, gazing at her and her jewelry.[5]

*Harper's Weekly* published a drawing of the meeting showing President Hayes in an armchair, and Carl Schurz seated next to Fanny and Elizabeth. A beautiful woman, Fanny was witty, intelligent, vivacious, and extroverted. Author Henry Adams used her as a model for his character Sybil Ross in his novel *Democracy: An American Novel* based on life in Washington at the time. Henry and his wife, Marian, moved into 1607 H Street off Lafayette Square and were friends and neighbors of the Chapman Lawrences, the de Hegemann-Lindencrones, and the Schurzes. Adams published the novel anonymously in 1880; his authorship was revealed after his death in 1918. He wrote about Washington society in a letter to Charles Milnes Gaskell, "this is the only place in America where society amuses me, or where life offers variety."[6]

Adams' description of Sybil most likely applies to Fanny Chapman too: "The imagination gave up all attempts to soar where she came. A more straightforward, downright, gay, sympathetic, shallow, warm-hearted, sternly practical young woman has rarely touched this planet."[7]

Fanny Chapman was twenty-nine years old when she and her sister started to "winter" in Washington; Carl Schurz was forty-six. There are no letters or indications of when or how they met; however, they were neighbors on Lafayette Square. The evening entertainments and the N.R.I club provided emotional relief to the widowed father of four, struggling as the Secretary of the Interior with the Indian affairs. He told Elizabeth Chapman Lawrence one night at one of their dinners that: he had been "lying [*sic.*] awake at nights" yet she reported, he was "going about in society as bright and as agreeable as ever."[8]

Schurz was able to leave the formal stance and professional appearance behind when he met with his friends, often entertaining them with his stories and his piano. In her letters, Elizabeth tells of Schurz's story of helping a Ute chief find a son he had lost twenty years earlier, which shows the caring humanitarian that the man was. Somehow, through the storytelling, piano recitals, fine wines, balls, and Washington society, Schurz and Fanny fell in love.

Despite the age difference of seventeen years and the disparate backgrounds, the relationship lasted until his death. Residents of Doylestown, Pennsylvania, whose oral family history overlaps the years and provides local gossip from the past, claim that Schurz and Fanny's relationship started while he was still married. They may have met in 1875 when Margarethe was in Germany; however, Schurz's letters to Fanny begin in 1880. The problem was Agathe Schurz, who hated the relationship and Fanny. The Schurz girls lived well in high society until their deaths in the 1920s; maybe they were afraid of losing inheritance or social position. Agathe had spent a year in the Moravian Seminary for Women, which taught "the female virtues" of the staid Victorian morality to the well-chaperoned girls. An unaccompanied woman in the presence of a male was unacceptable, and perhaps she felt that the relationship was immoral or disrespectful to her late mother. Perhaps the vivacious Fanny was a polar opposite of the serious Agathe; therefore, Agathe erased all vestiges of Fanny Chapman from Schurz's papers used by biographers and her father's *Reminiscences*. James Michener was Fanny's neighbor and boyhood friend.[8] He wrote:

> Of greater interest to me is the revelation made here concerning one of the grand old ladies of my hometown. As a boy, I knew and revered Fanny Chapman, younger half-sister of the dazzling Elizabeth. I remember her as kind, generous, aloof, a dear little old lady who had never married, pillar of her church and about the only respectable Democrat in town. She was the kind of winsome dear about whom I used to weave imaginary stories. In my version, she was always either knitting or doing good or serving tea or talking with the vicar.
>
> Now I find that she was the lifelong inamorata of Carl Schurz.[9, 10]

Fanny Chapman is listed as "Mrs. Schurz" in one of the Chapman family trees; were they ever secretly married? During their relationship, they exchanged and wrote over 1,000 letters.

# New York and the Gilded Age

Carl Schurz spent the last years of his life in and around New York City, living uptown and downtown, vacationing in the close and distant suburbs. He never held public office but turned his career to his first goal of journalism and writing, while remaining the unofficial leader and voice of the German-Americans. Money appeared to be an issue that was directly relative to his lifestyle. He lived in an expensive neighborhood with a *ménage* of four children, three or four servants, and assorted pets. He was realizing between $7,000 and $8,000 dollars a year from *Westliche Post* (approximately $190,000 in modern money). He also had some of Margarethe's inheritance but he was still thinking of going back on the lecture circuit to supplement his income.

He initially lived close to Dr. Abraham Jacobi on 34th Street. These two men had grown to be very close friends, nurturing a relationship that started in Revolutionary Germany and ended in New York. Both were pioneers and groundbreakers, who often fostered and supported humanitarian causes. Abraham Jacobi was a pioneer in pediatric medicine. His wife, Mary Putnam Jacobi, was a force in the establishment of women in medicine. The Jacobi children loved their "Uncle Schurz," and the Schurz children thought the same of "Uncle Jacobi."

Schurz was still seeking more employment at this time, when Henry Villard wanted to fund a newspaper in New York.[1] The wealthy financier and railroad owner was a fellow refugee from the Revolutions of 1849. His real name was Ferdinand Heinrich Gustav Hilgard; he left Germany without his father's knowledge and changed his name to Villard to protect his identity. He was a Civil War correspondent and a friend of Lincoln's. He had approached Parke Godwin (William Cullen Bryant's son-in-law), who wanted to sell shares of the *Evening Post,* with E. L. Godkin (owner of *The Nation*), Horace White (formerly of the *Chicago Tribune*), and Schurz. They were silent investors, letting a triumvirate manage the papers while a nervous newcomer, Carl Schurz, was the editor-in-chief.

The editors were able to use the paper as an organ for their individual ideologies. They were aptly named "Mugwumps" and were committed to remaining aloof from party politics. Schurz wrote on politics and foreign relations, while Godkin and White took on social affairs and economics. The position enabled Schurz to expound on his favorite interests, such as newly formed National Civil Service Reform League.

The James Garfield assassination attempt and his following death shocked Schurz. Staid Chester A. Arthur was now the president, much to his horror. However, Schurz praised him both privately and publicly for his veto of the River and Harbor Bill of 1882. Schurz praised the adoption of a Civil Service Reform measure and Arthur's veto of the Chinese Exclusion Act.

The *Evening Post,* under Schurz's guidance, began a campaign against the anti-Semitism that had begun in earnest in Russia and Germany. Charles Darwin's *On the Origin of Species* hit the world like an out of control thunderbolt in 1859. Evolution and the idea that man was descended from an ape was a highly controversial and popular topic of the age. Clergy called it "Evilution." Some scholars used it to promote their own negative, racist, and ethnic ideas. Francis Galton, a half-cousin of Charles Darwin, conceived of "eugenics," which professed a selective breeding program of superior races and individuals and the elimination of the inferior human beings. The movement, which started in England, reached the United States in the early 1900s. This theory, coupled with the anti-evolutionists, added to the movement for anti-immigration laws that turned the journalistic world into an open forum for all sides.

For many personal reasons, Schurz was a crusader against anti-Semitism. His first was his childhood experience in Liblar; he also had friends and associates who were not only Forty-Eighters but were also German Jews. He befriended Simon Wolf in Washington, a Bavarian by birth, who was active in Jewish educational and charitable movements and who was a friend of Presidents Lincoln, Grant, McKinley, and Woodrow Wilson. Wolf, the president of B'nai B'rith, was on the board of the Hebrew Orphan's Home in Atlanta, Georgia, and the Board of Children's Guardian's in Washington D.C. Schurz's Jewish German immigrant friends were the wealthy banker Isaac Seligman; Jonas, Louis, and Levi Strauss; and wealthy financier Jacob Schiff. They all shared a concern for children, charities, and the fight against the rising tide of anti-Semitism in America, Russia, and Germany. Abraham Jacobi, with Schurz's help, went to court over the conditions at New York's Foundling Hospital; he was influential in establishing a foster care program, again with Schurz. They also raised funds for the Hebrew Orphan's Home in New York.

Anti-Semitic discrimination in America had spread, including people who looked "Jewish" sounded "Jewish" or had Jewish names. On May 31, 1880, the *New-York Tribune* published an article on the "Ostracism of Jews:"

The Wife of Dr. Abraham Jacobi excluded from a Staten Island Hotel. Mrs. Jacobi, the wife of Dr. Abraham Jacobi of No. 110 West Thirty Fourth St. was refused accommodation St. Mark's Hotel on Staten Island because she bore a Hebrew name. She is Christian in faith, and is the daughter of the late George Putnam, the publisher.[2]

The article goes on to relate other incidents of anything or anybody Jewish being turned away from hotels and restaurants. The bigotry movement was revived in Germany and Russia. When Bismarck's opponent Eduard Lasker died suddenly in New York, Schurz used the eulogy as a bitter attack on anti-Semitism:

It sounds like a libel upon human nature when the report reaches us from the other side that the fanatics of this new persecution of the Jews, this empty mockery of the boasted enlightenment of the Nineteenth century, even now, after having darkened the last years of his (Lasker's) life, are seeking to vilify him in the coffin because he was a Jew. Let us pity them, for they realize not their shame and disgrace; in truth, it may be said, "They know not what they do!" But all the more willing and proud are we to stand here, American and German citizens of a free country, not of his faith, and with us stands every honorable man who respects a man's true worth, and remembering the noble heart, the great mind and lofty ambition of the departed, we reach the hand of brotherhood to him even beyond the grave.[3]

At the dedication of Montefiore Home for Chronic Invalids on Avenue A and 84th Street in Manhattan (now Montefiore Hospital in the Bronx), Schurz again lashed out at the anti-Semites:

The Jews have in proportion to their numbers done far more. I repeat this with all the greater willingness, as I have recently had occasion to observe the motive springs, the character, and the aims of the so-called "anti-Semitic Movement," a movement whose dark spirit of fanaticism and persecution insults the humane enlightenment of the nineteenth century; whose appeals are addressed to the stupidity, prejudice and the blindest passion; whose injustice affronts every sense of fairness and decency; and whose cowardice—for cowardice is an essential element in the attempt to suppress the competing energies of a mere handful of people—whose cowardice, I say, should provoke the contempt of every self-respecting man.[4]

His responsive attacks were not confined only to the hate mongers; he went after any "issues." He was called a "Mugwump" as were others who were apolitical. This name, applied to independents, was a derogatory definition of a person who sat on the fence with "the Mug on one side and the Rump on the other." Their political party detractors claimed them to be indecisive and that they vacillated constantly from one opinion to another. Due to his former positions, Schurz was open to vicious accusations about issues to which he had been connected or to ones that he openly criticized. He took on the railways and big money so much so that his position with *New York Evening Post* was in jeopardy.

Carl Schurz's New York of the nineteenth century, aside from its problems, was a center for the arts. He met the academic, medical, musical, theatrical, and wealthy denizens of the teeming city—dining with William Steinway at August Luchow's on 14th Street and Delmonico's on 44th Street and Fifth Avenue. As a member of the Author's Club, he met Mathew Arnold, Mark Twain, Oliver Wendell Holmes, Andrew Carnegie, Stephen Crane, Henry James, and other well-known authors. The Club met in a German restaurant, Sieghortner House, on 9 Lafayette Place in Manhattan. August Sieghortner opened it in the former William B. Astor mansion and served elaborate meals, including traditional German fare for the wealthy and famous authors and artists.

Schurz likely met Henry Irving when he was on tour in 1884. Irving loved the place, favoring terrapin and Saratoga Potato Chips. Schurz's son, Herbert, may have used the connection when he went to London to study with Irving. Schurz's musical side was satisfied with the affairs of the Liederkranz Club Singing Society. Schurz not only rubbed shoulders with the rich and famous; he became one of them. Fanny Chapman was close by, and they spent as much time together as they could; she had declared her love for him as he had for her.

When Schurz was forced to make a clean break with the *New York Evening Post* because of the conflict with the other editors, the loss of this position caused him to be in a poor financial position once again. A few friends tried to raise money for him; even his brother-in-law offered help, but Schurz refused them all, saying that he would make his living as a writer.

He continued to freelance, butting heads with candidate James G. Blaine, who failed in an attempt at the presidency; Grover Cleveland, the governor of New York, won the office. Schurz campaigned for the German-American vote again and bore the brunt of the usual "mudslinging" and accusations. He came through it all with President Cleveland realizing his contributions. Schurz continued on his path as an independent critic and "muckraker."

In 1884, after the election, financial problems became more acute for Schurz; he no longer had a steady income. He had to close down his household, move in with the Jacobis, and send his children to their relatives in Germany. He found some work editing an "export almanac." Fortunately, Schurz found a position as a representative for European bondholders of two American railroads. In 1888, he was made the American manager of Hamburg American Packet Company; he stayed with them for four years, until his lecture fees, publications, and investments allowed him enough financial stability to allow him to start on his scholarly literary career.

Schurz began to write independently for *Harper's Weekly*. His connection was George William Curtis, the president of the National Civil Service Reform League, who had written for *Putnam's Magazine*, which he helped found with George Palmer Putnam, Dr. Jacobi's father-in-law. When Curtis became ill in the 1890s, Schurz wrote anonymous editorials for the *Harper's Weekly*, and when Curtis died in 1892, he became part of the editorial staff. As a voice of the independent, he continued to barrage President Cleveland with letters of criticism and advice.

During the summer and fall of 1888, Carl Schurz returned to his homeland on business and for a family visit. He wanted to go to the Berlin archives for research on a book about the Civil War, meet with the European bondholders, and to visit his wife's relatives in Hamburg and Kiel. Germany was in a state of flux, during this period, because Kaiser Wilhelm I died of cancer after only ninety-nine days in office. His successor, Wilhelm II, cast a shadow over the country since there was no clear view of his policies. Schurz was again wined and dined in Berlin by the local officials. He even delivered a eulogy for the late departed Kaiser, whom he had despised during the Revolution. The speech reprinted on the continent and in the United States, reinforced Schurz's position as the leader of German Americans.

He visited Bismarck, the old Iron Duke, and got an ear full about the new emperor and his mother, Queen Victoria's daughter, who like her mother, Bismarck felt, was a poor influence on her regent husband. He kept Schurz for two and a half hours in the afternoon over a bottle of Rhine wine, then invited him back for supper, which was a "*gemütlich*" affair with Bismarck and his family. He met the new Kaiser in Hamburg aboard his ship. Schurz found him intelligent and robust. Ironically, this same man plunged the world into World War I, fostering the hatred of all things German in the early twentieth century.

Schurz returned home in November 1888 to his son, Carl Lincoln, who was ill and needed several operations. The trip was profitable for Schurz for he was now the American representative for the Hamburg American Line ($18,000 per year). The position resulted in two more trips to Germany in 1889 and 1890. His detractors, in the news, claimed that his trip was part of his disappointment with Cleveland's tax policies, and as the Mugwump leader, he had decided to stay abroad.

However, he continued to write, dictating in Pitman shorthand to a secretary. He completed a two-volume life of Henry Clay in 1887, edited his speeches, and prepared new articles. He never wrote a history of the American Civil War, although publishers would have liked to have had his views; he left this to a close friend, James Ford Rhodes, and started his own *Reminiscences* in 1887 as Schurz's stance as a politician was as a critical observer. He had lost all fear of repercussion, and while living well in New York, he was feted by the Commonwealth Club for his Civil Service Reform activities. Schurz began to speak out more publicly on contemporary concerns. In 1890, he spoke to the Forestry Association in Philadelphia on conservation.

Schurz only took a small part in the campaign of 1892 because he was suffering from gall bladder problems; he restricted his campaign comments to the newspapers until he was able to make a speech at Cooper Institute in German in support of Democrat Cleveland. His real interest now was his writing both books and weekly editorials for *Harper's Weekly*. His private life improved; he brought his family back to New York in 1885. He summered at the Jersey shore, probably in Elberton, N.J. with the Seligmans; in 1892, he purchased a house in the posh Pocantico Hills near Tarrytown, New York. The Summer Social Register of 1894 lists Carl Schurz and his daughters at their summer homes, along with those of the Rockefellers, Astors, Morgans, Roosevelts, and Vanderbilts.[5] The Schurzes were officially part of the Upper Crust. Schurz loved the countryside in Pocantico, inviting his friends for social events and walks in the countryside. He wrote, "How beautiful is the world, I hope it won't be necessary to depart from it for a long, long time to come."[6] He sold the house to his son. For a while, he lived on East 68th Street in Manhattan until he settled in on 24 East 91st Street, half a block off Fifth Avenue, next to his friend, Andrew Carnegie.

Abraham Jacobi convinced him to build "a cottage" near his in Bolton Landing, New York, which Schurz did, constructing a beautiful home 200 feet above the lake, below Jacobi's. Both houses are gone; Jacobi's burned down and Schurz's was torn down and replaced with a series of condominiums. However, they had beautiful days there; Schurz would take early morning walks with his three dogs; his daughters retired there, and the Jacobi children were very frequent visitors to "Uncle Schurz," who sat and played with them on the parlor floor. The two families took their meals together, sharing kitchen staff. Schurz could write in his room with a beautiful view of the lake. Many visitors were welcomed for his hospitality and company.

His relationship with Fanny remained as a major part of his life. He wrote to her frequently in the German "*alte Schrift*." She had learned German and the old script for him, and they communicated by mail. She sent her letters from him to a niece in Germany so that they would not be lost; her letters to him disappeared after his death. Their intimacy lasted over many years, but he regretted that he could not make her truly happy. The real reason for this could be attributed to Agathe's dislike of Fanny, their closeness in age, or the fact that Schurz's children resented her taking the place of their beloved mother, Margarethe. Although engaged to a man named Boker in 1870, Agathe never married, despite the urging of her father. She had offers in later life but focused on social causes. Marianne also never married; she was active in the New York *Damen Verein*. Both sisters were well-educated and trilingual. Even until the ends of their lives, they never wanted for anything. Carl Lincoln and Herbert both attended Harvard University. Carl became a lawyer.

In the late 1880s and 1890s, Schurz, in New York, followed his intellectual and artistic passions. He found musical companionship at the Liederkranz Club with William Steinway, the piano manufacturer, president of the Club, and a close friend. He attended the opera, theatre, and concerts. He performed at the Liederkranz. On one occasion, a pianist did not show up at Carnegie Hall; Schurz took over and played Chopin.

Grover Cleveland was re-elected for a second term and Schurz continued his letter and editorial barrage about Civil Service Reform. He took over the presidency of the National Civil Service Reform League that continually pressured and lobbied for reform of government offices. Schurz had no shame in "advising" the President of the United States about extradition treaties with Russia; ambassadors, most importantly those in Berlin; the repeal of the Sherman Silver Purchase Act; and the reappointment of Theodore Roosevelt as civil service commissioner. He kept a good relationship with Cleveland, traveling to Washington for a dinner with the President and his wife.

Schurz continued to battle Tammany Hall in New York, still pursuing reform that was successful when the Republicans won the City and the State; however, when Theodore Roosevelt was appointed police commissioner and began to enforce Sunday liquor laws, the German-American community was in an uproar over the absence of beer on the Sabbath. The new law forbade the opening of saloons on Sunday; there were more Germans in the city than were in Berlin, many of whom worked six days a week and looked forward to their Sunday beer, preferably in a "*Biergarten*." Roosevelt's legally closed taverns managed, via bribes, to stay open. This law made Schurz somewhat unpopular with the Germans; however, his increasing prominence and his status as the United States' "Mr. German American" solved many of the antagonistic feelings.

He spoke at German affairs, attended German Day, increased the use of Hamburg Line ships, and advised the German academic world. This position was difficult as the century wore on. Schurz was increasingly disturbed by the escalating tensions in his home country and the difficult relations between his new country and the old one. Concurrently, there was a conflict over interests in Samoa between the U.S., Britain, and Germany. Warships from the nations were gathering there. In 1889, German troops landed there destroying property and causing casualties among the populace. German Minister Count Arco-Valley called on Schurz in New York, looking for a solution, offering to end the bloodshed and contention in the islands and restore powers to Samoa; however, before any action could be taken, a hurricane destroyed all of the warships of the three powers and ended the issue.

Carl Schurz was never in favor of the annexation of any "foreign" land or province. He applauded Grover Cleveland's withdrawal of the treaty of annexation of Hawaii that had been negotiated by the previous administration, but he was upset by the President's intrusion with the dispute between Venezuela and Great Britain over the border of British Guiana. These were the first steps toward the formation of the Anti-Imperialist League.

# Elder Statesman
# The Final Years

The last ten years of the nineteenth century in New York City were a time of strife, corruption, inflation, murder, and mayhem. Prostitution, gambling, drinking, and bribery were a fiber in the teeming metropolis. Carl Schurz grew into the role of the wise, elder statesman of New York, writing and publishing a voice of reason in his chaotic world. The anarchists were on the move in Europe, and the world seemed to be falling apart at the seams. The Republican Party nominated William McKinley to run against William Jennings Bryan, on a "silver" platform, famous for his speech that ended with "you shall not press down upon the brow of labor this crown of thorns. You shall not crucify mankind upon a cross of gold."[1] Like the majority of German Americans, Schurz was opposed to inflation and took on the fight to preserve the gold standard of currency. Convinced that America was facing a crisis, he spoke out during the campaign, supported by the German Sound Money League and the National Sound Money League, returning to the Midwest to face German-American opponent John Peter Altgeld, who had taken the support of the gold standard and Bryan on the campaign trail.[2] Schurz was helped by the newspapers, who branded Altgeld a friend of the anarchists for pardoning men from the Haymarket bombing. He also refused to allow federal troops to handle the Pullman rail strike, led by socialist Eugen V. Debs. Schurz used McKinley's victory to continue to push for civil service reform in the federal government. During the dedication of Grant's tomb in New York, Schurz was able to meet the new president over a cigar at the Windsor Hotel. As cordial as McKinley was, and as important a voice that Schurz still had, the constant request and political maneuvering did not fare well. In 1897, much to Schurz's chagrin, New York Governor Frank S. Black (in the midst of his own Erie Canal scandal) signed a new civil service law delineating appointments on the grounds of merit and fitness. The fitness for a job was to be determined by appointment from the politicians overseeing each department. Schurz could not make any progress with the governor and was only able to continue his quest with the National Civil Service Reform League. He was further defeated when he came under attack by Jacob H. Gallinger of New Hampshire.[3] Others joined in on the attack; on May 29, 1899, McKinley ordered the exemption of over 3,600 positions from civil service regulations.

Although Schurz was horrified by McKinley's action, he was even more upset by the President's conversion to imperialism. In the last decade of the century, the world appeared to be possessed with the fever of conquest and annexation. In direct contrast was the advent of anarchy as a way of reform, beginning with the Haymarket Riot, terrorist bombings in France, the stabbing of the Empress of Austria, the assassination of Umberto I of Italy, and the assassination of President William McKinley. In the midst of protest and violence, Teddy Roosevelt and Henry Cabot Lodge were leading a movement for a "large policy" in reality the takeover of territories. The major world powers were on a quest for territory to produce economic advantage. Carl Schurz and his "Mugwump" cohorts were not only shocked and upset with the turn of affairs but were outraged. He was strongly opposed to "empire building" and wrote a letter to President McKinley "predicting that the incorporation of tropical islands would lead to the end of 'the Republic of Washington and Lincoln.'" He said:

> I am so firmly convinced of this that, cordial advocate of the civil service reform and of a sound currency as you certainly believe me to be, I would rather see … the whole civil service law repealed and a free silver coinage enacted than Hawaii annexed.[4]

The annexation of Hawaii did not occur because of a lack of a majority in the Senate, but as soon as that was done with, the "affair with Cuba" came to the fore. While war clouds gathered, Schurz—who abhorred the thought of war with the memories from Chancellorsville, Gettysburg, echoing in his head—wrote editorials against the intercession of the United States in Cuba against Spain. His former employee Joseph Pulitzer's *New York World*'s and William Randolph Hearst's *New York Journal*'s use of jingoistic language to urge the country into the war overshadowed his efforts. The "yellow journalism" outraged Schurz. Schurz went all out to halt the imperialistic rush as much as he could in his writings. The clash that he saw coming was with his old friend Theodore Roosevelt a firm believer in American annexation of territories.

The two men, the elder German-American political leader and the brash, outspoken war hero Teddy were bound to reach a parting of the ways. Roosevelt was a popular heroic figure, with his namesake "Teddy Bear" appearing in children's playrooms, and Schurz was still an old foreigner. In a speech at Newport Naval College, Roosevelt said:

THIS NATION cannot stand still if it is to retain its self-respect, and to keep undimmed the honorable traditions inherited from the men who with the sword founded it and by the sword preserved it.... No nation should ever wage war wantonly, but no nation should ever avoid it at the cost of the loss of national honor. A nation should never fight unless forced to; but it should always be ready to fight. The mere fact that it is ready will generally spare it the necessity of fighting.[5]

In the speech, he used the word "war" effusively, and Schurz quickly attacked Roosevelt in *Harper's Weekly,* refusing to support him as governor of New York and speaking out against him, supporting instead his opponent, Augustus van Wyck, although he was tied to Tammany Hall.

The division between the two old allies widened weekly. Schurz wrote copiously increasing his stance of anti-Imperialism, but he was too far away from the government to be effective; his only weapon was journalistic noise. Teddy Roosevelt was more confident of his position and began to call the "good government anti-imperialists: 'goo-goos.'" Schurz had publicly made clear that he was voting for Theodore Bacon for governor in 1898 and not for Roosevelt. *The New York Times* reported his action on October 23, 1898:

The chief of the reasons why Mr. Schurz reluctantly withholds his vote from Mr. Roosevelt is the manner in which that gentleman has advocated, in his own speeches, an extreme policy of expansion, involving not merely the risk but the threat of war. Mr. Schurz's analysis of Mr. Roosevelt's declared views on this subject is a model of courteously contemptuous statement. Even its victim can hardly resent it, though it is bound to make him very indignant.

To make matters worse, Roosevelt answered in a speech in 1899: "I don't care what that prattling foreigner shrieks or prattles." After the Spanish–American War was over, Schurz feared and predicted a violent outcome as an aftermath. The Anti-Imperialist League formed on June 15, 1898, with Schurz as vice president. The Treaty of Paris, which the League opposed, fearing the worst, was signed on December 10, 1898. On February 4, 1899, Schurz's prediction came true. Only two days before the Senate ratified the treaty, fighting broke out. American troops had invaded Puerto Rico in the summer preceding the treaty, but now the military presence was moved to the Philippines to stop a revolution against American presence there. The Philippine–American War of 1899–1902 war cost 4,200 American military lives, 20,000 Filipino insurgents, and over 200,000 more civilians to the "collateral damage" of war after the treaty had been signed.

An outraged Carl Schurz attacked President McKinley in the press and in private letters, calling the President a "miserable customer" without the "courage of his own convictions."[6] There was to be a national convention of the Anti-Imperialist League in Chicago. The author Mark Twain, credited with the founding of this organization, recruited George S. Boutwell as its first president, adding eighteen vice presidents to the executive board for credibility. Andrew Carnegie, Samuel Gompers, President Grover Cleveland, and Carl Schurz were more of the notable ones.

As the main speaker at the gathering of 160 delegates, Schurz demanded an armistice based on independence in the Philippines; he ended his speech with his very familiar saying: "Our country—when right to be kept right, when wrong to be put right." The gathering voted to propose a platform of armistice but, to Schurz's chagrin, did not include Philippine autonomous independence.

When the nominations for the presidential campaign of 1900 were beginning with each party, Carl Schurz and others were trying to form a new third party, attempts which heretofore had been unsuccessful. The German-Americans who supported the anti-imperialist cause would not vote for William Jennings Bryan, whom they detested. Schurz spoke once again at Cooper Union, trying to foster support for a candidate to oppose Bryan and McKinley; however, his friend Andrew Carnegie withdrew his promised $25,000 support donation because of the negotiations with the sale of his steel works. Therefore, the whole project was doomed and abandoned as Schurz had to bring himself to vote for William Jennings Bryan, who continually dodged support of the "Mugwumps." McKinley Republicans, promising a "full dinner pail," won the election.

Schurz's life in politics, in 1900, did not concern him as much as his personal life and tragedy did. As the years speed by in later life, colleagues and friends pass on. Age brings a sense of loneliness and one of being the last man standing. During the latter part of the century, he had lost his friends Henry Villard, William Steinway, both his brothers-in-law on his wife's side, and one on his side of the family. The greatest tragedy struck him in 1900: the death and burial of a child.

Herbert Schurz was a bright creative light at Harvard University, graduating in 1897. He was president of the German and French clubs, an outstanding student, a concert violinist, and a gifted performer, particularly in the Hasty Pudding Theatricals. A bespectacled, handsome young man, he received rave reviews for his performances from the *Boston Globe*, who said he had a "rare dramatic talent." He also had a comic talent and was selected as the "Ivy Orator" for the graduation ceremonies. His presentation was called "a hilarious influence" by *The New York Times* (June 27, 1897). In 1894, he appeared in French plays and operettas. In 1896 (his junior year), Herbert, as president of the *Deutsche Verein*, wrote a comedy, presented in German, and then went on to appear for the Hasty Pudding Theatricals in a three-act comic opera called *Branglebrink, or a Weary Wander's Woeful Wooing* as "Robert of Alles the gentleman who found the heart."[7] Herbert Schurz inherited his father's skills as an orator and was an excellent actor in three languages. In the fall of 1896, he appeared as Argon, the lead role in the *Cercle Français* performance of Moliere's *Le Malade Imaginaire* (*The Imaginary Invalid*). At Harvard, he was known as a performer and a man of humor, which he displayed as an editor of *Harvard Lampoon*. After he graduated in 1897, Herbert went to Columbia University Law School to follow his brother's and father's pathway. However, in the spring of 1900, according to reports, he was suffering from "overwork" before his graduation. He stopped his studies and accompanied a "sick" friend to the Bahamas, South America, Italy, Germany, and London, ostensibly to study acting with the famed Henry Irving. On July 24, 1900, he was found dead in his bed on 15 Bedford Place in the Bloomsbury area of London. His cause of death was listed as a stroke (cerebral hemorrhage) caused by overwork. His father received a telegram at Bolton Landing announcing his son's death; making it even more difficult for him were the letters from Herbert that arrived after his death. The *Harvard College Class of 1897 Fourth Report* printed an obituary, which read in part:

> Yet when all has been said that can be said of him, no one can describe the qualities that made him what he was to us. It was not his intellectual gifts, great as they were, nor the charm of his varying moods, nor yet his whimsical and delightful humor. It was rather the rare combination of all of these qualities which drew men to him, and which has made his death a direct personal loss to his classmates, and left a place among us no other can ever fill. F.A.B [8]

Herbert was only twenty-four years old; his letters are missing, and his travels remain a mystery. Agathe set up a memorial fund in his name at Columbia University.

However, there was more tragedy; Carl Lincoln Schurz was married to Harriet Tiedemann, the daughter of Dr. Frederick Tiedemann, who had died earlier in 1887. The couple was expecting a child, which was stillborn in 1900. Harriet Schurz never recovered from *postpartum* psychosis; Carl Lincoln, now part of a law firm, divorced her in 1920, remarrying a twice divorcee, Marie Hart, in 1922. Harriet died a year later. The year was a very sad one for a grieving Carl Schurz. He invited his sister, Toni (Antoinette), to stay with him at Bolton Landing. Despite his urging, Agathe remained single even after two proposals. He kept Fanny Chapman in his life at least on paper, sharing political views but not always in person.

Despite his own grief, Schurz picked up the torch of protest against American control of a protectorate in Cuba. Reports of atrocities were reported from the Philippines, where American soldiers were using a water torture method (in the modern world, waterboarding) to obtain information from prisoners. On July 4, 1901, authors Mark Twain and William Dean Howells issued an address against the Cuban protectorate and the atrocities in the Philippines. Their cause was shattered upon McKinley's assassination on September 6, 1901. Teddy Roosevelt took over, and although he ended the torture in the Philippines, he seized the Isthmus of Panama for a canal and announced his version of the Monroe Doctrine.

Schurz kept up with the New York City election of 1897, supporting reformer Seth Low as mayor. Once the election was over, he returned to writing about the anti-imperialist cause. Roosevelt was easily re-elected in 1904. Schurz's anti-imperialist protests were somewhat successful; during the first year of his term, Roosevelt was able to mediate and end the Russo Japanese War, no further territories were annexed, and the Philippines eventually gained independence.

There was increasing trouble on the home front. Southern bigotry and racial violence were increasing and the anti-imperialists stood to the task of crying out with a voice of reason. Schurz wrote frequently against Southern bigotry. He was asked to speak at Tuskegee Institute by Booker T. Washington, who became one of his admirers and a friend. Schurz believed that the Southerners themselves held the key to the solution of the problem by emphasizing education against prejudice. He wrote "Can the South Solve the Negro Problem?" for *McClure's Magazine* in 1904, resulting in the expected positive and negative reactions from both sides. The African-American community, led by Congressman George H. White, expressed his appreciation: "I feel that every American Negro owes you a debt of gratitude for your outspoken manly statement at this critical moment when public sentiment is being so strongly against our race."[9, 10]

As he slowed his life down and had trouble traveling, Schurz continued to write about causes and politics; he signed with *McClure's Magazine*, collaborating with editor Ida Tarbell, the well-known "muckraker." He opposed anti-Semitism, supporting the rally against the Kishinev pogrom in New York. He started his *Reminiscences* possibly knowing that he would not finish them. Most of all, he had become the symbol of all that was good with German Americans. He believed that American ideals and citizenship could be merged with all that was good from German culture.

At the fiftieth anniversary of the Liederkranz Club, Schurz's keynote address was "The German Mothertongue," where he repeated his belief that immigrants need not give up their native language. He said, "It means that we should adopt the best traits of the American character and join them with the best traits of the German character." There was a sign over the door at his home that read: "*Hier wird Deutsch gesprochen;*" the Schurz household spoke German when the family was alone. On his seventieth birthday, he was feted in Berlin and in Delmonico's in New York; a week later, the German Social Scientific Society of New York celebrated at the Liederkranz. The club was presented with a life-sized portrait of Carl Schurz, resplendent in formal dress and with a tiepin given to him by Fanny Chapman, painted by Julius Geertz. It still hangs in the entry hall of the Liederkranz in the twenty-first century. In 1902, he moved next door to Andrew Carnegie, where he could stroll in Central Park, particularly around the reservoir, gold-headed cane in hand.

His last golden days were filled with visits from the rich, famous, and political figures. He had recovered from ptomaine poisoning, gallstones, and bronchial infections, and Jacobi had ordered abstinence from his favorite wines. In November 1905, he lost his balance and fell off a trolley car, resulting in repeated headaches from a severe concussion. In May 1906, after returning from a speech in Atlanta, he thought he was suffering from his usual bronchitis, but it turned out he was more seriously ill and that the end was near. Dr. Jacobi, Mark Twain, William Dean Howells, and other visitors dropped by, but there was no hope as the old campaigner was fading quickly. "How easy it is to die," he said to the doctor who he finally used the familiar pronoun "*du*" with after all their years of close friendship. Carl Schurz died, after refusing Catholic last rites, on May 14, 1906.

# Epilogue

*He had a heart overflowing with sympathy for the two most unfavored races in America, because he himself had known what it meant to be oppressed and to struggle towards freedom against great odds. It is easier, however, from many points of view, to sympathize with a people or a race that has had an unfortunate start in life than it is to be frank and at the same time just.—to say the word and do the thing which will permanently help, regardless of the moment of whether words or acts please or displease. As Mr. Schurz stood before Hampton students, it was plain that he was a man who had been able to lift himself out of the poisoned atmosphere of racial as well as sectional prejudice. It was easy to see that here was a man who wanted to see absolute justice done to the Indian, the Negro and to the Southern white man.*

Dr. Booker T. Washington, in memory of Carl Schurz at Carnegie Hall,
November 21, 1906

Carl Schurz was laid to rest in Sleepy Hollow Cemetery in Tarrytown, New York, on a hillside overlooking a tree-covered valley, alongside Herbert. After his death, a private funeral was held on May 17, 1906, at his home on 91st Street. The pallbearers were George McAneny, executive officer of the New York City Civil Service Commission, later the executive manager of *The New York Times* and Dr. Jacobi's son-in-law; author William Dean Howells; Dr. Hans Kudlich, a German medical pioneer; Dr. Jacobi; Charles Francis Adams; Horace White; Andrew Carnegie; Isaac N. Seligman; Joseph H. Choate; Oscar S. Straus; and other notables. A brief memorial was held in the house with Felix Adler of the Ethical Culture Society delivering a eulogy in English and Dr. Jacobi delivering one in German while a quartet from the musical Arion Society provided the music. A funeral train from Grand Central station delivered Schurz's body to the cemetery, where Dr. Hollis Burke Frissell, the President of Hampton Institute (now

Hampton University), praised his contributions to African and Native Americans during a brief address. The old revolutionary, general, and rabble rouser's journey was then over.

On November 21, 1906, Schurz's memory was honored at Carnegie Hall. Frank Damrosch conducted the orchestra, playing funeral marches by Wagner and Chopin, with an all-star group of speakers, including President Cleveland and Booker T. Washington as the most prominent delivered eulogies. The memorial drew national attention and Schurz got the acclaim that he deserved.

Many memorials were created after his death followed this service. His works, many letters, and speeches were published. Before the "Great War of 1914," he was lauded as a great American. His children died during the early part of the century: Agathe in 1915 at age sixty-two, Carl Lincoln in Frankfurt of a heart attack, age fifty-three, in 1924, and Marianne at age seventy-two in 1929 in New York City.

His children were present for the dedication of two of his New York City memorials. George McAneny was instrumental in the creation of Carl Schurz Park, dedicated in 1910, covering 14 acres in the Yorkville area of Manhattan Island, overlooking the East River and the waters of Hell Gate near Gracie Mansion. In 1913, sculptor Karl Bitter used Schurz's death mask for his statue, "Defender of Liberty and A Friend of Human Rights," erected at Morningside Drive and 116th Street in New York City, dedicated by Count Johann von Bernstorff. Bitter's second monument was placed in Menominee Park in Oshkosh, Wisconsin. Memorial monuments were created in many parts of America and Germany. Parks and Forests in Bolton Landing, Merton, and Monches, Wisconsin, all bear his name. Schools in Texas, Chicago, and Wisconsin, as well as streets, carry on his legacy of human rights advocacy. Schurz, Nevada, set in the middle of a Native American Reservation, was named in his honor for his work with the tribes there. Mount Schurz, north of Eagle Peak and south of Atkins Peak in Yellowstone National Park, was dedicated to him because of his ecological and preservation efforts for the National Park System. The United States government honored his memory with a 4-cent stamp in 1983; World War II gunboats and ships carried his name.

Ironically, it was Adolf Hitler and his regime that caused the erasure of many of the contributions that Carl Schurz made to America. In 1927, the Carl Schurz *Vereiningung* was founded in Berlin, where, on the 100th anniversary of his birth in 1929, the *Reichstag* honored him. There was information linking this organization with the Nazi regime. The anti-German feelings still spilled over from World War I; to make matters worse, a German American Bund Camp was named after him in Michigan. During World War II, German clubs of any kind were shut down. The FBI was tracking down "German sympathizers" and spies, with neighbors reporting on neighbors. Some Germans were interred with no post-war reparation.

In the twenty-first century, the media is using the other "N" word again, connecting it to "right-wing" Conservatives and racists. The connection would have offended Schurz. His name is now unknown except to those closely studying American history. One museum curator, when asked, about a Thomas Nast exhibit, identified Schurz as the man who drew *Peanuts'* Charlie Brown. New Yorkers when asked about him reply that he's the guy who owned the "park."

The modern German Government, on the other hand, has honored the man who once was wanted as a revolutionary and a "jailbreaker." Berlin-Spandau, Stuttgart, Bremen, Erftstadt-Liblar, Heidelberg, Giessen, Karlsruhe, Cologne, Neuss, Rastatt, Wuppertal, Leipzig, Pirmasens, Paderborn, and Pforzheim all have a Carl Schurz Strasse. Schools in Rastatt, Erftstadt, Bonn, Bremen, Frankfurt am Main, and Berlin-Spandau are named after this former "criminal." His memory lives on in his native country on the walls of American and German Army barracks in Bremerhaven and Hardheim and on a bridge over the River Neckar. There is even a Carl Schurz Grill off Carl Schurz Strasse in Erftstadt-Liblar.

Carl Schurz would have relished taking on anyone who criticized his beliefs and causes; however, his voice is still extant in modern newspaper articles during the teen years of the new century. His relevant quotes have appeared coast to coast in modern American media. He was truly a renaissance man, whose multiple artistic talents have been lost in his personal political history. He predicted difficulties with Latin America, immigration, inflation, and civil service corruption. He was a talented, multilingual, artistic idealistic moralist whose memory needs to be preserved.

# Appendix:
# Schurz's Cast of Characters

Adams, Charles Francis (1807–1886): Writer, politician, and diplomat-son of John Quincy Adams.

Adams, Henry (1838–1918): American author and ambassador-grandson John Quincy Adams; his famous work is *The Education of Henry Adams*.

Altgeld, John Peter (1847–1902): twentieth governor of Illinois; German-born American attorney.

Anneke, Fritz (1818–1872): German Revolutionary socialist and American Civil War colonel.

Arthur, Chester (1829–1886): twenty-first president of United States (1881–1885).

Ashley, James Mitchell (1824–1896): Ohio representative in the House (1863–69), later Montana Territory governor.

Astor, William H. (1792–1875): wealthy merchant son of John Jacob Astor.

Barlow, Francis (1834–1896): lawyer, politician, and Union general in the Civil War.

Beecher, Henry Ward (1813–1887): clergyman, abolitionist, and brother of Harriet Beecher Stowe.

Benton, Thomas Hart (1782–1858): nicknamed "Old Bullion," senator from Missouri, and a leader of Western Expansion.

Bird, Francis William (1809–1894): abolitionist and business leader.

Blaine, James G. (1830–1893): Maine senator and Speaker of the House (1869–1875).

Bowles, Samuel (1826–1878): journalist who published the *Springfield Republican*.

Brown, Benjamin Gratz (1826–1885): twentieth governor of Missouri and United States Senator from Missouri.

Bryant, William Jennings (1860–1925): orator and politician; three times nominated for president of the United States.

Burnside, Andrew (1824–1881): general in the Civil War, invented sideburns, and the first president of the NRA.

Butler, Andrew (1796–1857): senator from South Carolina who authored the Kansas Nebraska Act, who resigned from the Senate after beating Senator Sumner violently and almost to death.

Carnegie, Andrew (1835–1919): industrialist and steel industry philanthropist.

Chambrun, Adolphe de (1831–1891): legal *attaché* at the French Embassy in Washington D.C.

Chandler, Zachariah T. (1813:1879): One of the founders of the Republican Party, mayor of Detroit, U.S. senator, and Secretary of the Interior under U. S. Grant.

Chase, Salmon P. (1808–1873): sixth Supreme Court Justice and governor of Ohio.

Cleveland, Grover (1837–1908): twenty-second and twenty-fourth president of the United States.

Crazy Horse Tȟašúŋke Witkó (His Horse is Crazy) (c. 1840–1877): Lakota leader of the Oglala.

Cockrell, Francis (1834–1815): politician from Missouri, senator, and Confederate general.

Cooke, Jay (1821–1905): financier of the Civil War and railroad mogul.

Curtis, George William (1824–1892): editor of *Harper's Weekly.*

Davis, Jefferson (1808–1889): U.S. senator and president of the Confederate states.

Debs, Eugene V. (1855–1926): American socialist and trade unionist.

Dönhoff, August Karl, Count von (1797–1874): secretary of the German legation in Washington.

Colfax, Schuyler, Jr. (1823–1885): Indiana representative, Speaker of the House (1863–69) and vice president of the United States (1869–73).

Fields, James T. (1817–1881): American publisher, editor, and poet.

Fletcher, Thomas Clement (1827–1899): eighteenth governor of Missouri.

Flickhardt, Frederick M.D. (c. 1830–?): doctor at Bethlehem Pennsylvania.

Garfield, James (1831–1881): twentieth president of the United States.

Gay, Sydney Howard (1814–1888): American attorney, abolitionist, editor of the *National Anti-Slavery Standard,* and an active participant in the New York City underground railroad.

Grant, Ulysses S. (1822–1885): eighteenth president and general in the Union Army.

Greeley, Horace (1811–1872): author, *Statesman* founder, and editor of the *New-York Tribune.*

Grund, Francis (1805–1863): Bohemian-born American journalist and writer; author of *The Americans, in their Moral, Social and Political Relations* (1837).

Hamlin, Hannibal (1809–1891): American attorney and vice president under Lincoln (1860–64).

Hancock, Winfield Scott (1824-1886): Union general in the Civil War and Democratic nominee for president in 1880.

Hayes, Rutherford B. (1822–1893): nineteenth president of the United States and Civil War general.

Hecker, Friedrich Franz, Karl (1811–1881): German lawyer and revolutionary, colonel in the Union Army.

Herzen, Alexander Ivanovitch (1812–1870): the father of Russian socialism.

Hillgaertner, George (1822–1865): editor, writer, and fellow revolutionary of Schurz's who had been condemned to death in Bavaria yet escaped first to Switzerland and then to Chicago in 1852 before settling in St. Louis.

Holmes, Oliver Wendell, Sr. (1809–1894): poet, physician, and writer.

Hooker, Joseph (1814–1879): "Fighting Joe" career military officer and general in the Civil War.

Jacobi, Abraham, MD (1830–1919): German revolutionary, first American pediatrician, and Schurz's best friend.

Jacobi, Mary Putnam (1842–1906): pioneer female physician, suffragist, and wife of Abraham Jacobi.

Jewell, Marshal (1825–1883): governor of Connecticut, ambassador to Russia, postmaster general, and Republican Party chairman.

Johnson, Andrew (1808–1875): seventeenth president, Lincoln's vice president, and slave holder.

Howard, Oliver Otis (1830–1909): career military officer, Union general in the Civil War, and founder of Howard University.

Lincoln, Abraham. (1809–1865): sixteenth president of the United States who drafted the Emancipation Proclamation.

Lincoln, Mary (1818–1882): Lincoln's wife and first lady of the United States.

Lincoln, Robert Todd (1843–1926): son of the Lincolns, lawyer, and politician.

Lincoln, William Wallace "Willie" (1850–1862), died of typhoid at age eleven in the White House.

Lincoln, Thomas "Tad" (1853–1871): tragically died of tuberculosis at age eighteen.

Lind, Jenny (1820–1887): known as Johanna Maria Lind, the "Swedish Nightingale," the nineteenth century's most popular vocal artist.

Lodge, Henry Cabot (1850–1924): Republican senator and member of New England's elite.

Lowell, James Russell (1819–1891): American Romantic poet; one of the New England Fireside poets.

Mahler, Franz (1826–1863): colonel in the Union Army who was killed at Gettysburg; a friend of Schurz in Rastatt.

Mason, James Murray (1798–1871): a United States senator from Virginia and a professed slavery advocate, who was later expelled from the country because of his involvement in the Trent Affair.

McClurg, Joseph W. (1818–1900): nineteenth governor of Missouri, slave holder, and colonel in the Union Army.

McKinley, William (1843–1901): twenty-fifth president of the United States and a major in the Union Army who was assassinated.

Meade, George G. (1815–1872): Spanish-born Union Army general and engineer-in-command at Gettysburg.

Meagher, Thomas Francis (1823–1867): Irish nationalist and Union general in the Civil War.

Olshausen, Theodor (1802–1869): German author, journalist, and politician; the Revolutions of 1848 forced him to America for ten years, left in 1865, leaving his share in the *Westliche Post* to be sold in 1867.

Paine, Halbert E. (1826–1905): lawyer and general in the Union Army and U.S. congressman from Wisconsin.

Paine, Byron (1827–1871): Wisconsin Supreme Court Justice, lieutenant colonel in the Union Army, 43rd Wisconsin Infantry Regiment, who helped obtain the right to vote for African-American freedmen.

Pope, John (1822–1892): career officer in the U.S. Army and general in the Civil War.

Preetorius, Emil (1827–1905): leader of the German American Community in St. Louis and a Forty-Eighter.

Pulitzer, Joseph (1847–1911): born in Hungary, journalist known for yellow journalism and the Pulitzer Prize, hired by Schurz in St. Louis, and owner of the *New-York Tribune.*

Randall, Alexander Williams (1819–1872): attorney, sixth governor of Wisconsin, abolitionist, and postmaster of the United States

Roosevelt, Theodore, Sr. "Thee" (1831–1878): American businessman and father of Theodore Roosevelt.

Roosevelt, Theodore, Jr. (1858–1919): twenty-sixth president of the United States and governor of New York.

Salomon, Edward (1828–1909): American politician, eighth governor of Wisconsin, and Union Army general.

Schiff, Jacob (1847–1920): Jewish-American banker and railroad magnate.

Schimmelfennig, Alexander (1824–1865): German revolutionary and Union Army general.

Sheridan, Phillip "L'il Phil" (1831–1888): general in the Union Army.

Sherman, William Tecumseh (1820–1891): general in the Union Army, businessman, and educator.

Seligman, Isaac (1834–1928): German-American Jewish banker.

Seward, William (1801–1872): Secretary of State (1861–1869) and U.S. senator from New York.

Shields, James (1806–1879): Irish-American politician, senator from three different states and general in the Civil War.

Sickles, Daniel (1819–1914): controversial general in the Union Army and the first man acquitted of murder for temporary insanity.

Sigel, Franz (1824–1902): revolutionary general in Germany and major-general in the Union Army.

Slocum, Henry Warner (1827–1894): general in the Union Army and House of Representatives member in New York.

Stanton, Edwin McMaster (1814–1869): lawyer, politician, and Lincoln's Secretary of War.

Stevens, Thaddeus (1792–1868): Radical Republican leader in the House of Representatives.

Steinway, William (Wilhelm) (1835–1896): German-born piano manufacturer.

Strauss, Levi (1829–1902): German-born businessman who was the first to manufacture blue jeans.

Sumner, Charles (1811–1874): United States senator from Massachusetts and Radical Republican abolitionist.

Tarbell, Ida (1857–1944) writer, journalist, and muckraker.

Tiedemann, Gustav (1808–1849): commander of revolutionary forces at Rastatt who was executed in 1849.

Tiedemann, Heinrich (Henry) M.D. (1813–1894): founder of Lankenau Hospital in Philadelphia.

Twain, Mark (Clemens, Samuel Langhorne) (1835–1910): American writer and friend of Schurz.

Tweed, William "Boss" (1823–1878): leader of Tammany Hall, New York, political machine.

Villard, Henry (1835–1900): American journalist and financier.

Von Bismarck, Otto (1815–1898): German "Iron Chancellor" who dominated Germany and Europe.

Von Gilsa, Leopold (1824–1870): Prussian general in the Union Army.

Walker, Francis A. (1840–1897): American economist and general in the Union Army.

Walker, William (1824–1860): the "Great Filibuster," an American lawyer, physician, participant on several private military expeditions into South America to circumvent American neutrality law, and president of Nicaragua (1856–7).

Washington, Booker T. (1856–1915): dominant African-American leader, former slave, and friend of Schurz.

Weed, Thurlow (1797–1862): with Seward, a leader of the New York Anti-Masonic Party and a newspaper publisher.

White, George Henry (1852–1918): African-American congressman during the Jim Crow era who founded Whitesboro, New Jersey.

White, Horace. (1834–1916): *Chicago Tribune* and financial expert

Wilberforce, William (1759–1833): English politician and abolitionist.

Wilhelm, Kaiser II (1859–1941): German Emperor, instigator of World War I, and grandson of Queen Victoria.

Wolf, Simon (1836–1923): Jewish activist, financier, and president of B'nai B'rith.

# Endnotes

Foreword

1. Schurz, C., *The Reminiscences of Carl Schurz, Vol. II, 1832–1863* (New York, Doubleday, Page & Co., 1909), p. 45.

Preface

1. Lubrecht, P., *New Jersey Butterfly Boys in the Civil War: The Hussars of the Union Army (Civil War Series)* (History Press: Charleston, 2011) and *Germans in New Jersey: A History (American Heritage)* (History Press: Charleston, 2016).

Chapter 2

1. Schurz, C., *The Reminiscences of Carl Schurz, Vol. I, 1829–1852* (New York, Doubleday, Page and Co., 1917), p. 5.
2. *Vorhin war ich in Hessenland/Von Gutenberg ein Wolf genannt,/Jetzt bin Ich durch Gottes Macht/Graf Wolf Metternich zur Gracht.*
3. *Burghalfen* is an old German term for estate manager, literally estate manager and tenant farmer. *Burg* is a castle and *halfen* is from half since the manager got half the crop that he supervised. It was originally hyphenated as *Burg-halfen*.
4. Schurz, C., *op. cit.* p. 21–22.
5. Schurz-Jüssen, A., "*Lebenserrinnerungen,*" *The German American Review*, Vol. XXIII (1957), pp. 22–25.

Chapter 3

1. Goethe, J. W., *Die Leiden des jungen Werthers* (1774).
2. Cargill, O., *Intellectual America: Ideas on the March* (MacMillan, New York, 1941), p. 22.
3. Schiller, F., *Die Räuber* (1781); *Wilhelm Tell* (1804).
4. Schurz, C., *The Reminiscences of Carl Schurz, Vol. I.*, p. 23.
5. Becker, H., *Universal History for the Young.*
6. Schurz, C., *op. cit.*, p. 257.
7. *Ibid.*, p. 26.

8. *Ibid.*, p. 29.
9. *Ibid.*, p. 31.
10. *Ibid.*, p. 33.
11. *Ibid.*, p. 34.

Chapter 4

1. Schurz, C., *The Reminiscences of Carl Schurz, Vol. I*, p. 40.

Chapter 5

1. Bone, H., *Deutsches Lesebuch für höhere Leranstalten, zunächts für die unteren und mittleren Klassen der Gymnasium mit Rücksicht auf scrifftliche Arbeiten der Schüler* (1840).
2. Schafer, J. (ed.), *Intimate Letters of Carl Schurz* (DaCapo Press, New York, 1970), p. 8.
3. *Ibid.*
4. *Ibid.*, p. 9.
5. *Ibid.*, p. 15.
6. *Ibid.*, p. 19.
7. Louis Philippe I (1773–1850) was king of France (1830–1848).
8. Schurz, C., *The Reminiscences of Carl Schurz, Vol. I*, p. 116.
9. *Ibid.*, p. 121.
10. Friedrich Wilhelm Ritschl (April 6, 1806–November 9, 1876) was a well-known German scholar, best known for his studies of Roman author Plautus.
11. Moritz August von Bethmann-Hollweg (1795–1877) was the author of *Der Civilprozeß des Gemeinen Rechts in geschichtlicher Entwicklung* (Civil Procedure in Common Law: A Historical Overview) and served later as Prussian minister of education. His grandson, Theobald von Bethmann-Hollweg, served as chancellor of Germany (1909–1917).
12. Schurz, C., *op. cit.*, p. 127. Schurz refers to him as van Calker, though his name was Friedrich Calker and his two major works were *Urgesetzlehre des Wahren, Guten und Schönen* (*The Original Teachings on the Law of the True, Good and Beautiful*; Berlin, 1820) and *Denklehre* (Logic; Bonn, 1822).
13. Johann Wilhelm Löbell (1786–1863) was a historian at Bonn who wrote *Gregor von Tours und seine Zeit* (Gregory of Tours and his times, 1839), a revision of Becker's *Weltgeschichte* (1836–38), *Weltgeschichte in Umrissen und Ausführungen* (World history outlined and explained Part I, 1846), *Die Entwicklung der deutschen Poesie von Klopstocks erstem Auftreten bis zu Goethes Tode* (The development of German poetry from Klopstock until Goethe's death, 1856–65), and *Historische Briefe* (Letters on history, 1861).
14. Adolf Heinrich Strodtmann (1829–1879) was a German poet, journalist, and translator. He wrote *Lieder eines Gefangenen auf der Dronning Maria* (Songs of a prisoner of the "Drowning Maria," 1848), *Lieder der Nacht* (Songs of the Night, 1850), and *Gottfried Kinkel Biography* (1850).
15. Sperber, J., *Rhineland Radicals: The Democratic Movement and the Revolution of 1848–49* (Princeton, Princeton Univ. Press, 1991), p. 190.
16. Schurz, C., *op. cit.*, pp. 138–139.
17. Felix Maria Vincenz Andreas Fürst von Lichnowsky, Graf von Werdenberg (April 5, 1814–September 19, 1848).
18. Joseph Maria Ernst Christian Wilhelm von Radowitz (February 6, 1797–December 25, 1853).

19. Schurz, C., *op. cit.*, p. 143.
20. Heinrich Wilhelm August Freiherr von Gagern (August 20, 1799–May 22, 1880).
21. Silenus was the Greek mythological companion and tutor to the wine god Dionysius, whose artistic portraits resembled, in Schurz's eyes, Robert Blum (November 10, 1797–November 9, 1848), who believed no one person should rule over another. He was executed in Vienna for his role and beliefs.
22. On October 6, 1848, an angry mob hung Theodor Franz, Count of Baillet von Latour (1780–1848) from a lamp post during the Vienna uprising.
23. Friedrich Wilhelm Count of Brandenburg (1792–1850) was a German soldier and Politician.
24. Otto Theodor von Manteuffel (1805–1882) was a conservative Prussian statesman and prime minister.
25. Schurz, C., *op. cit.*, p. 248.
26. Fritz Anneke (1818–1872) German revolutionary socialist and American Civil War colonel.
27. Schurz. C., *Lebenserrinnerungen, bis zum Jahre 1852* (Georg Reimer, Berlin, 1906), p. 184.

## Chapter 6

1. Franz Heinrich Zitz (November 18, 1803–April 10, 1877) was an attorney in Mainz who later moved to New York and joined the firm of Kapp, Zitz, and Fröbel. He returned to Germany when amnesty from his revolutionary activities was offered, and died in Munich.
2. Schafer., J., *The Intimate Letters of Carl Schurz* (Da Capo Press, New York, 1970), p. 248.
3. Gustav Adolph Techow (1813–May 25, 1890) was an author on gymnastics, who died in Melbourne, Australia.
4. Friedrich (von) Beust (August 9, 1817–December 6, 1899) was a communist who became a pedagogue in Switzerland.
5. Alexander Schimmelfennig (July 20, 1824–September 5, 1865) turned from the Prussian Army to the Communist League in opposition to Marx and Engels. After migrating to America, he became a Union Army general in the American Civil War.
6. Franz Sznayde (1790–1850) was born in Poland.
7. Louis Blenker (July 31, 1812–October 31, 1863) was a colonel of 8th Infantry Regiment, eventually becoming a brigadier general.
8. Ludwik Mierowslawski (1814–1878) was a Polish general, writer, and political activist in Poland, Baden, and Italy.
9. Franz Sigel (November 18, 1824–August 21, 1902) was a revolutionary general in Germany and a major general in the Union Army.
10. Dahlinger, C., *The German Revolution of 1849 Being an Account of the Final Struggle in Baden, for the Maintenance of Germany's First National Representative Government* (Putnam, New York, 1903), p. 266.
11. A Swiss refugee's account names Wilhelm Friederich Zobel (1816–1863) as the man who escaped with Schurz. In his memoirs, Schurz often gets names wrong and maybe Adam is a nickname or a mistake.
12. Kennecott translates *Bursche* as "servant," which could also mean a younger aide or a member of the "brotherhood." The term "servant" is unlikely in the revolutionary army.
13. Bancroft, F., *The Speeches Correspondence and Political Papers of Carl Schurz 6 Vols.* (New York: Putnam, 1913), p. 61.

14. Otto Julius Bernhard von Corvin (1812–1886) was a German author who covered the American Civil War and worked for Charles Dickens in London.
15. August Löffler was a farmer who immigrated to Canada, and contacted Schurz by letter to Washington D.C. in the 1870s; Schurz never reached him again.
16. Frederick Neustädter of the American Civil War, 1st Missouri Infantry, was a captain in the Baden Revolution.
17. Schurz, C., *The Reminiscences of Carl Schurz, Vol. I*, p. 244.
18. Dr. Hermann Becker (1820–1885) was a lawyer, publisher, and deputy to Germany's Upper Chamber and Mayor of Cologne.

Chapter 7

1. Sperber, J., *Rhineland Radicals: The Democratic Movement and the Revolution of 1848–49* (Princeton, Princeton Univ. Press,1992), p. 149.
2. *Ibid.*, p. 293.
3. *Ibid.*, p. 183.
4. Renner, H., *Die pfälzische Bewegung von 1848/49* (Landesbildstelle Rheinland-Pfalz, 1963).
5. Marx, K., and Engels, F., *Heroes of the Exile,* marxists.org/archive/marx/works/1852/heroes-exile/ch01.htm, Chapter I.
6. *Ibid.*
7. Meyer, *Die ganze Geschichte meines gleichgültigen Lebens. Band 2 1829–1849* (2017), p. 435.
8. *Ibid.*, p. 346.
9. marxists.catbull.com/archive/marx/works/1850/04/kinkel.htm.
10. *The Letters of Charles Dickens*, edited by his sister-in-law and eldest daughter, 1833–1870. Letter December 4, 1850, to Walter Savage Landor, p. 225.
11. Schurz, C, *The Reminiscences of Carl Schurz, Vol. I*, p. 253.
12, The use of invisible ink goes back to the Romans and Pliny the Elder, who used the milk of the tithymalus plant.
13. Hermann Becker started a newspaper, *Westdeutsche Zeitung. Democratische Politischer Tageblatt* in 1849, which was published until 1850 when the government shut it down. It reported on the labor movement.
14. The tribunal consisted of Appellate Judge Göbel as chairman, the District Court Council Ludowigs Schmitz, Assessor Landau von Riedenheim, Wohlers, and as an alternate, Mr. Möller of the Public Ministry.
15. The jurors who acquitted the defendants were Peter Schuler, Karl *v.* Aften, Kaspar Siegen, P. J. Odenbach, Herm. Breuer, J. A. Wahlers, Chr. J. Bartman, M. Breuer, Pet Berk, Br. Roesberg, and Johann Classen Neumacher.
16. Ludwig Meyer (1827–1900) was a German pioneer of non-restraint treatment in nineteenth-century psychiatry.
17. *Bonner Komitee für Besten der Kinkels' Kinder., Prozeß Verhandlungen von Gottfried Kinkel und Genossen zu Köln, an April bis 2 Mai 1830* (2019).
18. Christian Lassen was a professor of oriental philosophy at the University of Bonn when Schurz was a student there.
19. Markgrafen Strasse 26 is a parking garage today, located very near the center Berlin and Checkpoint Charlie.
20. Rachel Felix, Elisabeth Felix, or Mademoiselle Rachel was a famous French actress who was the mistress of Napoleon III and Napoleon Joseph Charles Bonaparte.
21. *Richmonder Anzeiger*, July 28, 1855, Vol. 2, p. 3.
22. Russian Baroness Brüning (1785–1858) was Dorothea, Princess Lieven, the wife of the Russian ambassador to England; she was involved Revolutionary activities;

mistress of Austrian Chancellor Metternich, and French statesman Francis Guizot; and later joined the refugees in London.

23. Schurz, C., *op. cit.* p. 304.

24. Karl (Carl) Petermann (August Carl Heinrich Ludwig) (March 26, 1807–September 23, 1866) was a local magistrate and had met Kinkel in Berlin at the Democratic Congress.

25. Moritz Karl Georg Wiggers (October 17, 1816–July 30, 1894) was a German politician and revolutionary. He was later tried and acquitted; however, in 1853 he was tried for conspiracy and imprisoned. By 1871, he was a representative to the German *Reichstag* for the North German confederation.

26. Wiggers, M., *Gottfried Kinkels Befreiung. Die Gartenlaube*, 1883. The complete account of the Romantic escape, in German, can be found at de.wikisource.org/wiki/Gottfried_Kinkel's_Befreiung.

27. Ernst Brockelmann (March 22, 1799–December 24. 1878) was born in Ratzeberg and died in Rostock; he was a member of the Mecklenburg Assembly of Deputies. In 1927, the steamship *Ernst Brockelmann* was named after him.

28. Schurz, C., *op. cit.*, p. 319.

29. *Ibid.*, p. 330.

30. *Philadelphia Enquirer*, April 18, 1853, p. 1.

31. Schurz, C., *Lebenserrinnerungen, bis zum Jahre 1852* (Berlin. Georg Reimer 1906), p. 339.

32. *Ibid.*

## Chapter 8

1. William Macready (1773–1873) a famous British actor known for his conflict with American actor Edwin Forest, causing the Astor Place Riot in New York; he was also responsible for the exit of John Wilkes Booth's father, Junius Brutus Booth, from the London stages.

2. Marie Catherine Sophie de Flavigny (1770–1819) was born in Frankfurt am Main to a French Viscount and a German banker's daughter. She married and divorced Charles Louis Constant d'Agoult, Count of Agoult. She lived with Franz Liszt and became friends with Chopin and Wagner. She had three children with Liszt and wrote under the name of Daniel Stern.

3. Schurz, C., *The Reminiscences of Carl Schurz, Vol. I*, p. 350.

4. DeVesme and Finch, *The Annals of Psychical Science. A Monthly Journal devoted to critical and experimental Research in the Phenomena of Spiritualism*, Vol. 4, July–December 1906, p. 255.

5. Reinhold Solger (1817–1866) was a German-born American novelist and political activist a from Roxbury, Massachusetts.

6. The Erard piano with "peculiar" mechanical actions applied to pianofortes and harps was introduced in the Great London Exhibition of 1851: a full sized Grand with seven octaves, "A" to "A," lieveverbeeck.eu/Erard_London_Expositions.htm

7. Arnold Ruge (1802–1880) was a German philosopher and writer that Schurz called a "political dreamer."

8. Schurz, C., *op. cit.*, p. 372.

9. *Ibid.*, p. 378.

10. *Ibid.*, p. 387.

11. Fanny Lewald (1811–1889) was German author and feminist, who was a close friend of Johanna Kinkel.

12. *The English Woman's Journal: Vol. II, February 1859* (1859), p. 306.

13. Malwida von Meysenbug (1816–1903) was a predominant author and feminist, whose friends included Richard Wagner, Romaine Rolland, and Carl Schurz.
14. Schurz, C., *op. cit.*, p. 399.
15. *Ibid.*, p. 399.
16. *Ibid.*, p. 401.

Chapter 9

1. Princess and Landgravine Augusta of Hesse Kassel was the great granddaughter of George II of Great Britain.
2. Abrams, L., "Finding the Female Self: Women's Autonomy, Marriage and Social Change in the Nineteenth Century," in Rüger, J. and Wachsmann, N. (eds.), *Rewriting German History: New Perspectives in Modern Germany* (Palgrave MacMillan, New York, 2015), Part II, Chapter 8.
3. *Ibid.*
4. *Ibid.*
5. Schafer, J., *Intimate Letters of Carl Schurz* (DaCapo Press, 1970) p. 109.
6. Schurz, C., *The Reminiscences of Carl Schurz*, Vol. II, p. 5.
7. Trefousse, H. L., *Carl Schurz: A Biography* (Knoxville: University of Tennessee Press, 1982), p. 49.
8. Malwida von Meysenburg (1816–1903) was a German writer, whose works include *Memories of an Idealist*. She was a friend of Friedrich Nietzsche and Richard Wagner; she met Carl Schurz in London and was the first woman nominated for the Nobel Prize for Literature.
9. Schurz, C, *op. cit.*, p. 16.
10. Lucretia Mott (*née* Coffin) (1793–1880) was a famous abolitionist and social reformer.

Chapter 10

1. During the Civil War, Vaughn was the surgeon of the 14th Mississippi Regiment and surgeon in chief for the state and the military hospitals.
2. James Shields (1806–1879) is the only man to serve as a senator for three different states: Illinois, Minnesota, and Missouri.
3. Francis Grund (1805–1863) was a Bohemian-born American journalist and writer, whose works include *The Americans in their Moral, Social and Political Relations* (1837).
4. Schurz, *The Reminiscences of Carl Schurz*, Vol. II, p. 29.
5. *Ibid.*, p. 31.
6. William Seward (1801–1872) was Secretary of State (1861–1869) and U.S. senator for New York.
7. Schurz, *op. cit.*, p. 33.
8. Thurlow Weed (1797–1862) was, with Seward, a leader of the New York Anti-Masonic Party and a political "manager," manipulating nominations while working as a newspaper publisher.
9. Salmon P. Chase (1808–1873) was the sixth Chief Justice of the United States and an abolitionist.
10. Schurz, C., *op. cit.* p. 33.
11. Charles Sumner (1811–1874) was a United States senator from Massachusetts and a Radical Republican abolitionist.
12. Schurz, C., *op. cit.*, p. 34.

13. Andrew Butler (1796–1857) was a senator from South Carolina who authored the Kansas Nebraska Act. He resigned from the Senate after beating Senator Sumner almost to death. He resigned as a result.

14. Schurz, C., *op. cit.*, p. 36.

15. Robert Augustus Toombs (1810–1885) was a lawyer, slaveholder, and senator from Georgia.

16. Schurz, C., *op. cit.*, p. 37.

17. James Murray Mason (1798–1871) was a United States senator from Virginia and a professed slavery advocate, who was later expelled from the country because of his involvement in the Trent Affair.

18. Schurz, C., *op. cit.*, p. 37.

19. Bancroft, F. (ed.), *The Speeches Correspondence and Political Papers of Carl Schurz 6 Vols.* (New York: Putnam, 1913), Vol. I, p. 11.

20. *Ibid.*

21. *Ibid.*, p. 14.

Chapter 11

1. Tolzmann, D, H., *Missouri's German Heritage 2nd. Ed.* (Little Miami, Milford, 2006)

2. Schurz, C., *The Reminiscences of Carl Schurz, Vol. II*, p. 41.

3. *Ibid.*, p. 45.

4. geni.com/people/Col-Edmund-J%C3%BCssen-USA/6000000011321445527

5. "Environment Has a History: How Hamburg became European Green Capital," hamburg.de/contentblob/2819910/c14c95c70a26523817be7aea56d3ab37/data/environment-has-a-story.pdf.

6. museumoflondon.org.uk/discover/londons-past-air.

7. Alexander Ivanovitch Herzen (1812–1870) was the father of Russian socialism.

8. Jenny Lind (1820–1887), Johanna Maria Lind, known as the "Swedish Nightingale" was the nineteenth-century's most popular vocal artist.

9. Malvern water comes from a spring in the Malvern Hills on the border of Hereford and Worcestershire in England. In 1842, it was incorporated into a clinic for any ailment.

10. Schafer, J. (ed.), *Intimate Letters of Carl Schurz* (New York: DaCapo Press, 1970), p. 158.

11. *Ibid.*, p. 163.

12. *Ibid.*, p. 171.

Chapter 12

1. Schafer, J., (ed.) *Intimate Letters of Carl Schurz* (New York: DaCapo Press, 1970), p. 163.

2. Whyte, W. F., "Chronicles of Early Watertown," *The Wisconsin Magazine of History*, Vol. 4. No. 3(1921), pp. 287–314.

3. William Wilberforce (1759–1833) was an English politician and abolitionist.

4. Halbert E. Paine (1826–1905) was a lawyer and general in the Union Army, after which he served as a U.S. Congressman from Wisconsin.

5. Thomson, *A Political History of Wisconsin* (Milwaukee: E. C. Wilson, 1900), p. 137.

6. *Ibid.*

7. Ellen Flavin (1847-1917) was the daughter of a neighboring farmer David Flavin, an Irish immigrant; later in life, she became a nun in a convent in Chicago.

8. Alexander Williams Randall (1819–1872) was an attorney, sixth Governor of Wisconsin, avid abolitionist, and postmaster of the United States.
9. Schurz, C., *The Reminiscences of Carl Schurz, Vol. II*, p. 83.
10. The famous Dred Scott Decision (formally *Dred Scott v. Sandford*) of March 6, 1857, declared that Dred Scott who lived in a free state was not entitled to his freedom, could never, be a citizen and that the Missouri Compromise of 1820 was unconstitutional.
11. Schurz, C., *op. cit.*, p. 88.
12. *Ibid.*, p. 90.

Chapter 13

1. Schurz, C., *The Reminiscences of Carl Schurz, Vol. II*, p. 88.
2. *Ibid.*, p. 89.
3  *Ibid.*, p. 90.
4. *Wisconsin Free Democrat*, Wednesday, February 2, 1859, Vol. XV, Issue 9. p. 2.
5. This speech "States Rights and Byron Paine" was not published in Schurz's collected works. It was taken from the *Milwaukee Daily Sentinel* March 24, 1859, pp. 2–3 and can be found at en.wikisource.org/wiki/State_Rights_and_ Byron_Paine.
6. Ironically, John Parker Hale, a staunch abolitionist, had a daughter, Lucy, who was courted heavily as a belle of Washington society. Her suitors included Oliver Wendell Holmes Jr. and Robert Todd Lincoln; her secret fiancée was John Wilkes Booth.
7. Address, Faneuil Hall, Boston (April 18, 1859).
8. *Boston Liberator*, Friday, April 29, 1859, Boston Mass. Vol. XXIX, Issue 17, p. 65.
9. Dawes, G., *The Historical Jesus Quest, Landmarks in the Search for Jesus of History* (Louisville, Westminster John Knox Press, 1999), pp. 77–79.
10. *Boston Liberator, op. cit.*, p. 65.
11. *Weekly Wisconsin Patriot*, Saturday, September 24, 1859, Vol. 6, Issue 27, p. 2.
12. *Cedar Falls Gazette*, Friday, June 15, 1860, p. 3.
13. *Weekly Champion and Press*, Saturday, October 13, 1860, Vol. 3, Issue 34, p. 2.
14. Trefousse, H. L., *Carl Schurz: A Biography* (Knoxville: University of Tennessee Press, 1982), p. 88.
15. Schurz, C., *op. cit.*, p. 194.
16. *New York Herald*, Monday October 1, 1860, p. 6.
17. *The Campaign of 1860 comprising the speeches of Abraham Lincoln, William H. Seward, Henry Wilson, Benjamin F. Wade, Carl Schurz, Charles Sumner, William Everts &c*, Albany (Weed, Parsons & Company, 1860).
18. *Albany Evening Journal*, Tuesday, December 11, 1860, Albany, NY, p. 2.

Chapter 14

1. *India Rubber World*, Pearson, H. C. (ed.), "Rubber Interests in Europe," Volume 33, (India Rubber Publishing Company, New York, 1905), p. 332.
2. Schurz, C., *The Reminiscences of Carl Schurz, Vol. II*, p. 250.
3. Bancroft, F., *The Speeches Correspondence and Political Papers of Carl Schurz, Vol. I* (New York: Putnam, 1913), p. 240.
4. *Ibid.*, p. 280.
5. *Ibid.*, p. 302.
6. *Ibid.*

Chapter 15

1. Schurz, C., *The Reminiscences of Carl Schurz, Vol. II*, p. 320.
2. *Ibid.*, p. 23.

Chapter 16

1. *Crisis*, Wednesday, June 11, 1862, Columbus, Ohio. Vol. II, Issue 20, p. 154.
2. Thomas Hart Benton (1782–1858), "Old Bullion," was a senator from Missouri and a leader of westward expansion.
3. *Regimental Journal of Colonel Eugene A. Kozlay: Commanding 54th Regt. New York Volunteers from June 30th 1861 to April 23rd 1866: Part One: 1861–1862* dmna.ny.gov/historic/reghist/civil/infantry/54thinfKozlayJournal.htm
4. Schurz, C., *The Reminiscences of Carl Schurz, Vol. II*, p. 367.
5. Salmon P. Chase (1808–1873) was the sixth Supreme Court Justice and governor of Ohio.

Chapter 17

1. Kettell, *History of the Great Rebellion, from its commencement to its close giving an account of the origin, The Secession of the Southern States, and the Formation of the confederate government, the concentration of the military and financial resources of the federal government from official sources* (Hartford, L. Stebbins, 1865), pp. 445–446.
2. Keller, C., *Chancellorsville and the Germans Nativism, Ethnicity, and Civil War Memory.* (New York, Fordham Univ. Press, 2007), p. 85.
3. Trefousse, H. L., *Carl Schurz: A Biography* (Knoxville: Univ. of Tennessee Press, 1982), p. 135.
4. Schurz, C., *The Reminiscences of Carl Schurz, Vol. II*, p. 431.
5. *Ibid.*, p. 433.
6. *Ibid.*
7. Dodge, T., *The Campaign of Chancellorsville* (Boston, Rand, Avery & Co., 1881), p. 102.
8. *Ibid.*, p. 4
9. *New York Herald*, Wednesday, October 12, 1864, p. 5.

Chapter 19

1. Lubrecht, P., *New Jersey Butterfly Boys in the Civil War*, (Charleston, History Press, 2013).
2. *The Philadelphia Enquirer*, March 9, 1864, p. 2.
3. Bancroft, F. (ed.), *The Speeches Correspondence and Political Papers of Carl Schurz* Vol. I. (New York: Putnam, 1913), p. 315.
4. *Daily National Republican*, Saturday, March 25, 1865, Washington D.C., p. 1.
5. Bancroft, *op. cit.*, pp. 326–327.
6. *Ibid.*, pp. 252–253.
7. *Ibid.*, p. 234.
8. Schurz, C., *The Reminiscences of Carl Schurz, Vol. III* (New York: Doubleday Page and Co., 1927), pp. 122–123.

Chapter 20

1. Bowers, C., *The Tragic Era: The Revolution after Lincoln* (Boston, Houghton Mifflin, 1962).
2. *Boston Daily Advertiser*, July 31, 1865, Issue No. 25, "Letters from the South by Carl Schurz Letter No. 1: The Sea Islands and Free Labor," p. 1.
3. Schurz, *Report on the Condition of the South*.1865. 39th Congress, Senate Ex Doc. 1st Session. No. 2. wwnorton.com/college/history/america-essential-learning/docs/CSchurz-South_Report-1865.pdf
4. Schurz, *The New South* (New York, American News Co., 1886, reprinted on demand; Forgotten Books, 2018).
5. *Ibid.*
6. *Ibid.*
7. *Ibid.*
8. Tiedemann, F., "On the Brain of the Negro, Compared with that of the European and the Orang-Outang." Philosophical Transactions of the Royal Society of London, Vol. 26 (1836), pp. 497–527.
9. Trefousse, H. L., *Carl Schurz: A Biography* (Knoxville: University of Tennessee Press, 1982), p. 160.

Chapter 21

1. Benjamin Gratz Brown (1826–1885) was the twentieth governor of Missouri and United States senator from Missouri.
2. Thomas Clement Fletcher (1827–1899) was the eighteenth governor of Missouri.
3. Dr. George Hillgaertner (1822–1865) was an editor, writer, and a fellow revolutionary of Schurz's who had been condemned to death in Bavaria and escaped first to Switzerland and then to Chicago in 1852; he then settled in St. Louis.
4. Sydney Howard Gay (1814–1888) was an American attorney, abolitionist, and editor of the National Anti-Slavery Standard; he was also active in the New York City underground railroad.
5. Adolphe de Chambrun (1831–1891) was a legal *attaché* at the French Embassy in Washington D.C.
6. Zachariah T. Chandler (1813–1879) was one of the founders of the Republican Party, mayor of Detroit, an U.S. senator, and Secretary of the Interior under Ulysses Grant.
7. Schuyler Colfax Jr. (1823–1885) was Indiana representative, Speaker of the House (1863–69), and vice president of the United States (1869–73).
8. James Mitchell Ashley (1824–1896) was Ohio representative in the House (1863–69), later becoming the governor of Montana Territory.
9. *Cleveland Leader*, Friday, September 7, 1866, , p. 2.
10. *Lecha County Patriot*, Tuesday, January 29, 1867 (Allentown, PA), Vol. 40, p. 4.
11. Emil Preetorius (1827–1905) was the leader of the German-American community in St. Louis. He was also a Forty-Eighter.
12. Theodor Olshausen (1802–1869) was a German author, journalist, and politician. The Revolutions of 1848 forced him to America for ten years. He left in 1865, leaving his share of the *Westliche Post* to be sold in 1867.
13, Primm, J. N., "The G.A.R. in Missouri 1866–1870," in *The Journal of Southern History*, Vol. 20, No. 3, August 1954, pp. 356–375.
14. *Der Freischütz* is a romantic German opera by Carl Maria von Weber with spoken dialogue.

15. Schurz, C., *The Reminiscences of Carl Schurz, Vol. III*, p. 264.

16. Stevens, W. B., *St. Louis, the Fourth City, 1764–1909, Vol. I* (St. Louis, S. J. Clarke,1911), pp. 848–849.

## Chapter 22

1. Schurz, C., *The Reminiscences of Carl Schurz, Vol. III*, p. 387.
2. *The Missouri Daily Democrat*, April 15, 1869.
3. Trefousse, H. L., *Carl Schurz: A Biography* (Knoxville: University of Tennessee Press, 1982), p. 188.
4. His speeches and letters on all the events of this year were printed and well documented in *Carl Schurz. Speeches Correspondence and Political Papers, Volume II*. (Bancroft (ed.), New York, Putnam, 1913)
5. Trefousse, *op. cit.*, p. 198.
6. *The Weekly Caucasian* (Lexington Missouri) Saturday, December 27, 1873, p. 4.

## Chapter 23

1. Francis William Bird (1809–1894) was an abolitionist and radical reformer, known as "The Sage of Walpole Massachusetts."
2. Trefousse, H. L., *Carl Schurz: A Biography* (Knoxville: University of Tennessee Press, 1982), p. 227.
3. *The New York Times*, March 19, 1876, p. 12.

## Chapter 24

1. Trefousse, H. L., *Carl Schurz: A Biography* (Knoxville: University of Tennessee Press, 1982), p. 241.
2. August Karl Graf von Dönhoff-Friedrichstein (1845–1920) became a friend of Schurz.
3. Thomas H. Tibbles (1840–1928) was an abolitionist, Methodist minister, and editor of the *Omaha Daily Herald*.
4. Trefousse, *op. cit.*, p. 247.
5. *Der Letzte Mohikaner* (*The Last of the Mohicans*) was published in 1826.
6. *Lowell Daily Citizen and News*, Wednesday, December 5, 1877, Vol. XXVII, Issue 6,700, p. 1.
7. *Evening Star*, Thursday, February 21, 1878, Washington D.C., Vol. 51, p. 2.
8. *Evening Star*, Wednesday, February 27, 1878, Washington D.C., p. 1.
9. *Cincinnati Daily Gazette*, Saturday, February 22, 1879, p. 1.

## Chapter 25

1. de Hegermann-Lindencrone, L., *The Sunny Side of Diplomatic Life: 1875–1912* (New York, Harper Bros., 1914), p. 71
2. *Ibid.*
3. In 1976, Helen Hartman Gemill discovered Elizabeth Chapman Lawrence's letters and papers in a breadbox in a museum in Doylestown Pennsylvania, and included them in a book, *The Breadbox Papers*, which includes Lillie's description of the N.R.I.
4. de Hegermann-Lindencrone, *op. cit.*, pp. 71–72.
5. *Ibid.*, pp. 79–80.
6. Adams, H., *Letters of Henry Adams*, letter from Henry Adams to Charles Milnes Gaskell, November 25, 1877, p. 326.

7. Adams, H., *Democracy: An American Novel* (New York, Penguin, 2008), pp. 10–11.
8. Gemmil, H. H., *The Breadbox Papers, The High Life of a Dazzling Victorian Lady: Biography of Elizabeth Chapman Lawrence. With an Introduction by James a Michener* (Doylestown, Tower Hill Press, 1983), p. 217.
9. James A. Michener (1907–1997) was a famous American author who was raised in Doylestown, Pennsylvania, where he knew Fanny Chapman. He wrote more than forty books, including *Hawaii, Texas,* and *Tales of the South Pacific.*
10. Gemmil, *op. cit.*, p. 21.

Chapter 26

1, Henry Villard (1835–1900) was a wealthy entrepreneur in New York with backing of rich German investors.
2. *New-York Tribune*, Monday, May 31, 1880, p. 2.
3. Cowen, P., "The Death of Carl Schurz," in *The Menorah A Monthly Magazine for the Jewish Home*, Vol. XL, Nos. 235–240 Independent Order of B'Nai B'rith, Jewish Chautauqua Society (New York, 1906), p. 320.
4. *Ibid.*
5. *Social Register, August 1894, Vol. VIII, No. 8.* It was issued quarterly and contained the summer addresses of residents of New York, Philadelphia, Boston, Chicago, and Baltimore (1894).
6. Trefousse, H. L., *Carl Schurz: A Biography* (Knoxville: University of Tennessee Press, 1982), p. 273.

Chapter 27

1. *Official Proceedings of the Democratic National Convention Held in Chicago, Illinois, July 7, 8, 9, 10, and 11, 1896,* (1968), pp. 100–105.
2. John Peter Altgeld (1847–1902) was the twentieth governor of Illinois and a German-born American attorney.
3. Jacob Harold Gallinger (1837–1918) was senator from New Hampshire and a homeopathic physician.
4. Trefousse, H. L., *Carl Schurz: A Biography* (Knoxville: University of Tennessee Press, 1982), p. 281.
5. theodore-roosevelt.com/images/research/speeches/tr1898.pdf
6. Trefousse, *op. cit.*, p. 284.
7. *Harvard's Graduates Magazine Volume IV 1895–96,* (Boston, The Harvard Graduates Magazine Association, 1896), p. 590
8. *Harvard College Class of 1887*, Fourth Report, June 1912 (Boston), p. 362
9. George Henry White (1852–1918) was the only African-American congressman to serve during the Jim Crow era.
10. Trefousse, *op. cit.*, p. 297.

# Bibliography

Adams, H., *Democracy: An American Novel* (New York, Penguin, 2008); *The Letters of Henry Adams*, Six Volumes (Cambridge, 1982-1988).

Anneke, M. F., *Mutterland: Memorien einer Frau aus dem badish pfälzischen Feldzuge1848–1849* (Munster:2007).

Ashton, R., *Little Germany: Exile and Asylum in Victorian England* (Oxford: Oxford Univ. Press, 1986).

Bancroft, F. (ed.), *The Speeches Correspondence and Political Papers of Carl Schurz 6 Vols.* (New York: Putnam, 1913).

Barrett, J. H., *Life of Abraham Lincoln presenting his early Political Career and Speeches in and Out of Congress also a General View of His Policy as President of the United States* (Baldwin New York: Moore, Wilstach, 1865).

Bartsch, F., *Erftstadt: Eine Reiche Kulturlandschaft vor der Toren Kölns* (Cologne: Greven Verlag, n. d.).

Beisner, R. L., *Twelve Against Empire: The Anti-Imperialists 1898–1900* (Chicago: University of Chicago Press, 1985).

Bittel, C., *Mary Putnam Jacobi the Politics of Medicine in Nineteenth Century America* (Chapel Hill: Univ. of North Carolina Press, 2009).

Boas, N. F. and Meyer, B. L., *The Alma Farm an Adirondack Meeting Place* (Bolton Landing: 1999)

Böhmert, V., *Erinnerungen Heinrich Christian Meyer: Stockmeyer für die famillie gesammelt von Heinrich Ad. Meyer* (Hamburg: Lütcke u. Wulf, 1900).

Bonner Komitee für Besten der Kinkels' Kinder, *Prozeß Verhandlungen von Gottfried Kinkel und Genossen zu Köln, an April bis 2 Mai 1830* (Bonn: Google Books, 2019).

Bowers, C. G., *The Tragic Era: The Revolution After Lincoln* (Boston: Houghton Mifflin Co., 1962)

Cargill, O., *Intellectual America Ideas on the March* (New York: MacMillan Co. 1941).

Dahlinger, C. W., *The German Revolution of 1849 Being an Account of the Final Struggle in Baden, for the Maintenance of Germany's First National Representative Government* (Putnam, New York,1903)

Dawes, G. (ed.), *The Historical Jesus Quest: Landmarks in the Search for Jesus of History* (Louisville, Westminster John Knox Press, 1999).

De Jonge, A. R., *Gottfried Kinkel as Political and Social Thinker* (New York: AMS Press 1966).

De Hegermann-Lindencrone, L. *The Sunny Side of Diplomatic Life 1875–1912* (New York: Harper Bros., 1914).

DeVesme and Finch, *The Annals of Psychical Science. A Monthly Journal devoted to critical and experimental Research in the Phenomena of Spiritualism*, Volume 4 July–December 1906,

Dodge, T. A., *The Campaign of Chancellorsville* (Boston, Rand, Avery &Co., 1881).

Domschcke, B. and Trautmann, F. (ed.), *Twenty Months in Captivity Memoirs of a Union Officer in Confederate Prisons* (Rutherford: Fairleigh Dickinson Univ. Press, 1987).

Duffner, W., *Der Traum der Helden 12 Nachrufe auf ihm Sommer und Herbst 1849 hingerichtete Kämpfer der Badischen Revolution* (Schauenburg: Verlag Moritz, 1992).

Easum, C. V., *The Americanization of Carl Schurz* (Chicago: Chicago University Press, 1929).

Efford, A. C., *German Immigrants, Race, and Citizenship in the Civil War Era* (Washington D.C.: Cambridge University Press, 2013).

Efford, A. C., *The Arms Scandal of 1870–1872: Immigrant Liberal Republicans and America's Place in the World* (Marquette University: e-publication, 2018).

Emerson, E., Jr., *A History of the Nineteenth Century Year by Year*, 3 Vols. (New York: P.F. Collier and Son, 1911).

Fast, H., *The Last Frontier: Exciting American Saga of the Cheyenne's Last Stand* (New York: Avon Books, 1949).

Flanders, J., *The Victorian City Everyday Life in Dickens' London* (London: Atlantic Books,2012).

Förderer, A., *Erinnerungen aus Rastatt 1849 Zweite Auflage* (Lahr, Baden: 1899 )..

Freitag, S. and Rowan, S. (ed.), *Friedrich Hecker Two Lives for Liberty* (St. Louis: University of Missouri, 2006).

Fuess, C. M. *Carl Schurz Reformer 1829–1906* (Port Washington: Kennikat Press, 1932).

Gates, W. P., *Old Bolton on Lake George N.Y.* (Bolton: Gates, 2006); *Millionaires Row on Lake George N.Y.* (Bolton: Gates, 2011).

Gemmil, H. H., *The Breadbox Papers: The High Life of a Dazzling Victorian Lady: Biography of Elizabeth Chapman Lawrence. With an Introduction by James a Michener* (Doylestown, Tower Hill Press, 1983).

Geschichte Nr. 3 *Die Revolution von 1848* (Der Spiegel: 2014).

Goedsche, C. B., *Carl Schurz Cultural Graded Readers German Series III* (New York: Van Nostrand, 1963).

Greeley, H. *The American Conflict. A History of the Great Rebellion of the United States of America 1860–1864 Causes, Incidents and Results Vol I and II* (Hartford: O.D. Case, 1864).

Greene, E. *Lieber and Schurz Two Loyal Americans of German Birth: War Information Series No. 19 October 1918* (Washington D.C.: Committee on Public Information, 1918).

Harvard College Class of 1887. Fourth Report, June 1912 (Boston,1912).

*Harvard's Graduates Magazine* Volume IV 1895–96, (Boston, The Harvard Graduates Magazine Association, 1896).

Helper, H. R., *Compendium of the Impending Crisis of the South* (New York: A. B. Burdick, 1860).

Hochbruck, W. and Erdogan, A., *Carl Schurz* (Freiburg: Carl Schurz Haus, n.d.).

Hoffmeister, G. (ed.), *The French Revolution in the Age of Goethe* (Hildesheim: Olms Verlag, 1989).

*India Rubber World*. Pearson, H. C. ed. Volume 33. October 1, 1905 (India Rubber Publishing Company, New York, 1905).

Jackson, L., *Dirty Old London: The Victorian Fight Against Filth* (New Haven: Yale University Press, 2014).

James, E. T. (ed.), *Notable American Women 1607–1950* (Cambridge: Harvard University Press, 1971).

James, H. *Washington Square* (New York: Penguin Books, 1986).

Jett, D. C., *American Ambassadors: The Past, Present, and Future of America's Diplomats.* (St. Martin's Press, 2014).

Kaufmann. W., *Die Deutschen amerikanischen Bürgerkriege (Sezessionskrieg 1861–1865)* (Munich: R. Oldenbourg Verlag, 1911).

Keller, C. *Chancellorsville and the Germans: Nativism, Ethnicity and Civil War Memory* (New York: Fordham University Press, 2007).

Kessler, W., *Carl Schurz Kampf, Exile und Karriere* (Cologne, Greven Verlag, 2006).

Kettell, T. P., *History of the Great Rebellion, From Its Commencement until its Close* (Hartford, L. Stebbins, 1865).

Kinzer, S., *The True Flag Theodore Roosevelt, Mark Twain and the Birth of the American Empire* (New York: Holt, 2017).

Lenox Hill School of Nursing, *Lenox Hill Hospital School of Nursing* (New York: n. d.).

Liederkranz 1947 History Committee, *History of the Liederkranz of the City of New York 1847–1947 and of the Arion New York* (New York: Drechsel Printing Co. 1948).

Manley, E., *Carl Schurz Jugendjahre in Deutschland Selections* (New York: Allyn and Bacon, 1932).

Marx, K., Engels, F., and Livingston, R. (ed.), *Heroes of the Exile* (online book).

Merkel, M., Suchows, R. P., *Der Harburger Binnenhafen* (Hamburg: Helms Museum, n. d.).

Meyer, F. S., *Die Ganze Geschichte meines gluckgüttigen Lebens Band 2 1829–1849* (Kiel: Solivagus Praeteritium, 2017).

Morris, R., Jr., *The Long Pursuit Abraham Lincoln's Thirty Year Struggle with Stephen Douglas for the Heart and Soul of America* (New York: Harper Collins, 2008).

Nicolay, H., *Lincoln's Secretary A Biography of John G. Nicolay by Helen Nicolay* (New York: Longmans, Green and Co., 1949).

Oberholtzer, E. P., *Jay Cooke Financier of the Civil War* 2 vols. (New York: Burt Franklin, 1970)

O'Brien, K., *The Great and Gracious on Millionaire's Row* (Sylvan Beach: North Country Books, 1978)

Paine, B., *Thomas Nast; His Period and Pictures American Men of Letters Series* (New York: Chelsea House, 1980).

Petig, W. E., "Carl and Margarethe Schurz: Their years in Wisconsin," *Yearbook of German Studies Volume 51*, pp. 29–82 (Wisconsin: The Society for German American Studies, 2016); "Margarethe Meyer Schurz: A Problematic Biography," *Yearbook of German Studies Volume 52*, pp. 43–54 (Wisconsin: The Society for German American Studies, 2017).

Presber, R., *Das Deutschland Buch* (Berlin: Franke Verlag, 1930).

Prucha, F. P. ed. *Americanizing the American Indians: Writings by the "Friends of the Indians* (Columbus: University of Nebraska Press, 1973).

Ruger, J. and Wachsmann, N. *Rewriting German History: New Perspectives on Modern Germany.Abrams,* L., "Finding the Female Self: Women's Autonomy, Marriage and Social Change in the Nineteenth Century," (Palgrave MacMillan, New York, 2015) Part II. Chapter 8.

Sandoz, M., *Cheyenne Autumn* (Columbus: University of Nebraska Press, 1953).

Schafer, J., *Carl Schurz Militant Liberal* (Madison: Historical Society of Wisconsin, 1930); (ed.) *Intimate Letters of Carl Schurz* (New York: DaCapo Press, 1970).

Schrader, F. F., *The Germans in the Making of America* (New York: Haskell House, 1972).

Schurz, C., *The Reminiscences of Carl Schurz: Illustrated with Portraits and original drawings*. Three Volumes (New York: Doubleday Page and Co., 1927); *The Life of Henry Clay in Two Volumes* (Boston: Houghton and Mifflin, 1887); *Life of Slavery or the Life of the Nation* (Ithaca: Cornell University Digital Collection, n.d); *Abraham Lincoln An Essay* (New York: Houghton Mifflin, 1891); *Abraham Lincoln. Riverside Literature Series*. (New York: Houghton Mifflin, 1919); *The New South* (New York: American News Co., 1886); *The Spoils System: An Address to the Civil Service Reform League* (Philadelphia: Henry Altemus, 1896); *Lebenserrinnerungen bis zum Jahre 1852* (Berlin. Georg Reimer 1906).

Shields, D. S., *The Culinarians Lives and Careers from the first age of fine dining.* (Chicago: University of Chicago Press, 2017).

Sperber, J., *Rhineland Radicals: The Democratic Movement and the Revolution of 1848–1849* (Princeton: Princeton University Press.1991).

Spielhagen, F., *Die von Hohenstein Roman* (Leipzig: Stackmann Verlag,1872).

Stamm, I., *Der „Verräter" der begnasdight wurde: Otto von Corvin(1812-1886) und die Revolution in Baden* (Rastatt: Aquensis Historik, 2012).

Stevens, W. B., S*t. Louis the Fourth City 1764-1911*, Vol I. (St. Louis, S. J. Clarke, 1911).

Stolz, G. *Das Leben der Margarethe Meyer Schurz Wegbereiterin des Kindergarten in den USA* (Husum,2007),

Stolz, G., *Heinrich Adolph Meyer und sein „Haus Forsteck in Kiel* (Husum: 2007).

Straus, O., *Under Four Administrations from Cleveland to Taft* (New York: Houghton Mifflin, 1922).

Swart, H. W., *Margarethe Meyer Schurz a Biography* (Watertown: Watertown Historical Society, 1967).

Terzian, J. P., *Defender of Human Rights Carl Schurz* (New York: Julian Messner, 1965).

*The Campaign of 1860 comprising the speeches of Abraham Lincoln, William H. Seward, Henry Wilson, Benjamin F. Wade, Carl Schurz, Charles Sumner, William Everts &c*, Albany (Weed, Parsons & Company, 1860).

*The Century Illustrated Monthly Magazine*, May 1887–October 1887 (New York: The Century Co., 1887).

*The English Woman's Journal Vol. II*, February 1859 (London: English Woman's Journal Company 1850: Google Books).

Thomas, J., *Universal Pronouncing Dictionary of Biography and Mythology* (Philadelphia: J.B. Lippincott and Co., 1882).

Thomson, A. M., *A Political History of Wisconsin* (Milwaukee: E. C. Wilson, 1900).

Thormann, B., *Die Bonner Burschenschaften in der Revolution 1848* (Rheinische Geschichte: 2019).

Tiedemann, F. M.D., "On the Brain of the Negro, Compared with that of the European and the Orang-Outang," *Philosophical Transactions of the Royal Society of London* Vol. 126 (1836) pp. 497–527 (London: Royal Society, 1836) jstor.org/stable/108042.

Tolzmann, D. H., *German-American Achievements: 400 Years of Contributions to America* (Heritage Books, Westminster, 2010); (ed.), *German Americana Selected Essays* (Milford: Little Miami, 2009); (ed.) *Illinois German Heritage* (Little Miami, Milford: 2005); (ed.) *Missouri's German Heritage 2nd. Ed.* (Little Miami, Milford, 2006).

Trefousse, H.L., *Carl Schurz: A Biography* (Knoxville: University of Tennessee Press, 1982).

Truax, R., *The Doctors Jacobi* (Boston: Little Brown, 1952).

Tusken, L., *Carl Schurz Tremendous Dutchman and True American* (Winchester: The Winchester Academy Press, 1983).

Twain, M. and Warner, C. D., *The Gilded Age A Tale of Today* (New York: Trident Press, 1964).

Valuska, D. L. and Keller, C. B., *Damn Dutch: Pennsylvania Germans at Gettysburg* (New Jersey: Stackpole Books, 2004).

Wallman, C. J., *The German Speaking 48ers Builders of Watertown Wisconsin* (Madison: Max Kade Institute for German American Studies, 1992).

Wersich, R. (ed.), *Carl Schurz Revolutionary and Statesman. His life in Personal and Official Documents and Illustrations in German and English* (Munich: Heinz Moos Verlag, 1979).

Werth, B., *Banquet at Delmonico's Great Minds, the Gilded Age and the Triumph of Evolution in America* (New York: Random House, 2009).

Whitridge, A., *Men in Crisis: The Revolutions of 1848* (New York: Charles Scribner's, 1949).

Whyte, W. F., "Chronicles of Early Watertown," *The Wisconsin Magazine of History,* Vol. 4. No. 3 (March 1921) pp. 287–314 (Madison: Wisconsin Historical Society), jstor.org/stable/4630310.

Will-Weber, M., *Muskets and Applejack Spirits, Soldiers, and the Civil War* (Washington D.C.: Regnery History, 2017).

Wust, K. and Moos, H., *Three Hundred Years of German Immigrants in North America 1683–1983* (Munich:300 Jahre Deutsche in Amerika, 1983).

Yearbook of German American Studies, Vol. 52 (2017).

Zacks, R., *Island of Vice Theodore Roosevelt's Doomed Quest to Clean Up Sin Loving New York* (New York: Doubleday, 2012).

# Index

1st N.Y. Lt. Artillery 99
4th N.Y. Cavalry 99
54th. N.Y. Regiment 99
58th N.Y. Regiment 99
61st Ohio Regiment 99
74th Penn. Regiment 99
75th Penn. Regiment 99-100
8th West Va. Regiment 99

Adams, C. F. 85
Adams, H. 146, 148, 181
Adler, F. 165
Altgeld, P. 157, 167, 182
Althaus, F. 28, 74, 76
Andrew, A. 85
Anneke, F. 36-38, 40, 42, 50,167, 173, 183
Anti-Imperialist League 156, 159, 183
anti-Semitic movement 151-152
Arco-Valley, Count 156
Author's Club 153

Bancroft, G. 97,123-124
Banks, Gov. N. P. 85
Barlow, Gen F. 109-110, 167
Barlow's Knoll 109
Beaufort, Madame Princess de 57
Becker, Dr. H. 43, 49-50, 171, 174
Becker, G. 38
Becker, K. 171-172
Benton, Sen. T. H. 99, 167, 179
Bethlehem, Penn. 111, 113-116, 121, 131
Bethman-Hollweg, M. A. 30, 172
Beust, F. 37, 42, 173

Bey, A. 147
Bird, F. W. 85, 136, 167, 181
Bischoff, C. 135
Bismarck, O. von 124-125, 152, 154, 170
Bitter, K. 165
Black, Gov. F. S. 157
Blenker, L. 38, 99, 173
Bloomsbury 44, 48, 58, 73, 82, 161
Blum. R. 32, 173
Bolton Landing 13, 155, 161, 165, 183-184
Bone, H. 24-25, 172
Bonn 25, 27-31, 33-36, 42, 44, 46, 48, 50-51, 61, 166, 174
*Bonner Zeitung* 27, 30, 34, 37, 45
Booth, S. 175
Bowles, S. 85, 136, 167
Brady, J. T. 112
Brahms, J. 135
Breier, E. 20
Brockelmann, E. 54-56, 175
Brodhead, R. 67-68
Brooks, P. 69
Brown, B. G. 121, 130, 132, 167, 180
Brown, J. 85, 87
Bruchsal 38, 47
Brühl 18-20, 22
Brune, G. 52-53, 55
Brüning, Baroness von 52, 55, 60, 174
Bryan, W. J. 91, 157, 160, 167
Bryant, W. C. 97, 137, 150, 167
Bucher, L. 124
Bühl, A. 50
Bull Run 94, 101

Burnside, Gen. A. 103, 114, 167
*Burschenschaft Frankonia* 27-29, 33, 88
Butler, A. 167

Caesar, J. 25
Cameron, S. 87, 112
Carl Schurz Park, N.Y. 165
Carnegie, A. 153, 155, 160, 164, 167
Carson, J. M. 141
Chapman, F. 13, 145-149, 153, 161-162, 182
Chapman-Lawrence, M. 13, 145-146, 181
Chase, S. 69, 102, 114, 168
Chief Joseph 140, 148
Chief Ouray 141
Citigo Creek 111
Clay, C. M. 92
Clay, H. 154
Cleveland, Pres. G. 153-156, 160, 165, 168
Cluseret, Col. G. P. 101
Cooke, J. 66, 114, 116
Cooper, J. F. 142
Cooper, P. 137
Corvin, O. von 40, 74
Crane, S. 153
Cuba 168
Curtis, W. 130, 154, 168
Custer, Gen. G. A. 122

Damrosch, F. 165
Davis, J. 67, 117, 129, 168
Dawes, Sen. H. L. 142, 178, 183
Debs, E. V.157, 168
Defoe, D. 20
Delmonico's 5, 126, 135, 153, 162
Dickens, C. 29, 48, 64-65, 145, 174,
Dietrich, A. 135
Disraeli, B. 135
Donoff, Count A. 141
Dorf Enge 42
Douglas, S. 67-69, 79-82, 90, 139
Doylestown, Penn. 145, 149
Drake, C. D. 126
Dred Scott Decision 178
*Dreikönigsgymnasium* 24
Dumming, C. 66

Edison, T. A. 144
Edmonds, J. W. 97
Eisenach 31-33, 73
Eliot, G. 86

Emancipation Proclamation 97, 102, 112, 169
Emerson, R. W. 85, 87, 91
Engels, F. 44-45, 173
Eugenics 151
*Evening Post* 150-151, 153
Evens, M. A. 85

Falkenthal, Dr. F. 51, 55
Faneuil Hall 84-85
Field, C. W. 137
Fields, J. T. 85
Fillmore, Pres. M. 59
Flavin, E. B. 78, 177
Fleischmann, F. 50
Flickhardt, F. 115-116, 168
Flying Dutchmen 12, 103-108
Fontane, T. 135
Forty-Eighters 72
Frankenstein Castle 38
Frankfurt National Assembly 45
Fredrick Wilhelm IV 34
Freiburg 40
Fremont, General J. C. 99, 101-102
French Arms Sale 136
Fredericksburg, Battle of 103-105
Fugitive Slave Act 84, 86

Garden of Women 137
Garfield, Pres. J. 102, 132, 144, 151, 168
Gellert, C. F. 23
Gettysburg, Battle of 105, 108-111, 158
Giddings, J. 88
Glover, J. 84
Godwin, P. 150
Goethe, J. 17, 20, 25, 28, 171
Gompers. S. 160
Grant, U.S. 110-111, 113-114, 119-120,
    122, 125, 127-131, 133-134, 136, 151,
    157, 167-168
Greeley, H. 91, 132, 168, 184
Griffin, J. Q. 85
Groth, K. 135
Grund, F. 68, 168, 184

Hale, Sen. J. P. 85, 178
Hamburg American Line 154
Hamilton, J. A. 96
Hancock, Gen. W. S. 112-114, 168
Hanna, E. P. 141
*Harper's Weekly* 130-132, 148, 154-155,
    159, 168

Harvard University 144, 147, 155, 160-161, 182, 184-185
Harvey, L. P. 78
Hasty Pudding Club 160
Hawaii 156, 158, 182
Hayes, Pres. R. B. 136-139, 142, 144, 148, 168
Hebrew Orphan's Home 151
Hecker, F. 65, 72, 111, 168
Hegermann-Lindencrone, L. 146, 181, 184
Herder, G. 23
Heroes of the Exile 45, 174, 185
Hoffmann, E. F. 99
Holmes, O. W. Jr. 85, 114, 153, 168, 178
Hooker, Gen. J. 102-108, 111-112, 114, 168
Houdini, H. 58
Howard, Gen. O. O. 103-107, 109, 111-112, 114

Indian Schools 140
Irving, H. 153, 161

Jackson, S. 99, 102, 104-106
Jacobi, A. 5, 11, 13-14, 51, 126, 136-137, 145, 150-155, 163-164, 168, 186
Jacobi, M. P. 152, 168, 183, 186
Jay, J. 137
Jewell, M. 125, 168
Johnson, Pres. A. 114, 116-119, 121-125, 168
Jüssen, E. 90, 128-129
Jüssen, M. 15-16
Jüssen, O. 73

Kaiser Wilhelm I. 92, 154
Kaiser Wilhelm II. 154
Kansas Nebraska Bill 69
Kant, I. 23
Kiel 125, 135, 154
Kinkel, G. 27-29, 31, 34, 37, 40, 42-61, 65-67, 70, 73, 75, 77-78, 82, 91-92, 124
Kinkel, J. M. 34, 44, 48-49, 52, 55, 59, 82-83
Kissinger, H. 11
*Kleinedeutschland* 64
Klopstock, F. G. 23
Know Nothing Party 72, 79, 84, 86, 93, 98, 105, 112
Körner, T. 20, 23
Kossuth, L. 60, 74

Kozlay, E. A. 100-101, 109
Ku Klux Klan Act 130, 133

LaFlesche, S. 142
Landor, W. S. 48, 74
Langbein, F. E. 23
Lankenau Hospital 65, 170
Lassen, C. 51, 174
Lenox Hill Hospital 11, 185
Lewald, F. 60, 135, 175
Liblar 12, 15-16, 19-23, 25, 31, 48, 133, 151, 166
Lichnowsky, Prince F. 32
Liederkranz Club of New York 11, 136, 153, 155-156, 162, 185
Lincoln, A. 11, 36, 68, 72, 79-97, 99, 101, 103, 111-115, 117, 121-122, 138, 150-151, 158, 169
Lincoln, M. 97, 114, 169
Lincoln, R. 169, 178
Lincoln, T. 169
Lincoln, W. 97, 169
Lind, J. 74, 146, 169, 177
Lobell, J. W. 30, 172
Lodge, H. C. 136-137, 158, 169
Lois, J. 144
Longfellow, H. W. 85
Longstreet, Gen. J. 102
Lowell, J. R. 85, 169
Lubrecht, C. T. 5, 11
Lubrecht, P. 171, 179
Luchow's Restaurant 153

Mahler, Col. F. 110, 169
Maison-aux Bains 75
Malvern 74, 177
Mandelbaum, S. 123
Mannheim 40
Manteuffel, O. T. 34, 173
Marx, K. 31, 36, 43-46, 56, 59, 61, 173-174, 185
Mason, J. M. 69, 95, 169, 177
May, K. 142
Mazzini, G. 60, 74
McAneny, G. 164-165
McClellan, Gen. G. 98, 103
*McClure's Magazine* 162
McClurg, J. W. 130, 169
Macready, W. 57, 175
McDonald, Gen. J. D. 129
McKinley, Pres. W. 151, 157-158, 160, 169

Meagher, Gen. T. F. 112, 169
Meeker, N. C. 141
Metternich, C. 12, 15-16, 19, 23, 29, 171, 175
Meyer, A. 62, 64, 135
Meyer, H. C., "Henry" 62-63, 74-75, 183
Meyer, L. 36, 50
Meysenburg, M. 66, 176
Michener, J. 13, 149, 182, 184
Milton, J. 23
*Milwaukee Atlas* 82
Missouri Compromise 67-68, 178
Montefiore Hospital 152
Montreux 74-75
Mugwumps 151-152, 154, 158, 160
Murg River 49

National Civil Service Reform League 156, 186
National Rational International Dining Club 147
National Sound Money League 157
Naugard Prison 47-49
Negro Question 117
Nepos, C. 25
Neustadt an der Haardt 38
*New York Tribune* 120-121, 132, 137, 151, 168-169, 182
Nez-Perce 140-141, 148
Nietzsche, F. 31, 61, 176

Oglala 142, 168

Paine, H. E. 77, 169, 177
Parker, H. D. 85
*Paulskirche* 32-33, 65
Perry, H. J. 93, 95
Petermann, C. 53, 175
Petrasch, T. 25-28, 35-36
Pfuel, Gen. E. von 33
Philippines 159-162
Phillips, S. H. 67
Pierce, E. L. 84-85
Pierce, Pres. F. L. 70
Pierce, H. L. 85
Ponca Tribe 141-144
Poncantico Hills 155
Pope, Gen. J. 101-102, 140, 169
Preetorius, E. 122-123, 125-126, 134, 169, 180
Prussian National Assembly 34
Puerto Rico 159

Pulitzer, J. 125, 158, 169
Pütz, W. 25

Rachel 51, 174
Radical Republican Party 122, 130, 170, 176
Radowitz, J. 32, 172
Rastatt 12, 35, 38-42, 44-46, 65, 109, 111, 166, 170
Reichenbach, Count O. von 60
Rey, G. 73
Rhodes, J. F. 154
Ronge, J. 16, 61, 63-64, 74, 78
Roosevelt, Pres. Theodore T. Jr. 156, 158-159, 161-162, 169, 182, 185, 187
Roosevelt, T. Sr. 137, 155, 169
Rothe, E. 73-74, 77, 83
Ruge, A. 59, 175

Schiff, J. 151, 169
Schiller, F. 17-18, 20, 25, 117, 171
Schimmelfennig, A. 37, 42, 60, 110, 169, 173
Schloss Gracht 12, 15, 25
Schlözer, de Kurd 146-147
Schumann, C. 135
Schurz, Agathe 14, 66, 73, 78, 98, 113, 116, 128, 133, 137, 143-144, 149, 155, 161, 165
Schurz, Anna 16, 27, 74, 122, 124
Schurz, Antoinette 14, 66, 73, 78, 98, 113, 116, 128, 133, 137, 143-144, 149 155, 161, 165
Schurz, Carl L. 14, 130, 133, 154-155, 161, 165
Schurz, Christian 16, 22, 25, 42
Schurz, E. 113, 116, 122
Schurz, Herbert 136, 143, 153, 155, 160-161, 164
Schurz, Heribert 18-19, 22, 123
Schurz, Margarethe Meyer 61-66, 72-75, 78, 82, 87, 91, 93, 95, 97, 102-103, 108, 113-114, 116, 121-123, 125, 128, 130, 132-133, 135-136, 149, 185-186
Schurz, Marianne 78, 98, 116, 128, 133, 143, 155, 165
Second Bull Run 101
Seligman, I. 151, 155, 164, 170
Selz 41-42
Seward, W. 69, 87-88, 91-92, 94-97, 117, 170, 176, 186
Shakespeare, W. 20, 25, 57

Sheridan, Gen. P. 123, 169
Shields, J. 170, 186
Sickles, Gen. D. 104-105, 170
Sidell, J. 95
Siegburg 35-36, 45, 49
Sigel, F. Gen. 38, 99-101, 103-104, 114, 129, 170, 173
Slave Trade Act 77
Slavery Abolition Act 77
Sleepy Hollow Cemetery 164
Slocum, Gen. H. W. 104, 114, 170
Spandau 43, 50-51, 53, 55-56, 124, 166
Spielhagen, F. S. 31, 186
Spraul, K. 99, 101
St. John's Wood 48, 58, 60
Stallo, Judge J. 132
Stanton, E. 102, 107, 112-114, 117, 170
Steinway, W. 11, 13, 137, 153, 155, 160, 170
Stockhausen, J. 135
Stockmeyer 62, 183
Strasbourg 42
Straus, L. 151, 170
Strodtmann. A. H. 31, 42, 51, 57, 172
Sumner, C. 69, 85, 87, 117, 129, 131, 134, 167, 170, 176-177
Swedish Nightingale 74, 169, 177
Sznayde, Gen. F. 37, 173

Tammany Hall 5, 112, 156, 159, 170
Tasso, T. 20
Techow, Capt. A. 37, 42, 173
*The Annals of Physical Science* 58
Third Division XI Corps 99, 103
Thirteenth Amendment 13, 126
Tibbles, T. H. 142, 181
Tieck, L. 20
Tiedemann, Dr. H. 65, 87, 91, 98, 117, 120, 170
Tiedemann, Dr. F. 120, 180, 186
Tiedemann, F. 99
Tiedemann, Col. G. 39-40, 46, 170
Tiedge, C. A. 23
Tilden, S. J. 137-138
Tolzmann, D. H. 10, 12, 177, 186
Toombs, R. A. 69, 177
Toups, A. 50
Tragic Era 116, 180, 183
Traun, C. 62-63

Treaty of Malmo 31-32
Trefousse, H. 14, 176, 178-182, 186
True Americanism 85
Tuskegee Institute 162
Twain, M. 13, 153, 160-161, 163, 170, 187
Tweed Ring 131, 137
Tweed, W. 131, 170

Ubstadt 38
Uhland, L. 33
Ungar, A. 50
Unger, L. 50
Ute Tribe 141

Veteran's Corps 113
Villa Forsteck 125, 135
Villard, H. 150, 160, 170, 182

Walker, Gen F. A. 143, 170
Wallenstein 25
Washington, B. T. 13, 162, 164-165, 170
Washington, Pres. G. 20
Watertown. Wisc. 73-74, 76-80, 121-122, 124, 177, 187
Webster, D. 86
Weed, T. 67, 69, 90, 170, 176
*Westdeutsche Zeitung Democratic Politischer Tageblatt* 43, 49, 174
Westendarp, W. 99
*Westliche Post* 169, 180
Whipple, E. P. 85
White, G. A. 162, 170
White, H. 136, 150-151, 170
Whittier, J. G. 86
Whyte, W. F. 77, 177, 187
Wide Awakes 88, 90, 192
Wieland, C. M. 20
Wiggers, M. 53-54, 56, 175
Wilberforce, W. 77. 170, 177
Willich, A. von 38-39, 45, 59-60, 66
Wilson, H. 84-85, 151, 177
Wisconsin Free Democrat 83-84, 178
Wolf, S. 170

XI Corps 12, 99, 103-109, 111

Zitz, F. 32, 37, 173
Zweibrücken 45